MW00681366

Issues on Race and Gender Politics: Antebellum to Present

Gerald E. Matthews

Australia • Brazil • Japan • Korea • Mexico • Singapore • Spain • United Kingdom • United States

Issues on Race and Gender Politics: Antebellum to Present

Gerald E. Matthews

Executive Editors:
Maureen Staudt
Michael Stranz

Project Development Manager:
Linda deStefano

Senior Marketing Coordinators:
Sara Mercurio

Senior Production / Manufacturing Manager:
Donna M. Brown

PreMedia Services Supervisor:
Joel Brennecke

Rights & Permissions Specialist:
Kalina Hintz
Todd Osborne

Cover Image:

Getty Images*

* Unless otherwise noted, all cover images used by Custom Solutions, a part of Cengage Learning, have been supplied courtesy of Getty Images with the exception of the Earthview cover image, which has been supplied by the National Aeronautics and Space Administration (NASA).

For product information and technology assistance, contact us at
Cengage Learning Customer & Sales Support, 1-800-354-9706

For permission to use material from this text or product,
submit all requests online at **cengage.com/permissions**
Further permissions questions can be emailed to
permissionrequest@cengage.com

ISBN-13: 978-1-111-00408-8

ISBN-10: 1-111-00408-0

Cengage Learning
5191 Natorp Boulevard
Mason, Ohio 45040
USA

Cengage Learning is a leading provider of customized learning solutions with office locations around the globe, including Singapore, the United Kingdom, Australia, Mexico, Brazil, and Japan. Locate your local office at:
international.cengage.com/region

Cengage Learning products are represented in Canada by Nelson Education, Ltd.

For your lifelong learning solutions, visit **custom.cengage.com**

Visit our corporate website at **cengage.com**

Printed in the United States of America

ISSUES ON RACE
AND GENDER POLITICS:
ANTEBELLUM TO PRESENT

by

GERALD E. MATTHEWS

About The Author

Gerald E. Matthews, Ph.D., LMSW is a full professor of Social Work and African American Studies at Ferris State University. He completed all of his studies and degrees at The University of Michigan. He has an earned BA, MSW, Ed.S. and Ph.D. degrees in the disciplines of Sociology, Social Work (Community Organization) and Educational Planning for Community and National Development respectively. Dr. Matthews is a former community organizer in Ypsilanti, Michigan, Mt. Morris Township/Beecher, Michigan, and Flint, Michigan. He has served as an administrator and Chief Executive Officer for eight years in a community health center located in Flint, Michigan. He has served on numerous community-based organization (CBO) boards, and has led workshops on administration practices and community organization for community individuals and CBO staff. He is a proud member of the Southern Poverty Law Center, The Urban League, the Rainbow Push Coalition, and the NAACP. His previous books are entitled:

- *Evangelism or Corruption: The Politics of Christian Fundamentalism* (2007) Cengage Publishers formerly Thomson Custom Solutions. Mason, Ohio.

- *Hegemony: America's Link to International Racism* (2004) Cengage Publishers. Mason, Ohio.

- *E Pluribus Unum: Justice, Liberty, and Terror* (An analysis of Western terrorism on people of African descent.) (2002) Cengage Publishers formerly Thomson. Mason, Ohio.

- *Journey Towards Nationalism: The Implication of Race and Racism* (First and Second Editions, 2001 and 1999). Thomson Custom Publishers/Cengage and Forbes Publishers, NY.

- *A Declaration of Cultural Independence For Black Americans: An Essay For Change and Growth* (1995). United Brothers and United Sisters, Hampton, VA.

FOR OUR YOUTH:

The Challenges of the

Future are yours.

To my wife Carolyn.

Prologue

Based on the events over the week of (April 13-17, 2009), when the Tea Party protests took place, it occurred to me that some may think that my issue with Obama is a matter of sour grapes because it is commonly known by my acquaintances and students that my candidate for president was Hillary. Therefore I have chosen to write this essay to clear up any misunderstandings that folks may have about my political philosophy. This is only important because I am Black, and therefore it is expected that I would walk lockstep with the president. And because I am critical of him and many of his policies, a search for the answer has led some to erroneously conclude that I am a Republican, heaven forbid, and/or that I am a social conservative, far from it.

I would have you know that I am a card-carrying democrat, and have been for years. I am what some would consider a social progressive, or "lefty" if you prefer because I am pro-choice, pro-women's rights, pro-gay/lesbian/transgender rights, pro-gun control, pro-affirmative action, anti-war, and anti-death penalty, a real "lefty" huh. But with that said, I probably have added to your confusion because at first blush one would think that my philosophical views are nearly in perfect unison with President Obama. But wait a second, I am also pro-The United States Constitution. But its interpretation is the primary factor here because of actions taken by certain authorities and various rulings coming from the Supreme Court. Of course, over the years I have written scathing essays about George W. Bush and his Papa, and strongly opposed the policies of Ronald Reagan, particularly when he chose to dismantle the Air Traffic Controllers Union, PATCO (G. Matthews, 2001, p.137). Couple these issues with the obvious fact that I am a Black man, would also lead one to the conclusion that I am a perfect candidate for Obamamania.

But once again, please wait. I am also against hypocrisy, deceit, and subterfuge as discussed in the Machiavelli and Alinsky Models where political expediencies are carefully weighed, which I speak to at length in this new book, because Obama is said to be a student of both theorists. And the intentional lies to mislead the populace that Machiavelli addresses in his 16th century pivotal work *The Prince*, should begin to shed light on my dissatisfaction with the double standards of my party. It is most difficult to encourage any egotist to dial down their desire to seek public praise and affection. In antiquity, according to Machiavelli, it was the lure of the coliseum; and in our modern times it is the attraction of the large arena with the added magnetism of the camera where competing interests must be hammered into submission. On this point Machiavelli wisely argues that "A man that is made a prince by the favour of the people must work to retain their friendship…" (p.34). But ego and arrogance are traits which will prohibit friendships to flourish. Thus recent events have brought my concerns to the boiling point where I felt the need to present my thoughts to you for the sake of clarity given the respect I have for you, my colleagues, students, relatives, and friends.

The approximate 2,000 demonstrations which took place around our nation were an expression by American citizens exercising their First Amendment Constitutional right of assembly and protest. They deserved far better treatment than they received in the national media, particularly NBC, and CNN. The only network that valued their citizenship right to protest was FOX. Of course FOX has the reputation, and deservedly so, of being a conduit for right-wing ideologies, therefore lending it incapable of making sound professional journalistic decisions, in the views of its critics and competitors. However I have recently found their work to be extremely informative, more so than my many years of viewing CNN; and if a "lefty" like me can find value in the work of Beck, Hannity, O'Reilly, and Greta, then I daresay that others may conclude the same if they would become more objective viewers. Naturally they do say some things which grind me, but they have guests which provide balance, and very lively debates and commentary. To illustrate this point there was the eloquent Patricia Ireland, the former president of the National Organization for Women (NOW), going toe-to-toe in a debate with the abrasive self-centered bully of FOX News, Bill O"Reilly. She held her own in making the case for women's rights, and the outrageous abhorrent murder of Dr. George Tiller who O'Reilly insists on referring to as Dr. Killer because he detests him for providing medical services to women seeking their right to an abortion. As a matter-of-fact there is evidence which suggests that O'Reilly, through his television influence and ability to reach those with extreme views, may have "fanned the flames of hate" that led to Dr. Tiller's murder (Mary Alice Carr, The Washington Post, 6- 5-09).

But with that said, what I found most troubling on the reporting of the "Tea Parties" by the other networks was not whether or not the citizens had made their protest grievances clear, which I personally thought they had, but rather it was the media's reaction of questioning the protesters right to assembly and protest at all. A democrat operative, Paul Begala, who I had previously thought to be a sound and fair critical thinker, surprised me by referring to the protesters as "wimpy whiners" and weasels, while actress Janeane Garofalo called them a "bunch of racists", and Ray Buckley of the New Hampshire Democratic Party said that the protestors were a "mob who didn't know what they were doing". And to make matters worse Garofalo also said that they were mostly "rednecks" that did not know their history, and that the Black Americans who had joined the protests with their White brothers and sisters were suffering from the "Stockholm Syndrome" (a condition brought on by captives and/or the oppressed, or kidnapped persons tendency to begin to identify with their captors/oppressors) (April 18, 2009, FOX News). No doubt there were some folks, both Black and White, who participated in these demonstrations who probably held dubious, and maybe even some bizarre views and motives; but to characterize all of the protestors in such strident negative and stereotypical language was beneath the dignity of any logical thinking, and rational person. Moreover censorship and a closed mind are relational characteristics and eschew the appreciation for the conceptual significance associated with hearing opposing views and philosophies. For after all a meaningful debate is quite different than the one-sided lectures that O'Reilly is known for, or *"grandstanding"*, as Ireland accurately characterized his interview style. The former will ultimately strengthen the knowledge base, and quite possibly one's social awareness which of course is not the goal of O'Reilly.

When Garofalo stated that the primary reason for the protests was that they hated the fact that a Black man was President, it provided me with a reinforced commitment to address my views on the matter because the last thing I need is for a White liberal to define my Black identity values for me no matter how well-intentioned she might be, or how well-informed she may be perceived by her peers and others. Similarly, I do not believe that those of us who are students of race relations need to be lectured by White or Black conservatives, for that matter, on the state of Black progress, or the so-called "post racial era" that they are so fond of stating. But in essence it is merely an indulgence in wishful thinking by historical neophytes brought on by the strength of Obama's election to the presidency. I grant you that it was a pivotal event in our nation's history, but the elimination of racism from the thoughts and hearts of our people, and the discrimination it spawns is still many generations away. For example, why are Jews still wary of their security while residing in their own nation, particularly when they have strong affiliations around the globe; could it be that anti-Semitism is a generational cultural dilemma in the diaspora that still exists in the aftermath of the Holocaust? This same dynamic holds true with the Black Holocaust known as slavery.

First of all, on the matter of hypocrisy, if dissent and protest are thought to be patriotic when we progressives organized and attended events during the Bush presidency, then the same should hold true for conservatives, and whether we agree with them or not is the exact purpose of the exercise, and the amendment which protects it. As the old expression goes, I may not agree with what you say, but I will defend your right to say it; violence however, is not part of this equation. Anything less than this smacks of hypocrisy, and my party members should know better; and of course they do, it is just that they don't give a shit. Furthermore, we were told that there would be a new openness in President Obama's administration, and transparency would be the rule of the day. We progressives howled when Vice-President Dick Chaney held his closed doors meetings with the energy interest groups of the Enron era, recall? And to no avail, attempts were made through one court challenge after another to secure the minutes of that meeting. Well in March 2009, Vice President Joe Biden held a similar closed door session with a special interest group comprised of union executives, and not one progressive voiced concern or disapproval, and it was only vaguely covered by the media. Another example of the hypocrisy is that the National Security Agency (NSA), under Bush, began wiretapping of American citizens which *candidate* Obama found highly unconstitutional and objectionable. However, *President* Obama finds this policy just fine, as his administration is not only continuing it, but is expanding it beyond what the Bush years had initiated. I ask you, where might be the progressive outrage on this new policy initiative?

But given the nature of politics, I have supported and defended my party's decisions when I thought them to be right and in the best interest of our nation, meaning the people. And likewise, I have stood in defiant disagreement with them, in both actions and publications, when I believed they have erred. For example, I believe that our gay/lesbian brothers and sisters deserved far better treatment from our military than the "don't ask, don't tell" policy initiated under the Clinton administration. Furthermore, the hypocrisy of my party is crystallized in the matter of pay equity for women, which is about 77 cents on the dollar of the pay for men doing the same job. Each democratic presidential hopeful campaigns on this issue, but upon election, the issue finds itself becoming less of a priority in terms of sustained vocalization, and legislative actions. As a descendent of slaves, I take exception to the lack of fair compensation for one's labor, as should we all. Again my party falls quite short on this matter. We also know that women are brutalized and murdered with regularity in our nation; however, the misogyny that was evidenced during the last political cycle, 2008, was at an unconscionable high level. This was mostly in evidence within the democrat party, with the progressives being the primary culprits; and continues to be shown as such in a Playboy article that denigrates conservative women in the expression of rape and abuse against them (June, 2009). By comparison, this is quite similar to the treatment that Sarah and Hillary both experienced throughout the 2008 political cycle, with the progressives again being the primary culprits, e.g., Jack Cafferty of CNN, actor Matt Damon, and the original founder and editor of Ms. Magazine, Gloria Steinem, to name a few. Thus racism and misogyny are two sides of the same coin, and are twin evils of American society; and both are exploited in the most despicable ways.

Also during the campaign, to gain political advantage, Obama stood silently by as his surrogates labeled Bill Clinton a racist, knowing all the while that the charges were blatantly inexcusable and false. This occurrence, in my humble opinion, is absolutely a detestable thing to do to a person, particularly here in America for a variety of very good historical reasons. Interestingly one Congressional Black Caucus (CBC) accuser has since apologized to President Clinton for making the false charge against him by using the excuse that "we just wanted to win so bad". First and foremost if a claim of racism is knowingly a lie, then the movement to eradicate hate from our society is harmed in the process. And what does it say about the character of those persons making the charge. That is, using the term racist as a descriptor of those who truly fit the mold becomes nearly insignificant if we continue to attach it to anyone at random whom we disagree with or do not like for one reason or another, i.e., if Bill Clinton is a racist, then how do we characterize members of various hate groups such as the *"KKK"* and *"Skinheads"*. There are no degrees of racism, a person, thing, or event is racist or it is not; the same as there is no such thing as being a little bit pregnant, you are or you are not. Those democrats who have labored for years in the cause of justice are well aware of this distinction; and various members of the CBC, Obama included, knew the harm they were doing to Hillary by marginalizing one of her major assets, Bill Clinton. Moreover there is no occasion where women should be referred to in the harsh language we heard often during the campaign of 2008. As in racism, the baggage of violence visited upon women is the concomitant product of learned behavior and derogatory language with the planned intent of reducing them to a status of inferior; so it was with former U.S. Senator Hillary Clinton, and Governor Sarah Palin. Unfortunately this is a relentless experience that still plagues them both as well as females in general throughout our nation from childhood to adult.

Obama once remarked to Hillary that at times he did not know who he was running against, her or Bill, as if Michelle and Oprah out campaigning for him were of lesser significance. The strategy then became very clear, they had to attack Bill, but on the other hand, Michelle was left unscathed because it had been previously established that family members would be off limits. Interestingly though Chelsea Clinton even experienced ridicule on the campaign trail. But Bill Clinton, mostly because of his stature I guess, was indeed the exception. Through Obama's words he served notice of his intention to stoop to a lower level of campaigning, which was his history in running for the state senate in Illinois, where his tactic to have his competition disqualified was determined by some to be dirty politics (Chicago Activist Interview, 2008). In the presidential contest, race and gender were carefully and strategically used as ploys to gain advantage over Hillary. This was coming from a crowd who used intimidation and "Chicago Style" politics of "*bait and switch*," and race and gender were just "*convenient tools of the trade*," which left a bad-taste in many mouths; and if this is an indication of "sour grapes," then so be it (R. Blagojevich Hearings, 2009). But the hypocrisy is real, for example if the democrats felt cheated by being disenfranchised during the 2000 presidential vote in Florida, likewise then we should have felt betrayed when the same occurrence took center stage by our own party in Michigan and Florida in 2008. How does the old saying go, "just because you are paranoid, doesn't mean that someone isn't out to get you"? The events taking shape at the national level today, are carbon copies of the gender and racial ploys used during the 2008 campaign, and Begala and Garofalo's reaction to the "Tea Parties" are but two examples of the strategy to neutralize the competition by charges of racism, which is easy to buy into given our nation's history, and the nature of adversarial politics. Where, I ask, do we draw the line? These types of tactics, we have long argued as progressives were the underhanded methods employed by Republicans, for it was them who used the experience of Willie Horton, a Black felon, against Michael Dukakis in the 1988 presidential campaign to help elect the first George Bush.

But soon these strategic ploys can be overplayed, and Blacks like others will grow weary of the excuse to assign race and racism to every criticism that one does not like. And of course, it does not escape the wary eye, in that the charge of racism takes on added significance when it is made by White Americans serving as allies instead of Black folks themselves. As a Black American I thank them for their vigilance; however I would like to add that the majority of Blacks see racism in a similar fashion. It is personally harmful, degrading, and corrupts the fabric of our nation's values. While our life experiences may be different, we are bound together by the inescapable fact that racism in America has touched us all, and therefore care should be taken in how charges are made to prevent a backlash by welcomed parties, as in "gotcha", when the logic of the event(s) fall short of close scrutiny. Such is the problem with the "Tea Party" criticisms which means that we all will lose in the long-run if this tactic of defying the First Amendment of our Constitution is not put in check.

I have written extensively on the Republican/conservative's shortcomings on issues of equal opportunity (Affirmative Action), including Title X which provides equality in athletic/academic scholarships in our nations colleges and universities, on gay/lesbian rights, gun-control, and pro-choice. As previously stated, these are issues on the progressive agenda, as well as the campaign against war and the death penalty. Now with the election of Obama we are seeing that the dynamic of race remains a great pernicious schism of American society. For centuries we have been divided as a people supposedly dedicated to the principle that we are "all created equal". My passionate belief in equality is fueled by the strength and dedication to the teaching of the Gospel by certain ministers of international acclaim who by name are: Joyce Meyers, Jesse Jackson, Jeremiah Wright, Al Sharpton, and Louis Farrakhan, to name a few.

I am not naïve about the nature of American politics, which means that I understand the games and lies that are endemic within the system in which some are convinced is an important part of the electoral process. I buy into this nonsense up to a point, but when it spills over into issues of the franchise, misogyny, death penalty, and race, I have zero tolerance for this type of political bullying and chicanery often referred to as gamesmanship, but in actuality it is the zenith of hypocrisy. This brings into focus another problem that I have with Obama, growing nearly in contrast to my aversion to the demagoguery of Bill O'Reilly, and the arrogance of my party to believe that it can continue to use race and gender as wedge issues to gain support for any policy, and to elect any politician, with justice to others be damn in the pursuit of these goals. We absolutely hate it when some Whites exploit race to gain advantage; therefore the same principles and standards should apply by progressives when we see race used in such an uncompromising fashion. Despite what others may have heard, reported, or written, both Machiavelli and Alinsky argue very effectively that trust is garnered through positive consistency in weighing political options which is a measurement of true activism by those leaders dedicated to serving the *greater* good of a nation, and *not* themselves. Thus to promote trust through activism is the antithesis of lies, deceit, self-service, or engaging in de-humanizing claims and unnecessary ridicule of one's adversaries. In this regard respect is earned, over time, through both words and deeds. When put in this context, a troubling pattern has emerged which, in my view, reflects poorly on the character and decision-making of Obama and his top advisers. The following represents a list of my major grievances, the Constitution notwithstanding:

1) Obama did not attend the major national political rally in support of the Jena Six in Louisiana (the Black teens who were being persecuted for their protest against racial injustice at their school in Jena, Louisiana). I can give him somewhat of a

pass on these events because he did write an effective piece on the injustice visited upon the teens. But as a leader his presence would have spoken volumes, given that he was beginning to position himself for a run for the presidency. However, I believe that he was counseled that his visible support for such a volatile Black issue would have damaged his image as a *non-racial* candidate, and therefore his campaign may not have been able to gain traction.

2) Also as a candidate he did not attend the Black Forum on race in New Orleans after Hurricane Katrina sponsored by the well-known activist Tavis Smiley. If you do not know of Tavis or Tom Joiner, it is an indication of ignorance of the contemporary Black experience insofar as Black and White relations are concerned. Bush was assailed by both White and Black progressives for his lack of response to the Hurricane's victims and its aftermath (can you recall the date when thousands of Americans, more than the official tally of 1800, were killed and/or left displaced and homeless across Louisiana and Mississippi, the effects of which are still in existence today)? They were first inappropriately called refugees by the media and the administration, until those doing so were reminded of the simple fact that these were Americans who had become victims of America's greatest natural disaster, mostly Black, and many were of other ethnicities, but all were mostly poor. They then became known as evacuees, who were worthy of our sympathy, but not much else, as they still struggle yet today to recover from the hurricane that struck that region of our nation on August 29, 2005, which in the minds of some is not nearly as relevant as 9-11-2001. This was a piece of the puzzle that Tavis hoped to

address by inviting the presidential candidates to the Forum which both Hillary and McCain attended, Barack offered to send Michelle.

3) He is not a strong supporter of Affirmative Action as his views shift from time to time depending on the political current that he finds himself in; and has stated as much by saying that he does not want his daughters to be beneficiaries of it which can be interpreted in at least two different ways. My question to him, and to other like minded Blacks, is: how does he think that he matriculated to Harvard, then Congress, and the Presidency, if not for the principles of Affirmative Action which opened the doors for his advancement through the laws of equal opportunity. The same can be said for Clarence Thomas, Ward Connerly, Juan Williams, and Condolezza Rice, all of whom are enjoying the benefits provided by Affirmative Action while holding it in disdain and abeyance for others.

4) He laughingly referred to himself as a "Mutt" as a reflection of his biracial heritage (mother=White, father=Black Kenyan/African). This term is both insulting and degrading because it undermines the generations of hardwork, sacrifice, and the untold loss of life by both Blacks and Whites who struggled to bring our nation and the world out of the ignorance, misery, and hate in which Blacks were seen as subhuman, akin to animals. This remains a belief and a family value of a multitude of White supremacists, (a.k.a. racists), in America today. Of course others also shared in the humor who attended his news conference, as he spoke of the dog he wanted to purchase for his children. Upon reflection I think he may have chosen his words more carefully because by extension it reflects poorly on his daughters,

whom I believe he would not want to be considered "one-quarter mutts" as in Jim Crow parlance.

5) He is a supporter of the death penalty which is not commonly known; but is a political decision in America shared by many candidates who are attempting to demonstrate that they are tough on crime, thus pandering to the emotions of revenge by a population educated to believe in its value. The death penalty is neither a practical or functional deterrent to crime. Rather it is state sanctioned murder, and has been used to enforce discriminatory laws and policies by the powerful in exercising their supremacy over the powerless, who tend to be minorities, and poor. For instance the data tells us that a person is more likely to be sentenced to death if the victim is White than if the victim is Black, which suggests, in America, there is more of a premium on White life than Black life. The American Civil Liberties Union is very adamant on this point. They present the following data and cogent argument, "While White victims account for approximately one-half of all murder victims, 80% of all Capital cases involve White victims. Furthermore, as of October 2002, [only seven years ago], 12 people [had] been executed where the defendant was White and murder victim Black, compared with 178 Black defendants executed for murders" where the victim was White (2003). And, presently of course, the data are still mounting. Additionally, it can be stated that in America we rarely, if ever, put to death those who are wealthy because they can afford to mount an excellent defense with a team of lawyers and investigators to match or exceed the resources of the state. And for those who would use Judeo-Christian beliefs in the "eye for an eye" passage always conveniently omit the

second part which states "vengeance is mine so sayeth the Lord". Additionally, over the centuries, literally millions of innocent persons have been killed by one nation state after another, in *"judicial murders"* for political crimes of avarice, power, and/or hate which they did not commit. As a vivid example let's begin with the execution of the Greek philosopher Socrates, for the charge of heresy, 400 years before the *trial* and crucifixion of Jesus, then the burning of Joan of Arc for sedition, the genocidal gassing and burning of six million Jews and others in the brutality of the Holocaust (WWII Nazism), and likewise the centuries of genocidal beatings, burnings, and lynching of millions of Blacks/Africans in the slave trade and the Jim Crow Era up through today, the 1995 hanging of Ken Saro-Wiwa, a Nigerian activist, and eight other Nigerian patriots who protested the abuse of the Ogoni people by the oil cartels and the nation's leaders, the genocide in Darfur by the Sudanese leaders existing still today dispatching mercenaries known as the Janjaweed (soldiers on horseback). Then there were the numerous apartheid killings in South Africa up until 1994 when a new Constitution was written outlawing such practices (but at first they were being dismantled by the White leadership under deKlerk who by "1991 had repealed all apartheid laws"), the 20th century Russian Stalag deaths, the 1989 Tiananmen Square massacre of thousands of Chinese students in Beijing, China under the leadership of Deng Xiaoping (pronounced "done shopping"), the 1975 "Killing Fields" by the Communist Khmer Rouge, "led by Pol Pot" who seized control over the Cambodian government, with more than two million Cambodians killed and/or executed (genocide), the 1992 Bosnian Civil War and Serbia "ethnic cleansing program" (genocide) to "remove Bosnian Muslims and Croats from newly independent Bosnia-Herzegovina", and the millions of Native American/Indian people killed here in the western hemisphere, and in our country at the behest of the expeditionary forces dispatched by the imperialistic power(s) here and abroad in acts of genocide, the same holds true for the Hawaiian and Philippine Islands' populations. Then there was the 1994 civil war in Rwanda where the Hutu people killed more than 500,000 Tutsis. But the Tutsis "eventually regained control of the country, forcing two million Hutu to flee. Rwanda becomes closely associated worldwide with genocide carnage and violence…It lost 20-40 percent of its population to slaughter and exile" (N. Kogan, 2006, pp. 366-390). Some will say that these are unconnected events to our death penalty. But I beg to differ. Is it because we no longer engage in mass executions, favoring more serial events on subsequent days of the month while ignoring the death toll that mounts year after year, or is it because we consider ourselves to be more *"civilized"* than the aforementioned nation states. To be certain, during his six year term as Texas Governor, George W. Bush approved over 152 executions, more than any governor in modern times (Sr. Helen Prejean, 2005). How then do we characterize these sequential accumulated planned killings by the state. Are they to be dismissed simply as executions? Revolutions and civil wars throughout the history of humankind have resulted in untold deaths of the innocents including women and children in state sanctioned violence euphemistically referred to as *"just collateral damage"*. Our persistent denial of this carnage, executions and collateral damage, is of course an example of our arrogance, which is underscored by our reluctance to change an antiquated practice that should have been banned years ago and remained unconstitutional as DNA evidence regularly demonstrates. It is splitting fine hairs when a person argues that America's system of putting its citizens to death is not related, in part, to the thinking that drove these other tragic aforementioned events. Those in power can generally present an adequate argument for the legitimacy of their punitive authority over others. However are we to let Obama off the hook, and give him a free pass because this scourge of our society was not discussed during the campaign season due to the fact that each candidate held similar beliefs on this pernicious issue? I, for one, think not! The question still to be asked and answered, particularly insofar as America is concerned, "Why do we kill people, who kill people, to show that killing is wrong?"

6) My next issue with Obama is that in prosecuting the war in Afghanistan, Obama's verbiage for its justification is reminiscent of that of George W. Bush and Lyndon B. Johnson, as he seeks congressional authorization of funding, and in essence approval for his actions. An organization of American veterans who served in Afghanistan now have taken a strong stance in opposition to Obama's claim that it is necessary to send troops to fight and die in Afghanistan. Their argument is that *"boots on the ground"* in Afghanistan is counterproductive to America's stated interest of peace and waging a war against terror; and the language of *terror* has now been euphemistically altered by Obama for some arcane reason. The veterans maintain that the "unintended consequences" of war where civilians are harmed and even killed does more to promote terror than any good we can do through military engagement (*Mike Malloy, Sirius Left Radio*, 6-8-09). This is the same situation

that we find ourselves in with the Iraq campaign, which is often compared to Viet Nam. Furthermore the Bush Administration gave serious consideration to further expanding the war in Afghanistan, but the argument that there were no available *"targets"* there of any consequence prevailed, so they shifted their aims to invading Iraq, which became the centerpiece of Obama's campaign for president. We do know that the quagmire in Iraq has been argued for years, and will be debated for many more. It appears that we have learned absolutely nothing from the Iraq venture, nor have we gained any particular knowledge from the Soviets who invaded Afghanistan in the 1980s. We ran a covert campaign to aid the Afghans in ridding themselves of the Russian invaders, and at the time we found the Afghans to be fierce combatants. What exactly has changed from then, and now? Absolutely nothing except that we are the ones there instead of Russians, and civilians are still being killed on a regular basis, now by us, which naturally angers the hell out of the Afghan people. Remember this old truism, "One person's terrorist, is another person's patriot". We are finding many more patriots in Afghanistan, than we initially believed, so therefore we must send thousands more troops to that war-torn nation; more war, more money, more death. Where does it end? This has, in tragic reality, become Obama's War.

7) Then there is the matter of Reverend Dr. Jeremiah Wright. He is a well known scholar and minister of both national and international acclaim. The respect for his humanitarianism transcends the many segments of the Black community. I have had personal correspondence with him, and actually met him at a church revival in Southfield, Michigan. As a matter-of-fact, because I wrote of his work, I was

honored to present him with a signed copy of one of my books entitled, *Evangelism or Corruption: The Politics of Christian Fundamentalism.* This occurred before Obama was a prominent fixture on the radar screen; but certainly while he was a member of Trinity United Church in Chicago where he received political support and spiritual guidance for years because he was befriended by Reverend Wright (G. Matthews, 2007). Obama's condescending speech in which he betrayed his long-term pastor, mentor, and friend for calculated political reasons, in my mind, stands as another testimony to his character. And now as president he is beginning to acquire quite a reputation for callous ruthlessness among the Washingtonian elite which may not bode well for the long-term interest of his administration. In my letter to Reverend Wright, after the betrayal, I expressed my deep sadness for what Obama had done to him. Of course his being portrayed in the media as some vile anti-American ogre is something that Black activist/ministers like him, and Reverends Jackson and Sharpton, and Minister Farrakhan are accustomed to, but having a Judas in one's congregation with ambitions of grandeur, is an altogether different matter. Reverend Wright's humble response to me was one of gratitude; while he expressed forgiveness for his long-time friend and confidant, Barack Hussein Obama. There are literally millions of Americans who have suffered abuse and oppression in our nation, but are unaware of the great personal sacrifices that these pastors of the cloth have made on their behalf, and the people of the world. Indeed we pay homage to Reverend Dr. Martin Luther King, Jr. for these very reasons. And it was the FBI Director J. Edgar Hoover who attempted to tarnish his reputation, by accusing him of un-American activities rooted in Communism. However, aside from Dr. King, the great majority of Americans lack knowledge of the humility and compassion of the others in their call to service for humanity. Moreover, the majority of Americans, also through ignorance harbor an extremely negative view of Malcolm X, quite similar to Reverend Wright. And with respect to Reverend Wright, he is only known to the majority of American citizens by the sound-bites they now occasionally hear and see on the newscasts; but which once had predominated the TV screen night-after-night during the 2008 campaign. Unfortunately, the primary spokesperson who could have set the record straight, then, and now, is Obama, had he remained true to his original conviction of refusing to yield to political ambition over friendship and loyalty. However, in retrospect, it could be argued that the ends justified the means, he became president. And when taken in this context, this philosophy does not run to far counter from the political activist models of leadership and integrity put forth by both Machiavelli and Alinsky in that they both argue for the weighing of personal values with actions that are determined to be in the best interest of the people. But it does require a person with a very large ego of sorts to assume that they are the best answer for the majority, and that those they wish to serve will applaud their decisions no matter who the victim(s) of their actions might be; while others who may disagree with their political philosophy and/or actions are legitimately relegated to the dissenting minority for having lost the favor of the people. But as Alinsky and Machiavelli cautions it takes a lot of hard work and a great deal of excellent strategic calculations, combined with some luck, to maintain the support of the majority when one's integrity and moral compass have been comprised. In the words of

Alinsky, "History is made up of moral judgments based on politics" (p.28), and competence and experience are central factors in this political paradigm, with little "wiggle-room" for error.

8) Obama has defunded Historically Black Colleges and Universities (HBCUs) to the tune of $85,000,000. Even George W. Bush maintained their funding level in his budgets. Recent reports have cited that certainly there are problems within the fiscal management of some HBCUs, however these issues can be addressed without removing them from the budget altogether. Nsenga Burton, a former HBCU instructor eloquently argues that "President Obama insists on letting it be known that he is not checking for Black folks during his presidential tenure. A few weeks ago he gave 'back pay' to Filippino WWII Veterans, which he should have done, in spite of adamantly stating that he would never support reparations for Blacks. Now, he is cutting funding for HBCUs (and Native American tribal colleges/universities), while increasing funding for Latino Universities [and appointing a Latina to the Supreme Court, clearly in a calculated political move to garner the votes of this large and growing population]". Burton continues by adding that these are important initiatives that the President should support, but that "…he does not believe that Blacks should be made to pay because our President looks like us. It is shameful that a Republican president like Bush recognized the economic need of HBCUs, while President Obama ignores it…Shame on President Obama for cutting the funds, and shame on Obama for continuing to make an example out of us, while allowing others to run amok" (http://www.the loop21.com).

9) And finally, what is up with all of these "*czars*" Obama is appointing; far more than any previous administration. These are persons with expansive powers, with no congressional oversight because there are no public hearings for confirmation, thus the Senate's Constitutional role of "Advise and Consent" is compromised. So therefore these folks do not give their Oath of Office to the American people, they serve only at the pleasure of the president, and owe allegiance to him alone. They are operating with a budget of taxpayer's money, and once again the transparency that was promised is an illusion. Wall Street Journal's Charles Payne, and FOX News' Neil Cavuto label the czars as "hand-picked puppets… answerable only to the 'hand', [and they] worry that they will do their job through threats, intimidation, new rules, new regulations, and new taxes". And Adam Lashinky, senior writer of Fortune Magazine has this to say, "…the czars [numbering about 20 and counting], are doing the work of cabinet members." Gary Kaltbaum's concern is that the czars will have a deleterious effect on the market, and that there appears to be no end to their numbers in sight. He adds, "This is all about putting too much power in too few hands". A few of these posts by name are: "A pay czar, regulatory czar, border czar, cyber czar, and Great Lakes Czar (who bears the responsibility for cleaning up the Great Lakes, [how ridiculous, this is cronyism gone wild]." Finally, Cavuto states that Obama did not mention czars at all in his bid for the presidency, and that the numbers of them he has appointed is not in the best interest of our nation (Lauren O'Reilly, Business & Media Institute Website). And for someone who ran on fiscal accountability, these czars certainly do not reflect that message. Quite the

contrary, they signal an expansion of government and the continuing of a power-grab which was a criticism of Bush.

For some time now, with respect to the Obama administration, I have maintained that many of their political decisions are very troubling. Not only is there a pattern of marginalization for those who have been historically disenfranchised, there is also the age old problem of taking Black votes for granted. The hypocrisy of my party is quite evident throughout these events. While I am a "lefty," I do believe in providing an opportunity for my students and others to hear my criticisms of those who claim to be progressives or otherwise. Certainly for the years of 2000-2008, many have heard and read sharp critiques of the Bush years. As a scholar I believe that I must also hold Obama accountable to the same standards, if not higher, because he *is* a member of my party who got my vote. We are all aware that race is a factor in our collective consciousness insofar as Obama is concerned. I have observed with great interest the interplay of Whites and Blacks on both sides of the political spectrum attempting to sort out the dynamic of race as they tread lightly around its edges before darting full bore into the fray like Begala and Garofalo. They make the classic mistake of many White liberals in that they think they can speak to the Black experience because "some of their best friends are Black". It really doesn't work that way, but at least I give them credit for their clumsy attempt. However careful study and diligent research will help to remedy their problem of ignorance. In this book I too make a similar effort by speaking on the issue of misogyny and trying to be a male spokesperson of sorts on this serious matter. As an ally of the feminist movement, in which the great author bell hooks speaks so eloquently of as a role for men, I hope that I have achieved what she academically spoke to, and have lived up to her standards. Furthermore I hope that my treatment of the issue, here and in my book, is helpful and not condescending to the millions of women who have been so victimized. In the final analysis, I pray that my learning curve on gender equality is not nearly as long as the one being experienced by some of those persons who have decided to speak out on race.

Throughout this treatise I have maintained that Obama and the Democratic Party could have done much better in promoting him without betraying others and many of our progressive values in the process, i.e. ends justifying the means. Certainly in my view, Dr. Reverend Wright deserved far better, and if you don't know the man, then you really have no legitimate basis to argue otherwise. As we move forward, I know my party can do much better than embracing the hypocrisy of the past. This is the case that I have attempted to address in this new text entitled: *Issues On Race and Gender Politics: Antebellum to the Present (2009), Cengage Publisher*. I hope the reader will agree, and will have learned something in the process.

GEM

Prologue Endnotes

Alinsky, Saul (1971). *Rules For Radicals: A Pragmatic Primer for Realistic Radicals.* Vintage Books, NY.

American Civil Liberties Union (2-26-03). *"Race and the Death Penalty"*. Website, www.aclu.org.

Burton, Nsenga k. (2009). *"Cutting funding to HBCUs just isn't fair"*. Website http://www. theloop21.com.

Carr, Mary Alice (June 5, 2009). *The O"Reilly Factor, guest just can't do it anymore, after killing of Dr. George Tiller,* FOX News.

Fox News Network (2009).

Illinois Legislature: Quid Pro Quo Hearings (2009). *"Prior to felony charges brought against Governor Rod Blagojevich",* March 2009.

Interview of Chicago Activist (October 2008). Name to be held Anonymous.

Ireland, Patricia (June 2009). *Interview on Bill O'Reilly, The Factor.* Fox News.

Kogan, Neil, editor (2006). *Concise History of the World: An Illustrated Time Line.* National Geographic,Wash. D.C.

Machiavelli, Niccolo (1516). *The Prince.* Translated with notes by George Bull. Penguin Books,1999. London, England.

Malloy, Mike (6-8-09). *"Veterans Against Afghanistan".* Sirius Left Radio.

Matthews, Gerald E. (2001). *Journey Towards Nationalism: Implications of Race* and *Racism,* 2nd ed. Cengage Publisher, Mason, Ohio.

_____.(2007). *Evangelism or Corruption: The Politics of Christian Fundamentalism.* Cengage Publisher. Mason, Ohio.

_____ .(2009). *Issues On Race and Gender Politics: Antebellum to Present.* Cengage Publisher. Mason, Ohio.

O"Reilly, Lauren (6-8-09). *Obama's Czars, 'Hand Puppets,' and 'Evil Despots,' Oh My!* Business & Media Institute, Website, http://www.businessandmedia.org.

Prejean, Helen, Sr. (2005). "Death In Texas". January 13th (examine website).

Preface

"...It should be noted that one can be hated just as much for good deeds as for evil ones; therefore a prince who wants to maintain his rule is often forced not to be good, because whenever that class of men on which you believe your continued rule depends is corrupt, whether it be the populace, or soldiers, or nobles, you have to satisfy it by adopting the same disposition; and then good deeds are your enemies" (N. Machiavelli, *The Prince*, 1519 Reprinted Penguin Books 1999, p. 63). I chose to open to open this treatise with the previous quote adopted from the great medieval philosopher, politician, and military strategist and tactician Niccolò Machiavelli. It was not by happenstance that my research on this book uncovered the writings of Machiavelli; I was led to him by one of my primary text authors whose works I have studied for years in graduate and post-graduate education, Saul Alinsky.

Interestingly concentrating on Community Organization in grad school provided me with the opportunity to sit with professors who found Alinsky's work central to our discipline, and therefore we used his theories and methods extensively in classroom and field education. The importance of this information is critical in that it parallels portions of the academic background of Barack Obama and Hillary Clinton in that they both, according to author Jerome Corsi, were students of Alinsky's methods. Indeed Saul's methods are unorthodox, and can be argued that they are far left of the political center. For example, to bring attention to the misdeeds of a slumlord, Saul encouraged his pupils to organize a protest in front of his home or church. And then employing a tactic to disrupt a meeting in which their grievances were not being addressed, he suggested that the group eat plenty of beans just hours before the meeting, then the loud rumblings of their bellies and the passing of gas was enough to get the attention of those persons in charge, aside from the unpleasant odor that filled the room.

I chose to write this book for the exact same reason that Machiavelli articulated in the opening quote. Leaders can be corrupted no matter how decent they would like others to believe they are in the discharge of their duties. When those they surround themselves with are persuasive in advising the leader to go against his/her core value(s) of doing the right thing, then the wrong becomes their value(s) no matter how many attempts they may make at rationalizing it away. Certainly political expediency comes in all forms, but the convenient strategic lies, the conspiracy and betrayals, the degrading treatment of one's adversary(ies), and the methods used to define the debate to gain an advantage either through subterfuge, deceit, or misdeeds all taint the political process and have been extensively used in one campaign after another, and the 2008 presidential election is no exception.

Logically for 2008, the question of race and gender took center stage by reason of the candidates matched in the contest. But unfortunately, however, the aforementioned negative traits of expediency also predominated the political landscape to the degree that both groups, racial and gender, were degraded and harmed in the process. It also must be understood that in America race does trump gender insofar as civil rights are concerned which will be demonstrated throughout this treatise.

Chapter One is the Introduction for the ensuing discussion. It offers a critical assessment and overview of race and gender theories and their significance for study in the context of American socio-political thought. As a society, true progress can only be accomplished when we come to grips with the realities of our discriminatory practices, owing to stereotyping and judgmental attitudes. Americans have created such a hateful environment in which the playing field of patronage and privilege, is so unequal with respect to race and gender, that the battle for a larger share of the shrinking distributional pie is being waged at the level of the presidency. And because of the presidency this debate is loud and visible to the degree that the entire world can witness how terribly degrading our so-called enlightened society truly is in these contemporary times.

Chapter Two is a backwards glance to our slave past (antebellum), and the political and civil rights initiatives which may have factored into the nuances of race and gender. For example, the discontinuation of the Atlantic Slave Trade by the Constitutional Compromise of 1787, precipitated a decrease in the numbers of slaves that were available to perform an increasing amount of work. Black women were then used more as breeders, like walking, talking baby manufacturers, to create more slaves which was still not enough to supply the growing demand for slave labor which brought about a call for a constitutional amendment to resurrect legal slave importation.

Chapter Three is a Post Bellum historical to contemporary analysis of initiatives and trends on Race and Gender. This chapter encapsulates the previous two by comparing and contrasting the evolution of the initiatives in their primary stages to their present form. Furthermore there will be an additional treatment of data as it relates to the initiatives which were thought to bring justice and equality insofar as race and gender are concerned.

This then brings us to Chapter Four which examines Political and Community Organization Strategies as well as Traditional Efforts that were used in the 2008 Presidential Election. As was mentioned in the Preface, I am a student of Community

Organization (CO) Theory and philosophies of which I have used a great deal over the years in my professional work and community services. I have a better than average working knowledge of CO principles and theories employed by field professionals which contribute to a successful registration and get-out-the-vote-effort. Furthermore analyzing the debate on the role that socialism and communism play in our contemporary thinking as well as understanding a few other popular "isms" e.g., feminism, "manism = man-up," racism, criticism, sexism, and schism will be explored in the context of the redistribution of scarce resources; and achieving justice and equality as well as demonstrating responsible advocacy for oneself and others in need are important links in this paradigm. And then, too, analyzing negative stereotypes associated with social welfare and bottom-up vs. top-down economic strategies as analogs to our conceptual dilemma, are worthy of our examination particularly as they were made a crucial part of the 2008 campaigns.

This brings us to Chapter Five as a continuation of our previous discussion on the institutional problems resulting from ignoring our distant past and recent history with respect to Disenfranchisement. This analytic discussion first appeared in the second edition of my text entitled *Journey Towards Nationalism*. When I first wrote this chapter to be included in that edition, it was done so in response to the voting, election, and legal decisions of the 2000 Presidential Election that gave George W. Bush his first term in office. I have thought it applicable to revise it for inclusion in this text, largely due to the similarities of the 2000 and 2008 campaigns as they both were associated with disenfranchisement, and their organizational responses perceived as attempts to remedy the problem. Furthermore, there were legal challenges in both elections, for political adversarial reasons to redress grievances of disenfranchisement for the first, and charges of registration and possible voting fraud for the second. Nevertheless, I believe the reader will find the discussion as significant today, as it was when I first wrote it a few years ago with some necessary changes of course.

Chapter Six begins a more expansive in-depth examination on the specifics of race and gender as put forth in previous chapters. It is in this chapter that I share with the reader the problem of gender relations, or better put, the challenges that Senator Hillary Clinton faced in her campaign for the Democratic nomination. Untoward discrimination, much of it bordering on misogyny, made the goal of the first woman to be nominated by a major party for president nearly impossible to achieve. But even given certain problematic events, which I will elucidate in this chapter, Senator Clinton still earned the majority of popular democratic votes, but she fell short in the delegate count to then Senator and now President Barack Obama.

As we turn our attention to the Republican Party, we sadly find many of the same, if not more egregious examples of double-standards and cases of misogyny that even exceeded the problems experienced by Senator Clinton. Governor Sarah Palin, the Republican nominee for Vice President had to battle through enormous odds related to visceral name calling, family degradation, and other extreme personal attacks coming from all sectors of society, including from within her own party, as did former Senator Clinton. I will compare and contrast Governor Palin's and Senator Clinton's experiences with those of President Barack Obama in this election cycle; thus arguing my primary thesis, that in America, race trumps gender.

In Chapter Seven I will address three major themes as they relate to Barack Obama's ascension to the Presidency of the United States of America. Of course, everyone acknowledges that this was an event of enormous historical proportions, with a magnitude of about 7.5 on the Richter Scale. While oceans didn't swell, the ground certainly shook under the stamping feet of jubilation expressed by scores of millions of his supporters in the United States and around the world. However, certain issues came into play on his way to the Democratic nomination, and then during the presidential competition which must be discussed in the interest of literary honesty and scholarly assessment. For example, exactly what does this concept of "change you can believe in" mean; and at what cost is it to be realized as it relates to the American public, our institutions, fairness, and the candidate himself in terms of leadership, honesty, and integrity.

Chapter Eight represents the Epilogue to the treatise. It serves not only to wrap up this book, but also provides some very cogent questions and concerns which I believe must be dealt with as we look to the future. Indeed there will be other Black Presidents which is the nature of firsts; for as one is confirmed, others who follow will find the path somewhat easier to tread. However as it relates to women, the first one must still work her way through the myriad of stereotypes and misogynist attitudes and beliefs.

The reader will learn a great deal about each president of our nation by reviewing their biographies in the appendix. The appendix was adopted from the American Heritage Dictionary, encyclopedia and web sources to ensure an accurate depiction of their background, and major initiatives. Throughout our history, and with the number of years in the presidencies, gender issues appear only briefly in the 19th Amendment to the Constitution. However it should also become crystal clear to the reader that race problems and initiatives along with legislative objectives were more significant and overshadowed the issue of gender. Historically then, political agendas omitted gender as a priority, because, as I make the case, race trumps gender. And not until gender equality can become a major initiative by male dominated administration(s), which President Obama supports, or within our nation in general, women will continue to struggle for justice. Leadership is critical to progress, and only time will tell if our future leadership is up to the challenge.

I would like to take this opportunity to thank my new publisher Cengage, and my editor Curt Ketterman, and all of the professional staff who helped bring this book to fruition. Once again I offer a special thanks to my typist, colleague, and friend Rosalyn Jorgensen whose patience and care with my work is always so appreciated. Thank you so much, Elz, for coming through for me. And another very special thanks to my sons, Gregory and Corwin, for challenging my ideas and providing me with a perspective on the 2008 election that was consistent with their Uncle Larry's. Yes my brother, our many hours of debate were informative; and then thanks to the tailgating gang Clarence, Woosie, Jim, and my sister-in-law BAM. To my daughter McKenzie, thanks for your artistic insight and recommendation of films which I have found useful for teaching, and crystallizing literary ideas. To my students and colleagues, thanks for the many hours of challenging discussions. And last but not least I would like to thank my wife Carolyn who is my confidant and very best friend. The fruit of our many hours of discussion is represented in the foundation of this book. This book as my others is dedicated to the memory of my mother Cassie. The significance of my beliefs and faith in God rests with her.

Table of Contents

CHAPTER ONE

Theories and Overview on Race and Gender

Introduction

It is incredibly difficult to present issues on race and gender, without at times sounding redundant. But it is a necessary function of this type of discourse because there are so many overlapping concepts and merging paradigms which are designed to help us to understand the dual nature of these dynamic terms. To assist us with the development of our thesis, I will rely, in part, on the writings of the extraordinary professor and author bell hooks (sic). She has presented her work at seminars, conferences, and the classroom where students and others have benefitted from her insightful contribution on gender and the feminist movement. My methodology, resting on extensive research, will be to bridge the gap between race and gender, while also moving between the historical and contemporary issues that have brought us to this place and time in the progress of our nation. In some respects there can be no denying of our nation's growth, while in others we can see the same tired positions of consternation, retrograde behavior, and negative reactions to social justice. The literature search and secondary data analysis herein helps to shed light on the flux in historical politics as well as the ideological positions associated with the 2008 Presidential race. In this regard, the works of Niccolo Machiavelli and Saul Alinsky will be of critical importance.

On Race

It is clear that judging from the title, and reading the preface, this book will be an examination on the effect that race and gender has on the political landscape, in particular

1

the 2008 Presidential election. And inasmuch as current events will logically lead us to one realization, that America's 2008 political cycle was vastly different than others in the past, but in essence it had little effect on changing the way we really think about race and gender. Moreover there are those who will readily argue though that the election of America's first African American president is an indication of a shift in race relations where racism has been pushed aside by the more practical reality of economic survival, with support of a younger more tolerant multi ethnic population. According to a *Fox News* poll, 47% of those surveyed believe race relations will get better in the next few years compared to 14% who says that it will worsen (11-4-08). But what is telling is that 23% stated that they will be scared if Obama wins the presidential election (Ibid.).

Therefore, with Obama's victory, the worse fears of that 23% may come to pass if hegemony cannot be conquered. For example prior to the reconstituting of the Truth and Reconciliation Commission in South Africa, after the collapse of apartheid, the White population feared that Blacks would begin to treat them as they had treated Blacks for generations. Their fears of course, over the years, have proven to be unfounded, and there has been a lessening of racial tension in their nation. Certainly the extreme hate, brutality, and hegemony has been replaced with the Black majority achieving political dominancy and electing Black leadership whose roles have reversed from promoting race inferior policies to more worthwhile endeavors.

This comparison is not intended to suggest that policies America has pursued under White presidents for hundreds of years have been with the *total* intent of undermining the progress of the Black population. Nor is the comparison intended to suggest that a Black president would be more culturally or racially sensitive than many of his predecessors. However there is the flux of two inescapable facts which comes with the election of Obama, which is that externally America portrays itself differently than it has in the past, and therefore its international image has changed for the better. Within this context a racial dichotomy will be explored, which in part, represents my thesis. There has been somewhat of a sea-change in established voting patterns in that more White Americans voted for a Black candidate than they have in the past, including Reverend Jesse Jackson's candidacy, or Shirley Chisolm's bid for the presidency. It was, however, a coalition of ethnic groups and the youth vote which combined to elect Obama.

White Americans have the largest voting bloc of any group in America, which indicates they have the ability to shape policies and the political spectrum in ways that are not possible by other ethnic groups. Therefore Obama, as any other president for that matter (see Appendix), must consider whether or not they are being responsive to the greater electorate, but not at the expense of others who have cobbled together a partnership to elect them/him to office. To reaffirm this interconnected political effort, a couple of myths must be refuted in demonstrating that while the Black American vote was important to Obama, it was the White vote that made his candidacy possible. Political strategist Dick Morris on the Sirius Patriot Station commented that "121 million people voted in 2004, the same as the numbers who voted in 2008, so this dissolves one myth of the unprecedented voter turnout. The second myth is that young people voted in overwhelming numbers over 2004; …in that year 11% of the vote was attributed to the youth the same as those who voted in 2008" (Sirius Radio, 11-7-08).

When we juxtapose the above data with an argument on prevailing views, and assumptions, we gain a much clearer understanding of the implication of race insofar as

3

voting patterns are concerned. For example, Orlando Patterson in *Newsweek* puts it this way, "...a substantial proportion of Whites, especially younger ones have no objection to closer relations with Blacks" [as the 2008 exit polls clearly shows] (*Newsweek*, 11-10-08, p. 41). He continues by adding, "[But] even if we make the most conservative assumption, that only a minority of Whites hold such racially inclusive views, the fact that, [and this is crucial], Whites outnumber Blacks about six to one means that [those with such views will still] greatly outnumber Blacks ...and [they are hoping that] Obama policies [will] improve the economic condition of all disadvantaged Americans. [And], there are strong hints from his speeches, and writings, that he will use the bully pulpit of the presidency to encourage Blacks to embrace those mainstream cultural values and practices that have served *him* so well" (Ibid.).

This added benefit of a Black president, is as Patterson condescendingly argues, serves as a role model of sorts, for all Blacks and disenfranchised persons. It is his belief that Blacks will emulate Obama, and the charges of America as a racist nation will disintegrate with the increasing acceptance of Blacks into the mainstream of society because they now will *behave* appropriately. Two arguments on this very issue were made by conservative commentators. The so-called liberals or progressive pundits would not dare raise the issue because of its condescending and paternalistic tone. It was Laura Ingraham, a conservative talk show host sitting in for the brutally honest and irritating egotistical Bill O'Reilly on *Fox*, when she had this to say in ridiculing Reverend Jeremiah Wright, that Obama's election proves that we are living in a "...post-racial America." She also makes the observation held by Obama himself that there is no longer a need for the Afro-centrist/Black Nationalist sermons preached by Reverend Dr. Wright,

4

because as she sees it, and no doubt speaking on behalf of millions of White Americans and a significant number of Blacks, that America has entered a new age of "post racialism" ("The Factor" on *Fox*, 11-7-08).

What is incredibly absurd, is that not once did it occur to Ms. Ingraham that she knows absolutely nothing about the Black church, and less about a theology with rich historical roots reaching back into antiquity. The oppression that Reverend Wright speaks of is the Philistines reincarnated; and the long suffering of Blacks through slavery, and contemporary discrimination cannot be washed away with the single, albeit momentous act of America electing a Black president. As I listened to Ms. Ingraham, I was struck by the fact that her only interest was in pressing her agenda of divisive conservatism (see Chapter Four on "isms"). Given the opportunity and means that she and others have on both sides of the political spectrum to offer a cogent analysis of the Obama victory, what is offered instead is ideological rhetoric embroidered with paternalistic views on patriotism as if Reverend Wright, and those who believe in his message of redemption through hard truth and faith, will need to attend the refresher Barack Obama workshop on race.

This school of paternalistic thought on elevating Black behavior to be more like the Obama model may prove to become more of an albatross around the neck of Blacks, pulling them down like an anchor in deep water, as opposed to buoying them up by enlightenment on the truth of the Black experience in America. For example, it is Mike Reagan who gives us the hard factual data and analyses why conservatism won on November 4, 2008, which may be a surprise to most, given the size of Obama's victory. He notes that Democrats hijacked conservative values, and by a three-to-one vote self-described conservatives believed that it would be Obama that would cut taxes, and that McCain would raise them. And that people saw in the Obama's an intact nuclear family, a man who has never been divorced, and a man with two beautiful daughters, and they thought this picture was a better depiction of America than what McCain offered. Mike Reagan, of all people, speaking on the Black psyche stated that when Blacks see Obama they think, "If I act properly, stop wearing baggy pants, get out of Air Jordan shoes, put on a shirt and tie, and talk properly, I too can be anything, or do anything I want in America" (Sirius Patriot Radio, 11-10-08). A totally exacting paternalistic view of the Black experience, insofar as progress is concerned.

Coupling these conservative views, along with the data, helps to demonstrate how a rehashing of values that were once made popular which ushered in George W. Bush, can now be used to lecture Blacks on appropriate behavior. Interestingly though it was John McCain who held onto his values which would not permit him to take cheap shots at Obama by using Reverend Jeremiah Wright against him. Urgings by various members of his campaign, and other advisors, did not budge him from his position on the matter. Character and honor are personal traits that are exceedingly rare within the political arena. Although a 527 political action group aired a portion of Reverend Wright's sermon, Senator McCain himself did not endorse it. He understood that the sermon was not just a reflection on Obama, but rather it was a reflection on each member of the Trinity United congregation, and the Black community in general. He questioned how one could make a case against Obama by using his minister, without indicting other Blacks who came to worship on Sunday. For some persons, including Obama himself, that fine point of character did not matter, but on McCain it wore very well. According

6

to McCain, "...the ad degrades our civics and distracts us from the very real differences we have with the democrats" (H. Bailey, *Newsweek*, 10-24-08, p. 44). In the final analysis it was argued that, "The debate over [Reverend] Wright within the campaign [was] part of a larger conflict over how negative McCain should go ... but to McCain he believed that he did the right thing" (Ibid.), which is what matters in the first place.

Gender

In the previous section, I spoke of an important value, as embraced by John McCain, of "doing the right thing." Certainly over the course of one's lifetime there are "things" which we may come to regret, and many of these "things" relate to our treatment of the opposite sex in terms of personal relations or competition of some sort. But some of the most intense transgressions occur among those of the same gender, particularly as they vie for positions of power, status, and/or a reward of some type. There are some philosophies or maxims which may help to guide us so that we learn to treat others with kindness, which may be asking too much of some folks; but certainly to treat others with respect is within all of our potential. Even if a person does not have a religious value base to live by, the Golden Rule of "Do Unto Others As You Would Have Others Do Unto You" sounds reasonable doesn't it? Why then is it when we speak of gender relations, how did it become one of the saddest chapters in American society. It is also etched, as such, into our everyday lives, and frames part of our conscious and unconscious behavior.

The danger zone for women often comes from an unexpected place or source; therefore they must be alert and prepared to protect themselves while striving to live a normal life. Women must achieve a strict balancing act in reaching their full potential

7

while maintaining their feminine appeal and/or expression of the self as a feminist. Also the source of the threat to their well-being can be quite evident, and known to the woman, as in spousal abuse after the initial shock has abated from the first terrible experience. But when the attack(s) originate from another woman or women, I imagine that it is just as difficult to deal with even if a man were the culprit. I make this observation for a variety of reasons because womanist theory as it relates to "…race, class, and gender oppression" is reflected in the ideologies of our society, as well as in the "…hierarchical divisions that generate conflict and struggle" (S. Koyana, 2002, p. 35). Furthermore, within the domain of family, politics, and the larger interconnectedness between systems, it is theory on socio-political behavior that helps us to better understand the whys of the unique challenges faced by women, thus negating the bizarre work of conservative political pundit Ann Coulter. Her race and class biases, as they relate to justice for women, are quite evident in her book entitled *Guilty*.

From her own mouth, Coulter engages in feminist betrayal and misogyny. She indicts women who do not measure up to her standard of female values, particularly if they happen to be single mothers. Coulter uses slanted incarceration data analyses as evidence to vilify single moms; but of course she neglects to mention that our prisons and jails are overwhelmingly populated by Blacks which might present a dilemma of racial fairness, not to her, but to her audience. She also refuses to make the argument, that if a case is made against single mothers, what then does that suggest about the obligation of the fathers; and the added neglect of the author herself to discuss this issue compounds this obvious oversight which clearly shows the Coulter historical agenda of making outrageous assumptions based on the exploitation of others. In essence she couldn't care less about those she harms with her vicious attacks so long as her name remains in lights, and she receives her lucrative book deals (see my *Hegemony* text, pp. 271-273 for additional discussion on Coulter). For example, she even made the tactical error of loudly snapping at fellow conservative Sean Hannity on his *Fox* TV show to make an irrelevant point to another guest (4-09).

Also, appearing on the *Fox* "Bill O'Reilly Show," and ABC's the "View," while making her rounds to promote her book, Coulter made the ridiculous claim that data does not lie as she attempts to offer explanations and support for her misogynist arguments. However it is common knowledge, or at least it should be, that people manipulate numbers to their own advantage on a regular basis. No better examples are partisan policy issues, e.g., "No child left behind." While the Republicans see the dismal data on children achievement tests as evidence of teacher failure, while on the other hand, Democrats, by and large, interpret these same data as an indication of system and institutional problems. Moreover, income tax returns each year reflect financial data that are "massaged," if not downright misrepresented to present an income picture that will lessen the filer's tax bill, as demonstrated by a number of Obama appointees.

I wonder when was the last time Coulter was completely honest in filing her tax returns. Of course using the thesis of her book *Guilty*, in which she states that data doesn't lie, she might very well be right, but people certainly do, as the millions of tax returns filed each year will attest, Coulter's included. But also, tragically lost in her diatribe against single moms is a testimony to the strength and courage of these women in overcoming tremendous odds as they care for their families, and struggle against the hostility of persons like Coulter (S. Koyana, 2002, p. 35), which cuts across socio-political and cultural lines.

It is a reported fact that on average twenty-one women are murdered weekly in our society. This is an average of three per day, sixty-four per month, and an astonishing 23,360 per year if we use the three per day statistics. However in a "Did You Know" section of *Diverse Magazine* it was reported that, "Domestic violence is one of the most chronically underreported crimes. Thirty percent of Americans say they know a woman who has been physically abused by her husband or boyfriend in the past year. And women of all races are about equally vulnerable to violence by an intimate; in the year 2000 there were 1,247 [reported] women killed by an intimate partner. [By comparison], that same year, 440 men were killed by an intimate partner, [thus demonstrating that women are much more susceptible and at risk to violent attacks and to being] killed by an intimate partner. Also, in 2000, intimate partner homicides accounted for 33.5% of the murders of women, and less that 4 percent of the murders of men" (March 20, 2008, p. 15).

Clearly, no woman, or anyone for that matter, should have to live their life in fear for their personal safety; nor should they be subjected to hostility or ridicule simply because they hold views which are different or unpopular by those views held by others. It is these types of attitudes and responses to diversity which forms the basis for misogyny. What is compelling is that this is the antithesis of the foundation of the feminist movement, and many women have gone on the personal attack of other women simply because of ideology and/or party affiliation (see also Chapter Five).

By now the reader may be wondering why is it that a male is writing on Feminist Theory, and addressing issues germane to the women's movement. Well according to bell hooks, the prolific author and activist who happens to be Black, sees men involvement in the struggle for women's rights beneficial to the movement, she writes, "Not all women, in fact, very few, have had the good fortune to live and work among [both] women and men actively involved in the feminist movement" (2000, p. VIII). Furthermore, at this juncture it is important to present bell hook's work as central to my thesis because she not only presents cogent arguments on the matter of race, she discusses the duality of race and feminism from both the Black and White perspective.

Dr. hooks also brings into focus an understanding of intra-gender ostracism, particularly as it relates to differences in political ideology, which Governor Palin and Senator Clinton fell victim to during the 2008 election cycle. Those 18 million cracks in the proverbial "glass ceiling" that Senator Clinton so proudly spoke of did not come without some cost to her. As difficult as it was, these were costs and sacrifices I am certain that she was glad to have made in her ongoing contribution and struggle for women's rights. And the same, I am sure, can be said of Governor Palin, even if a significant number of women, and men, have chosen to take an opposing view.

It was bell hooks who observed these phenomena, as she labored within the women's rights movement with a primary goal of gaining recognition for Black women in gender studies within, and outside the classroom. The feminist movement had long been devoid of Black female representation, or even acknowledgment of a potential synthesis of a trans-racial women's coalition, along with the advocacy of men as contributing factors for women's rights. Again bell hooks speaking with the authority of scholarship, and the experience of a Black woman, provides support and purpose for forging such coalitions, and the challenges faced by men to become supportive once the onus of hate has been removed from their hearts and minds. It is on this issue, within this section, in which I will spend a significant amount of time because of its importance to the feminist thesis, and because I have dedicated a separate chapter to Hillary and Sarah.

Dr. hooks has the foresight to recognize the importance of male support to the feminist movement. She also understands that men who embrace feminism and are "...honest about sexism and sexist oppression, [and] who have chosen to assume responsibility for opposing and resisting it, often find themselves isolated." And with respect to Black men who are supportive of women's rights, the question is more intense in challenging his right to even have a position on the problem. It is asked, "What kind of man is he?" But a cogent response is, "I am a Black man who understands that women are not my enemy. [However], if I were a White man with a position of power, one could [seemingly, as contradictory as it may sound] understand the reason for defending the status quo. [But] even then, the defense of a morally bankrupt doctrine that exploits and oppresses others would be inexcusable" (b. hooks, p. 81).

To be clear, the isolation that men experience for given support to feminist ideals can come from women as well as from men. This was quite evident in the 2008 race for the White House. While men took on other men, criticizing their support for the women in the race by using standard arguments such as lacking qualifications, not having the mental toughness, and/or conflict with family obligations; but some of the most ardent critics came from within the ranks of women themselves. Sadly they argue the same positions as men, but they do so with the added effect that as women the potential for

12

gender discrimination is minimized or made a moot point. Dr. hooks amplifies this argument by stating, "Feminism has its party line, and women who feel a need for a different strategy, a different foundation, often find themselves ostracized and silenced. Criticisms of, or alternatives to established feminist ideas, are not encouraged, e.g. …controversies about expanding feminist discussions of sexuality" (Op. Cit., p. 11).

With the above statement we now see the ostracism of women, before that we learned of the ostracism of men, particularly Black men, which in essence leaves us with only one racial gender group with an inclusionary right to have a legitimate opinion on feminism, which is White males. This is not uncommon, because in America White males have the sway on many institutional, public or private issues, movements, or protests. Furthermore this is the primary reason why it is important to receive White male support or sanction for initiatives important to a group, whether it is in the area of progressive ideals, policymaking or civil rights. Historically speaking, this has been an American truism, and to the credit of many White males, each time there has been a critical constitutional or civil rights challenge, they, as a group, in great numbers have supported justice for those in protest against injustice (b. hooks, p. 83). But with respect to women's rights, the schism of male support has been to the degree that yet today women still only earn approximately 77 cents on the dollar of what men earn in terms of wages, and ascension to the highest office in the land is still met with tremendous controversy and opposition. A further insult to women is also reported in a recent study that found "…female candidates need good looks more than men" (The Associated Press, 10-31-08).

13

And tragically, there remains another serious gender issue to be discussed which is misogyny. It represents a most shameful and ongoing chapter in American society. Professor hooks addresses hatred of women as a multifaceted human rights problem with serious institutional and international implications. It retards the progress of a society in that it prevents harmonious gender relations thereby effecting the youth, the family, and other institutions which contribute to the betterment of a society. Again bell hooks speaks with praise for social progress when men work with women. She refers to them as comrades, and that "Feminists have recognized and supported the work of men who take responsibility for sexist oppression," and she uses their work with batterers as an example (Op.Cit., p. 82).

This brings me again to the issue of my support for feminism, for who better to understand the psyche and inner turmoil of a batterer than a recovered batterer. The sickness, or rather disease of self hatred is translated to a hate for others; and therefore is an explanation, in part, for the batterer who has lost the ability to reason and maintain self-control. The behavior then is rationalized by blaming the person who is the target of their insecurities. The target can be his wife, girlfriend, partner, siblings, and in many cases, his children. The tenets of feminism helped to save me from myself, and the beneficiaries have been my wife, children, and to a degree, other males and women in general.

Certainly conquering the disease of alcoholism and substance abuse and writing about it, is another critical link in the therapeutic catharsis of self transformation, (a term which we will become more familiar with in later chapters) with a hope for the future that others may benefit from my experiences; particularly because gender equity is necessary

14

for our social progress. But more so, it is depressing to witness, and then to realize that there is a dual personal tragedy associated with misogyny in that it takes away from the humanity of the perpetrator, as they attempt to destroy their victim. It is (misogyny), also an invisible product of class, as well as gender privilege, as the perpetrator(s) refuses to acknowledge its existence or any consequences for their behavior. Hate is rarely an attribute to be proud of in one's character; nor is it a trait that one generally brags about, unless of course they happen to be a member of one of America's many hate groups.

Given the fact that abusers of women, whether it is physical or emotional in the power and control matrix, cannot help themselves, or so it may seem, but to be abusive, for the invisible psychological nature of the disease is unrecognizable to them as it is in other addictions. This lack of recognition of the hate within oneself, and the strong desire to maintain the status quo, is a very interesting phenomenon, in that some women will even be complicit partners in the abuse of other women. They will use similar reasons that men use for acting on irrational impulses to control, demean, and destroy a woman who, in their view is not deemed as being "worthy" of being treated as an equal.

The victim/target must be destroyed, or at the very least, she must be made to submit (one of Carolyn Matthews' favorite phrases), and/or have her dignity destroyed. In this regard, I do find it troubling to observe women treating other women with callous disregard and disrespect as men have done to women for generations and even centuries. Therefore women do not only seek refuge from men, they also seek refuge from other women. The constant struggle for acceptance from one's own gender must be maddening to women that have worked hard to take care of a family, some of which are working outside the home which means they have an added responsibility of a second or third job.

15

And then the reward for their hard work is criticism, and/or ignoring their need for additional support and understanding by other women. Professor hooks also put this in the context of race where Black women are not part of the strategies or thinking that takes place to assist the progress of White women. Therefore when race is added to the social equation that gives rise to misogyny, a complicated problem is made that much more difficult to address. For example, East Indian politician, Jayanthi Natarajan, expressing her thoughts on the issue of race and gender, had this to say about this not so-unique Amreican phenomena. "She believes that in a showdown between race and gender," which essentially was the focal point of the 2008 Democratic presidential contest, "…that race is clearly the more compelling justification in the minds of most Americans…and that a heavy sexist bias emerged throughout the campaign" (H. Boyd, 2008, p. 114).

To put an end to this foolishness will require that men take an active role as advocates for feminism, as I have previously argued. And hooks correctly observes that, "Separatist ideology encourages us [women] to believe that women alone can make feminist revolution, [they] cannot. Since men are the primary agents maintaining and supporting sexism and sexist oppression, they can only be successfully eradicated if men are compelled to assume responsibility for transforming their consciousness and the consciousness of society as a whole" (p. 83) (underline mine). Then bell hooks adds this strategy which has led to the ostracism of some men by their peers. She states, "Men who advocate feminism as a movement to end sexist oppression must become more vocal and public in their opposition to sexism and sexist oppression [underline mine]. Until men share equal responsibility for struggling to end sexism, feminist movement will reflect the very sexist contradictions [that women] wish to eradicate" (p. 83).

16

Chapter One – Endnotes

Bailey, Holly (2008). "Do the 'Wright' Thing," in *Newsweek*, Vol. CLII, No. 17, p. 44.

Boyd, Herb (2008). "Obama and the Media," in *The Black Scholar*, Vol. 38, No. 4, Oakland, CA.

Diverse Magazine (2008). "Domestic Violence Facts," March 20, 2008.

hooks, bell (2000). *Feminist Theory: From Margin To Center*, 2nd Edition, South End Press, Cambridge, MA.

Ingraham, Laura (2008). "The Factor," Bill O'Reilly Show on *Fox* Television.

Koyana, Siphokazi (2002). "The Heart of the Matter: Motherhood and Marriage in the Autobiographies of Maya Angelou," in *The Black Scholar*, Vol. 32, No. 2, Robert Chrisman, Editor-in-chief.

Morris, Dick (2008). Sirius Patriot Radio Station. Conservative Talk Show.

Patterson, Orlando (2008). "The New Mainstream," in *Newsweek*, Nov. 10th. Vol. CLII, No. 19.

Reagan, Mike (2008). Sirius Patriot Radio, November 10, 2008.

Steinem, Gloria (2008). Governor Sarah Palin critic who once commented that the only thing Palin has in common with Senator Hillary Clinton is a chromosome. How sad when Steinem was at the forefront of the feminist movement to give women a voice and equal opportunity, the epitome of Sarah Palin's achievement in her home state of Alaska, and now throughout the nation. Steinem is listed in the American Heritage Dictionary as a feminist and the founding editor (1972) of *Ms. Magazine.*

CHAPTER TWO

Major Antebellum Political/Civil Right Initiatives

Section I: The Colonial Years

As we continue to sort through the major issues of race and gender as they relate to the political climate in America, there are historical considerations which must be taken into account. And as we begin to examine our past, it certainly will shed light on our present circumstances as well as our potential to be a more socially tolerant nation. Racism and misogyny did not just evolve in America as two separate ideologies of hate. They were transplanted from Europe along with a class structure where a system of separatism and privilege existed as the foundation of national commerce/mercantilism and oligarchy. Therefore, here in America, the Bacon Rebellion of 1676 led by English aristocrat, Nathaniel Bacon, was soon followed by the chattel enslavement of Blacks and an apartheid system of slave codes adopted by state after state as a means of exerting total control in the adoption of the "peculiar institution" (Kenneth Stampp, *Peculiar Institution*, 1956).

According to Hine et al., Bacon had "recently migrated to [the colony of] Virginia," and became embroiled in a conflict with the governor over Indian policy, "…and his followers were mainly White indentured servants, and former indentured servants who resented the control exercised by the tobacco planting elite over the colony's resources and government. That Bacon also appealed to Black slaves, to join his rebellion, indicates that poor White and Black people still had a chance to unite against the [so-called] *master class*" (p. 56). Bacon dies soon thereafter, but his rebellion signaled to the elite (upper class) that there was a real danger in grievances shared by lower class Blacks and Whites within the indentured system. Permanent

18

enslavement became the answer as it reinforced the inferiority of Blacks and moved Whites closer to each other in spite of their class differences; and so it is in America today. However as the thesis of this book reveals, the 2008 election cycle gave the impression that a unique Baconess coalition had once again emerged. But the poor and working classes, at odds with the upper class, today is far more complex than during the time of Bacon; yet the similarities of antebellum and post-bellum America as far as 2008 is concerned is worthy of our examination. Then the only other antebellum distinction is the one of gender which was of lesser importance than race and class, but nevertheless, it had to be dealt with because women could become quite cantankerous when they chose to interfere in the men's only political system.

Cokie Roberts, in her book *Founding Mothers*, describes the impact that White women had on the pre and post Revolutionary period, and antebellum as a whole. Women, then and now, if they so choose can exert an enormous amount of pressure on the males in society, while fulfilling their role as wife, mother and in some cases, girlfriend or "concubine." In this regard it is said that "pillow-talk" is an effective form of communication between couples, with or without the marital contract. The influence that one partner has on another has contributed to nation building, ending civilizations, and of course determining the policies of an American President. The following represent a few famous pairs in history with the first name being the most well known or dominant partner is of course debatable: Cleopatra and Mark Antony, John Smith and Hiawatha, Franklin and Eleanor Roosevelt, Ronald and Nancy Reagan, Bill and Hillary Clinton, Barrack and Michelle Obama, and Sarah and Todd Palin. No doubt the reader can recall others which would be an important exercise to demonstrate your grasp of the concept(s) of which I speak.

Returning now to the original point on journalist Roberts' book, she cites the following on the influence status and role of women in pre-Revolution America, "Almost all of the women who mothered and married the Founders were of the wealthier classes, and even if they had no formal education, they did know how to read and write [which of course could not be said of those women belonging to the lower class], and many of them, like Abigail Adams, read extensively, though they never went to school. [And Abigail herself] never got over the injustice of excluding girls from proper schools, and she advocated vociferously for women's education...[while many] of the marriages were true partnerships, the women had no legal rights. Under a system called 'couverture,' their husbands essentially owned women. They had some rights to inheritance...but in the context of the marriage itself they owned nothing not even their own jewelry" (p. 13). And while some involved themselves in the Revolution alongside their husbands, it was also clear that "Despite their lack of legal rights, many pre-Revolutionary women still ruled the roost" (p. 14).

With respect to the Revolution which was a conflicted challenge for the colonies in the struggle for justice and a tug-of-war of good vs. evil, the political hypocrisy was addressed by women insofar as their rights and slavery was concerned. Attempts at patronizing women and keeping them at bay to prevent them from dabbling in politics was proving to be an exercise in futility. As a matter-of-fact it was, on some levels, encouraged because it was they who did the shopping, so protests over the injustice of taxation was taken up by an organizational effort called the "Daughters of Liberty." But imbedded within a poem printed in 1768 in the *Pennsylvania Gazette* lay the seeds of the struggle that was at hand with the British, and the inconsistencies of justice insofar as slavery and women's rights were concerned. It stated, "Since the men from a party, on fear of a frown, are kept by a sugar-plumb, quietly down.

20

Supinely asleep, and deprived of their sight, <u>are stripped of their freedom, and robbed of their right</u>. If the Sons (so degenerate) the blessing despise, let the <u>Daughters of Liberty</u> nobly are" (C. Roberts, p. 38). [Underline mine.]

As women became more and more involved in the struggle for independence and moving beyond "their place," it was rightly observed by Roberts that, "No political campaign can succeed without propagandists. In modern times armies of public relations firms and media buyers spend millions to bring a candidate or a cause to the voters via television, direct mail, or the internet. In colonial times the pamphlet was the delivery system of choice, and one of the great pamphleteers of that time was a woman – Mercy Otis Warren" (p. 45). It was Mercy who underscored the legitimate role that women could play in politics and also the power of "pillow talk." She characterized it in one of her correspondences to a friend this way, "you see madam I disregard the opinion that women make but indifferent politicians…When the observations are just and honorary to the heart and character, I think it very immaterial <u>whether they flow from a female lip in the soft whispers of private friendship</u> [underline mine], or whether thundered in the Senate in the bolder language of the other sex" (p. 51). And according to Roberts, "Mercy's private friendships were with some of the most influential men in the land" (Ibid.). Here Roberts seems to suggest that Mercy "got around," and maybe was a colonial mistress of sorts.

Whatever the case, Mercy Warren was indeed an influential spokesperson for women's rights, and that she believed it was quite possible for a woman to raise respectful children while pursuing a professional career. And according to Roberts, "Mercy clearly saw herself as someone with a political role to play," and too, it was her brother who asked the profound question "Are not women born as free as men" (p. 49). Then to raise the precarious analogy to the "Peculiar Institution" he added, "Would it not be infamous to assert that the ladies are all slaves by nature" (Ibid.) [underline mine]. Then again it was another of Mercy's friends,

Catharine Macaulay, whose so-called scandalous behavior was talked about on both sides of the

Atlantic. She too was an ardent supporter of women's rights; and between the three of them,

Abigail Adams, Mercy Warren, and Catharine Macaulay, they maintained a constant

correspondence often discussing the political issue(s) of the day (pp. 47-54). Their connections

to men of that time period, e.g., John Adams, George Washington, Thomas Jefferson, Alexander

Hamilton, and Elbridge Gerry rivaled any noted political figures of today. And therefore their

influence was deeply connected (p. 46).

Inserted into this drama of female correspondence and influence on "War, politics and

independence" (p. 59) was the female poet and slave Phyllis Wheatley. It has been argued that

Ms. Wheatley was a proponent of "Providential Design," meaning that she believed as did many

White slave owners of that day that it was the Will and Providence of God which brought them

out of the "darkness" of Africa into the light of America, albeit as slaves. And in this view, as

she freely acknowledged, Wheatley would much rather be a slave in America than free in Africa.

Certainly the effect which slavery has on the mental psyche of the slave him/herself is an

important consideration as we attempt to understand the behavior of both, slave and slave owner

in terms of policy formulation. But it must also be noted that Wheatley was just a young child, 7

or 8 years of age, when she was "fresh off the boat" from the continent of Africa. Enslaved, and

then afforded an education by her slave masters, was a benevolent conscience salving act for a

gifted child. The boat, by the way, which she was "fresh off," as put by Roberts, was a slave

ship. And the crossing of the Middle Passage was one of the most cruelest experiences suffered

by any human beings.

To further emphasize the perverted interplay between master and slave, no matter how compassionate the slave master attempted to be in their paternalism, Thomas Jefferson drives this point home: "The whole commerce between master and slave is a perpetual exercise of the most boisterous passions, the most unremitting despotism on the one part, and degrading submissions on the other. Our children see this, and learn to imitate it; for man is an imitative animal. This quality is the germ of all education" (*Hegemony*, Matthews, p. 271). The eloquence of the author of our Declaration of Independence, and he himself a slave owner, Thomas Jefferson certainly should be considered an authority on slavery and hypocrisy. Certainly a child alone, that has just endured, or rather survived the hardship and horrors of the Middle Passage, must have experienced indescribable fear. It is natural, and would be expected, that Phyllis Wheatley, or any child for that matter, would cling with fondness to anyone that had plucked them out of that misery.

After attending a political rally in Boston held for George Washington, Wheatley became caught up in the political moment, and was inspired to pen a poem about the soon to be first President of the United States. She wrote, "Proceed, great chief, with virtue on thy side, Thy ev'ry action let the goddess guide. A crown, a mansion, and a throne that shine, With gold unfading, WASHINGTON! Be thine" (p. 57) Once again Ms. Wheatley demonstrates the psychologically challenged subservient nature of those enslaved, and their seemingly affinity to the slave owners. We must remember at the time of Macaulay, Warren, Adams, and Wheatley, the colonies were experiencing a century of slavery. All four could be described as modern day feminists, with the inclusion of the Black female slave, theirs is the epitome of the foundation of our American disparate socio-political structure and its institutions.

I believe this colonial scenario as far as bell hooks would be concerned, is the pernicious underpinning to the sexism and even misogyny of today. She effectively argues that "Being oppressed means the absence of choices" (p. 5). And choice, as the reader must know by now, has been a bellwether term, if not a rallying cry for feminists since the "bra burning" era beginning in the nineteen sixties. Interestingly enough White colonial women attempting to achieve respect, while Black slaves longed for their freedom, is not unlike the values that America has embraced as democratic principles throughout its history. These were the principles of freedoms and rights which Jefferson wrote about in the Declaration of Independence, and are the same values for which we fight international wars, and then strive to achieve equality and security at home.

Section II: The New Nation

The slave codes which were put in place to reinforce the inferior status of Blacks, and the perverted power of White supremacy, became the mantra for the Southern Tradition; it then ironically ushered in a new mantra of "change" which was effectively used by the 44th President of the United States that secured his place in history. While slavery specifically, and Blacks in general, were at the core of the requisite for change in the national direction, it was originally the Tenth Amendment of States Rights that precipitated the growing and lingering tension within the nation. And now with our first Black/African American (The Nomenclature Cultural distinction will be discussed in a subsequent chapter) President, the nation is said to have, at long last, resolved its divisive race problem. I am far from convinced of this assumption due to the remarkable data that demonstrates the existence of a race dilemma of great magnitude.

For example, our nation's schools are more segregated now than they were in 1954 when the Supreme Court ruled that "Separate is not Equal," in *Brown v. The Board of Education,*

24

Topeka, Kansas; thus destroying the Principle of American Apartheid – the 1896 *Plessy v. Ferguson* Supreme Court ruling. Also while Blacks are just 12% of the nation's population, they represent nearly 50% of those incarcerated in our nation's prisons and jails, job discrimination remains an ongoing problem, and college admissions for Blacks are disproportionally lower than those for Whites (for data and discussion on these and other troubling facts, see the *State of Black America 2007* published by the National Urban League with a foreword by then U.S. Senator Barack Obama). Other such disparate facts are: "White male felons are more likely to get probation than Black male felons…[and] as a percentage of arrests, there are three times as many Blacks that become prisoners…and seven times as many Black Americans in prison, as a percentage of the population compared to Whites…murder rate for Black males is over six times that of White males…and Blacks are five times more likely to be the victim of a murder than Whites" (pp. 36-37).

The Urban League further notes that the troubling thing about the murder statistics is that they paint a rather grim picture of Black-on-Black crime. This is an historical socio-political problem that calls into question the fairness of a society that gives predators within a group an advantage over law-abiding citizens, and the criminal mentality flourishes because of a lack of opportunity of legitimate means of economic-financial support. The very popular and now deceased mayor of Detroit, Coleman Young, once commented, that a man is less likely to turn to crime if he has a decent job, or an opportunity to secure one. The historical nature of these problems are related to American White supremacy, and linked to the policies resulting from the belief that one group is inferior to another. We also see this same problem in the manner in which women are treated, and the ever-present misogynist views held by many in the population.

25

To better understand this phenomena, Frantz Fanon in his book, *The Wretched of the Earth* effectively argues that an oppressed people will act out against each other in a violent way. They also have a tendency to passively submit to abuses perpetrated against them by the power structure, but will quickly strike out against members of their own group for little or no reason. Fanon termed this type of behavior and violence which is directed within the group as "collective auto-destruction." Also, Fanon notes that while the oppressed group members will display psychological behavior patterns of avoidance of any obstacles placed in their path by the dominant group, they will become extremely agitated and impatient with members of their own group to the extent of indifference or random killing (p. 54). Simply put, the theory holds, when we are made aware of oppressive situations we should not be surprised to also see concomitant psychological disorders among the oppressed which can vary from mild to severe depending upon the circumstances and/or situations. These disorders may manifest themselves to the degree which can defy rational logic; such as a woman's approach/avoidance, fear and/or hesitation to leave an abusive man. Or, a slave's tendency to adopt perverted behaviors of their White masters, or a Jews tendency to embrace the cruel madness of their Nazi tormentors, and Black-on-Black crime.

But in direct contrast to Fanon's scientific analysis on the predator-victim premise, and even the prolific theoretician Lawrence Shulman's work on the subject; the racially tinged and stereotypical view given of the violence attributed to Black males, to promote White indifference, came of course from a former aide of George W. Bush, the 43rd President of the United States. It was the conservative writer John Dilulio...who introduced the detrimental term of "Super-predator to describe these Black males." And by way of explanation, as noted by Black activist, author, and TV reporter Tavis Smiley, "To incite fear, those who advocate for harsher penalties for law violators have used the term [Super-predator] relentlessly, which in turn provides support for a flawed justice system" (2006, p. 50).

So therefore returning to the advent of this nation through the Declaration of Independence, and examining our Constitution which breathed life into our democracy, will help us to better understand our present dilemma of race and gender inequity, beginning as we have seen with the Trans-Atlantic slave trade. This Black Holocaust set into motion the series of actions and counteractions which pitted Black against White, and male against female in a struggle for economic survival as well as political recognition. For what is politics, but rather a means to control and distribute scarce resources with the power to determine who the primary recipients will be, and to what extent there will be an adherence to policy, law, and the United States Constitution. The fuss over promoting the general welfare and protecting this nation are to be examined in the context of trashing the 1781 Articles of Confederation which were powerless to provide the federal government with the power to govern.

The Revolutionary wartime individuals, some soon to become the Congressional leadership under the new Constitution, had choices to make; and the pernicious manner in which those decision were made and carried out are being felt today by those who had no voice at the table, i.e., Blacks, other minorities, and women. In drafting the Constitution they pondered, to a great extent, the means of taxation and representation until it became abundantly clear that the big elephant in the room which they could not ignore was slavery. The ensuing debate which became known as The Compromise of 1787 led to the final drafting of The United States Constitution. The Northern policymakers used the only leverage they had to convince the Southern contingent to agree to a compromise, which was their belief that the South would go to

27

great lengths to protect and continue their "Southern Tradition" of enslaving Blacks, and maintaining White supremacy which of course had many Northern sympathizers.

The "Compromise" consisted of three primary parts. First the North operated on the accurate assumption that the South wanted protection for its slave owners whose slaves ran away to the North. The South wanted assurances that in this case there would be no safe haven for the runaway(s), and when found they would be returned to their owner. Second, the North believed that the South had a strong wish to "replenish its supply" of slaves through the Trans-Atlantic slave trade. And finally the North believed that if the South were to be given ample time to "replenish its stock," they would compromise on the other points as well; and therefore sign off on the Constitution sections for representation and the levying of taxes. The South did indeed agree, with the stipulation that the Trans-Atlantic trade would continue for twenty years until 1808 when the legal importation of slaves would come to an end. Thus supposedly ending an ugly chapter in American society (see Antebellum Timeline).

The South did agree to the Constitutional Compromise. However there was a major embarrassing glitch in terminology and practice with the philosophical and moral acknowledgment of slavery as an institution, inconsistent with the Declaration of Independence, which hypocrisy could only be addressed by not mentioning the word slave or slavery in the original Constitution. The "founders" resorted to using language such as the following: for slaves and slavery the euphemism became "those who owed service," and those "bound to service" (Article I, Sect. 2, 8; Article IV, Sect. 2). Additionally the other major problem could not be fixed by changing terminology, the founders had to resort to determining that for the apportioning of taxes and representation they declared that Blacks were not whole human beings.

ANTEBELLUM TIMELINE

1619	17th Century	1776	1787	1808	1820	1860-61
First Blacks land in Virginia	Began U.S. slavery	Declaration of Independence Hypocrisy "All Men are Created Equal"	Constitutional Compromise 3/5ths of a man Black Inferiority and White Supremacy	Official end of Trans-Atlantic slave trade (No More importation of slaves from continent of Africa.)	Missouri Compromise No expansion of U.S. slavery into territories.	Southern states secede from Union. Eleven states total (CSA).

1850's Three Pernicious Laws/Move to Repeal Constitution Compromise

1850's	1854	1857	1850's	1858	1860
Fugitive slave law	Kansas-Nebraska Act repealed. Missouri Compromise	Dred Scott Supreme Court ruled - Chief Justice Taney - Scott is not a citizen.	Resume Trans-Atlantic slave trade debate.	Lincoln declares Blacks are inferior in debate with Stephen Douglas.	Lincoln elected President

April 12, 1861	1861-62	1863	1865	1868-70
Attack on Fort Sumpter – Civil War begins.	Congress passes Confiscation Acts.	Lincoln present Emancipation Proclamation. End slavery in states in rebellion.	Civil War ends. Lincoln assassinated. 13th Amendment – Constitution – ending slavery.	Citizenship and equal protection Black males voting rights.

POST-BELLUM
JIM CROW TIMELINE

1865 — Reconstruction Era
Civil War ends.
Jim Crow Era begins. Slave codes changed to Black codes.

1877
Hayes bargain ends Reconstruction

1896
Plessy v. Ferguson Supreme Court ruling

Separate but Equal
Confirms American apartheid.

1920
Women's voting rights. 19th Amendment to Constitution

1954
Brown v. Board of Education ending separate but equal.

2008
Senator Ted Kennedy proposed expansion of Civil Rights Act.

Civil War Amendments

1865 — 13th
Officially end slavery.

1868 — 14th
Granted citizenship and equal protection under law.

1870 — 15th
Granted voting rights to Black men.

1964
Civil Rights Act

1965
Voting Rights Act

1967
LBJ expanded Affirmative Action to include women.

30

In the original Constitution, Blacks had become, in the minds of all who signed it, an inferior people valued at three-fifths of a person.

Therefore it was written in the founding document of this land, for all to see, and for all who wished to believe that Blacks were an inferior people; the stain of being less than human as characterized by those who had also stated that "all men are created equal...and endowed by their creator with certain inalienable rights including among these are life, liberty and the pursuit of happiness. This is the ultimate in hypocrisy, and Thomas Jefferson was quoted to have said, that if there is a God, we will pay for what we have done. The power the founders had was supreme in that they held life and death of others in their hands; and they chose to place Blacks at risk for abuse, degrading acts, and all sorts of mayhem and mischief which has been perpetrated upon a people because the founders, for expediency sake, decided that one group was unworthy to share in the beauty of freedom, equality, and liberty that they demanded for themselves. And moreover, to compound the problem, women had no rights guaranteed in the Constitution, and Indians were mentioned as an afterthought as though something altogether separate was to decide their fate (see aforementioned cited Articles). It is not surprising then that given the institutionalization of inferiority of certain people, our nation has struggled with this dilemma for generations, and will do so for generations to come (The reference for this discussion is taken from B. Quarles, see end notes).

Section III: Feminist Movements (Antebellum)

In further examining women's rights and the issues which predominated feminist attention during the time of Antebellum, was not much different than what we have observed in the Colonial Period. However we would do a disservice to progressive activism if we did not discuss five of the most prolific feminist figures during the early to mid 1800's. Susan B.

Anthony is probably one of the most well known early feminist who took on the major challenge of championing women's suffrage. While other issues of the time, namely the Tenth Amendment to the Constitution (States Rights), and of course slavery, overshadowed women's voting rights, Susan B. Anthony would not be deterred. As an early proponent of suffrage, she was cut in the same mold as Mercy Warren and Catherine Macaulay, meaning that she was an educated outspoken advocate for women's rights. And at times her outspoken independence caused controversy as when she complained about the Fourteenth and Fifteenth Amendments to the Constitution which guaranteed rights to Blacks, particularly Black males that White women did not have at the time.

Two separate biographies of Anthony's works and achievements argues this very point by stating, "In 1872, Susan demanded that women be given the same civil and political rights that had been extended to Black males under the 14th and 15th Amendments. Thus, she led a group of women to the polls in Rochester, New York to test the right of women to vote [a full 47 years before women were to receive the franchise]. She was arrested two weeks later and while awaiting trial, she engaged in highly publicized lecture tours, and in March 1873, she tried to vote again in city elections. After being tried and convicted of violating the voting laws, Susan succeeded in her refusal to pay the fine. From then on she campaigned endlessly for a federal woman suffrage amendment through the National Woman Suffrage Association (1869-90), and the National American Woman Suffrage Association (1890-1906), and by lecturing throughout the country" (http://www.history.rochester.edu). However one of the most damning comments attributed to Anthony appeared in her writing which could be considered "…quite racist by today's standards, particularly those when she was angry that the Fifteenth Amendment wrote the word 'male' into the Constitution…permitting suffrage for freed men. She sometimes argued that educated White women would be better voters/citizens than 'ignorant' Black men or immigrant men. In the late 1860's she even portrayed the vote of freed men as threatening the safety of White women. [And her's and Elizabeth Cady Stanton's newspaper named *The Revolution* was financed by a noted racist] (http://womenshistory.about.com).

It is also important to note that the racist claims against Ms. Anthony must be measured not only by the time period in which she lived, but also by other pertinent facts about her life. For example, not only was her "first involvement in the world of reform was the Temperance Movement [to be discussed] ...When she gave her first public speech for the Daughters of Temperance in 1849, [November] in 1851 she went to Syracuse to attend a series of antislavery meetings...In 1854, she devoted herself to the antislavery movement from 1856 to the outbreak of the Civil War in 1861 [see Antebellum Timeline]" (Ibid.).

Some Susan B. Anthony's Accomplishments

- *Founded the National Woman's Suffrage Association in 1869 with lifelong friend Elizabeth Cady Stanton. Together they worked for women's suffrage for over 50 years [Stanton is the second feminist of the four that I previously mentioned].*
- *Published 'The Revolution' from 1868-1870, [with Elizabeth Cady Stanton], a weekly paper about the woman suffrage movement whose motto read, 'Men their rights and nothing more, women their rights and nothing less.*
- *First person arrested, put on trail and fined for voting on November 5, 1872. Unable to speak in her defense she refused to pay 'a dollar of your unjust penalty.'*
- *Wrote the Susan B. Anthony Amendment in 1878 which later became the 19th Amendment giving women the right to vote (1920).*
- *Helped found the National American Woman's Suffrage Association in 1890 which focused on a national amendment to secure women the vote. She served as president until 2900.*
- *Compiled and published 'The History of Woman Suffrage' (4 Volumes, 1881-1902 with Elizabeth Cady Stanton and Matilda Joslyn Gage.*
- *Founded the International Council of Women (1888) and the International Woman Suffrage Council (1904) which brought international attention to suffrage.*
- *An organization genius – her canvassing plan is still used today by grass root and political organizations [underline mine].*
- *Gave 75-100 speeches a year for 45 years, traveling throughout the United States by stagecoach [during Jim Crow Era – Blacks could not ride on stagecoaches with Whites], wagon, carriage and train [separate cars were made available for Blacks].*

33

- *Led the only non-violent revolution in our country's history – the 72 year struggle to win women the right to vote (http://www.1kwdpl.org).*

Susan B. Anthony was born in Adams, Massachusetts on February 15, 1820. She died March 13, 1906 without ever seeing her lifelong work of women's suffrage ever being enacted as law of the land by Constitutional Amendment (XIX Amendment, 1920). It is said that her last words made in public were "Failure is impossible" (Ibid.). This phrase became the rallying cry for the Suffrage Movement throughout the nation (Ibid.). These facts on Ms. Anthony are critical to our discussion because they demonstrate that there was a significant national effort in place battling for women's rights during the Antebellum and Post-Bellum Eras (see the timeline); but even with the buzz created by the feminist movement and the media exposure, women's issues were still overshadowed by the Abolitionist Movement, and the effort to achieve justice for Blacks via the Civil War Amendments. The step backwards for Blacks was the 1896 *Plessy v. Ferguson* Supreme Court Ruling confirming American Apartheid – Separate But Equal.

The second major initiative of this time period led by feminists was the Temperance Movement. This movement also provides an opportunity to discuss the third woman activist important to our discussion – Frances Elizabeth Caroline Willard. Ms. Willard was a popular and long serving president of the Woman's Christian Temperance Union (WCTU – 1879-1898). The "WCTU was organized by women who were concerned about the destructive power of alcohol and the problems it was causing their families and society…these activities are often referred to as the Woman's Crusades" (http://www.wctu.org). (See Women's Suffrage and Temperance Timeline.) Additionally, Ms. Willard, as long term president of the WCTU, oversaw an organization that had a major mission in stamping out alcohol abuse and places where it was sold because it was believed that these businesses were ruinous to the family. Also the Temperance Movement was "an issue that grew up in tandem with the Suffrage Movement

34

…in fact, many women who were involved in one issue were involved in the other. [And] Temperance had even greater respectability, as it was clearly more within the traditional women's sphere [where] home and family were regarded as the legitimate terrain ruled by women" (http://www.oldstatehouse.com). The mission of the Temperance Movement made it and its members a natural ally of the Suffrage Movement and Susan B. Anthony (see timeline) (Ibid.).

And from another supporting historical and somewhat different perspective, according to the *Universal World Encyclopedia*, "By 1834 the auxiliaries to the American Society for the Promotion of Temperance which was organized at Boston in 1826, numbered over 5,000 persons and included over one million pledges. In 1836 the society adopted a platform seeking to have abstinence enforced by law, and by the time of the Civil War many of the northern and western states had passed prohibition laws [thus demonstrating the power and influence of women when organized a like cause]. Although most of these laws were repealed after the [Civil] War, a revival of temperance agitation occurred with the founding of the Woman's Christian Temperance Union in 1874. [This represented] the first effective organization of church forces on a national scale [that brought] into existence or the formation of the Anti-Saloon League in 1894. By 1917 two-thirds of the states had adopted prohibition, and in 1919 the 18th Amendment to the Constitution initiated prohibition on a national scale. The obvious failure of the experiment led to its repeal in 1933" (p. 4861).

However this failure did not deter the work of the WCTU. From 1874 through 2008 the past/current presidents have all been women: in the WCGU website; 1874-1879 (Annie Turner Wittenmyer), 1879-1898 (Frances Willard), 1898-1914 (Lillian M. N. Stevens), 1914-1925 (Anna Adams Gordon), 1925-1933 (Ella Alexander Boole), 1933-1944 (Ida Belle Wise Smith),

WOMEN'S SUFFRAGE & TEMPERANCE TIMELINE

1849	1851	1868-70	1872	1878	1879	1881-1902
Susan Anthony first public speech for the Daughters of Temperance	Anthony attended series of antislavery meetings	Anthony and Elizabeth Cady Stanton published weekly paper *The Revolution*	Anthony demanded that women be given the same rights extended to Black males under $14^{th}/15^{th}$ Amendments	Wrote the Susan B. Anthony Amendment which later became the 19th Amendment granting women voting rights	The most famous member and second president of the WCTU was Frances Willard who served from 1879-1898 (her death)	Compiled and published *The History of Women Suffrage*

1888	1904	1920
Anthony organized International Council of Women	Anthony organized the International Women's Suffrage Alliance	19th Amendment to the U.S. Constitution ratified

36

1944-1953 (Mamie White Colvin), 1953-1959 (Agnes Dubbs Hays), 1959-1974 (Ruth Tibbits Tooze), 1974-1980 (Edith Kirkendall Stanley), 1980-1988 (Martha Greer Edgar), 1988-1996 (Rachel Catherine Bubar Kelly), 1996-2006 (Sarah Frances Ward), 2006-Present (Rita Kaye Wert). The length of terms vary either by policy or "burnout." But based on past performance Ms. Wert should serve at least until 2012.

The fourth woman that should receive much consideration is the American Indian Sacagawea (Sacajawea). Her role as a feminist was carved out in the new western territory as explorer and guide to the federally mandated Lewis and Clark expedition. President Thomas Jefferson, in 1803 from a congressional appropriation, authorized Meriwether Lewis and William Clark to lead an expedition and chart the area from the Mississippi River to the Pacific Ocean. Sacagawea served as one of the translators for the two year mission. She was born of the Shoshone people, and her infant son (a single mom who would not be appreciated by Ann Coulter) accompanied her on the expedition. As "the only woman on the trip [characteristically] she cooked, foraged for food, sewed, mended and cleaned the clothes for members of the expedition." According to historical records she was an enormous help on the trip and national recognition attests to her contributions (http://womenshistory.com).

And last, but certainly not least, is the fifth woman in our feminist profile during Antebellum, Araminta Ross, a.k.a., Harriet Tubman. Ms. Tubman was born into slavery in 1820 and died on March 10, 1913. She became affectionately known as the "Moses of her people" because she was responsible for shepherding hundreds of slaves to freedom. Over a ten-year period, her route over what became known as the "Underground Railroad," was legendary in that the risks she took without regards to her personal safety was done because of her passionate disdain for slavery and belief in her people. While a former slave, she was physically beaten and suffered a permanent head injury from a blow which led to a chronic case of narcolepsy (uncontrollable frequent sleep disorder).

Harriet's bravery and fearsome demeanor was shown on numerous occasions. At one time she pointed a gun at a slave's head who was displaying fear of the trip, and told him that she would rather see him dead than to remain a slave. "She once proudly pointed out to Frederick Douglass that she never lost a single passenger." And it was Douglass who commented "Excepting John Brown – of sacred memory – I know of no one who has willingly encountered more perils and hardships to serve our enslaved people than Harriet Tubman." And it was John Brown who made the comment about the person he called General Tubman that, "she is one of the bravest persons on this continent." During the Civil War she served as a cook, nurse, and a spy for the Union. Harriet has served as an inspiration to many Americans and in "1995 she was honored by the federal government with a commemorative postage stamp bearing her name and likeness" (Library of Congress and Africans in America website).

By no means is this short list of dynamic feminists exhaustive of all those we could have chosen. Each of these women have worked with other women who, in their own right, would have been an excellent choice for this discussion. However, given my purpose for the selection of those named above, meaning that regardless of gender, each brings a unique set of qualities and credentials to their hard work and commitment for the betterment of our nation. Also overcoming stereotypes and the unnecessary attacks on their character did not deter them from promoting the principles of justice and equality. For example I could just have easily replaced Harriet Tubman with Ida B. Wells-Barnett, who herself was born into slavery, and worked hard to eradicate lynching from our society in which the disproportionate vast majority of the victims were/are Black men, but White males and Black women were also murdered in this vicious manner. Or I could have written more extensively on Elizabeth Cady Stanton who collaborated with Susan Anthony on the publication of the newspaper *The Revolution*. She was in her own right a powerful feminist who was a tremendous force in helping women to seek justice in America. The choices I have made, however, will stand on their own merit.

Now that I have discussed the issue of the Feminist Movement, primarily during the Antebellum years, it will be tucked neatly between Antebellum and Post-Bellum as a demonstration of the difficulty that women have endured in America when issues of race are in competition. "Greatness sometimes comes in the form of sacrifice," so said Jeff Bridges playing the part of the President in seeking confirmation of a woman for the Vice-Presidency" in the film ("The Contender," 2000). Women have sacrificed much throughout our history, and it is totally unfair and even unjust for one group to be expected to place their receiving of equal rights on hold at the expense of their dignity, while America decides which group is more worthy. We have witnessed this phenomena of *hierarchical degradation* throughout our history, whether it is American Indians, Immigrants/Latinos/Haitians or others, e.g., gays/lesbians, women or Blacks. All groups should be able to equally drink from America's fountain of justice and fair play, and this is exactly what this book is about.

The Civil War Years

Prior to the 1860s, when the Civil War began, there were at least four separate events or legislative acts that directly influenced decisions which made the Civil War inevitable. While these events were taking shape, as we have seen, women's issues were ongoing. Therefore simultaneously, there were two or maybe three or four groups, if we count the American Indians and Latinos that had grievances with America which for years had gone unaddressed. But insofar as my thesis is concerned we will continue to deal solely with Black and gender issues.

However we must keep in mind that the degrading circumstances and policies of exploitation which made genocide of the American Indian a reality, while pushing Latinos from land they had occupied for hundreds of years, is the root cause of the thinking that has given rise to hegemony and misogyny in America.

It does not require much profundity of thought to conclude that there would eventually be a clash of wills in terms of a national power struggle. This conflict was in the making well before Lincoln made the pronouncement that this nation could not survive half slave and half free. Years before he came to that conclusion, he was a hardcore White supremacist who only changed his policies, while his ideological views on Blacks remained, over the years, fairly consistent. In his 1858 debate with Stephen Douglas, he ensured the nation that his thinking on the question of Black inferiority would be the foundation of the policies of his administration. The careful speech maker Lincoln was not unlike the politicians of today who will say most anything to get elected, including castigating a group of people, or betraying a trust. Why, one might ask, did the campaign for the 1860 Presidential election hinge on race and Lincoln. Given the temperament of the nation, after the Constitution was drafted and signed, there existed two separate thoughts on slavery; one was that it was a beneficial institution, and the other was that it is a dying plague on the nation.

The South felt quite comfortable that the Tenth Amendment of States Rights shielded it from any untoward actions by the government; and that any interference in how they managed their affairs would be met with a stern rebuke from the South's congressional contingent. There was a reason that the South became more emboldened in their position, it was because it had in 1850 been successful in passing the Fugitive Slave Law which was also called the Bloodhound Bill or Man Stealing Act. While it permitted the violation of habeas corpus in the arrest and detention of Blacks thought to have escaped from slavery, it also violated the Fourth Amendment against illegal search and seizure (B. Quarles, 1987). Furthermore the 1854 passage of the Kansas-Nebraska Act repealed the 1820 Missouri Compromise preventing the expansion of slavery. A third development took place in 1857 when the Dred Scott Decision was handed down by the United States Supreme Court in which Chief Justice Taney wrote the majority opinion.

Taney ruled that Dred Scott was not a citizen of the United States and that his master had the right to take him anywhere he chose in American Territory regardless of whether the state or territory was free or pro-slavery. An examination of the timelines and appendix demonstrates that aside from publications, the issue of women's rights did not have anywhere close to the same magnitude or degree of development or national support and interest as black issues.

The nation's attention was captured by the question of slavery, particularly when there happened to be a constitutional challenge to bring about the continued subjugation of a people. The importation of slaves via the Atlantic Slave Trade was made unconstitutional after 1808 by the 1787 Compromise (see Chapter Six). However, it was soon discovered that the domestic trade was not enough to meet the needs of the plantation owners, therefore they asked that the ban on importation to be lifted, which in essence would mean some sort of amendment to the Constitution. It is important to keep in mind that the pro-slavers had already won three major victories in the 1850's, and now this push for reopening the importation of slaves was nearly all the abolitionists could bear. And to make matters worse, while Lincoln was sounding increasingly like an advocate for slavery, he was, after all, a member of the Free Soil Party founded in 1848 which opposed the expansion and continuation of slavery. In 1854 it morphed into the Republican Party. So it should be clear as to why there were those who were confused by Lincoln's stand on Black inferiority, and why he was not believed no matter how passionate he pleaded for understanding, and no matter how many speeches he made on the subject (see Lincoln in the Appendix).

Soon after Lincoln's election in 1860, the Southern states began to secede. Eleven states in total left the Union in the fall of 1860 and spring of 1861, and the Confederate States of America was formed by the first five to secede. Of course there were no women's issue(s) that could come close in comparison to the tension, conflict, and then bloodshed of the Civil War. Certainly this is not to advocate violence as a means of having grievances heard, it is a statement of fact on America's history. While the contemporary stature of Lincoln has grown to almost mythical proportions, in reality he never really provided leadership in the struggle to end slavery. As a matter-of-fact he was once quoted to say that if he could keep the Union intact by supporting slavery he would do it, and on the other hand, if freeing the slaves would preserve the Union he would do that, meaning that the plight of slaves was not his primary interest or concern. The same was true with his great general Ulysses Grant, who commented that if the war was about slavery he would surrender his sword to the enemy (B. Quarles). Moreover, as far as the North was concerned, upon the passage of Lincoln's 1863 Conscription Act, riots broke out in New York and a number of Blacks were lynched in protest to the draft.

To demonstrate that Congress actually led in the struggle to end slavery, it passed two major pieces of legislation, the First and Second Confiscation Acts in 1861 and 1862 respectively. The first gave the military the authority to confiscate any property that was being used in the war effort, and if that property consisted of slaves, they should be set free. The second act was broader in scope in that it charged the military with the responsibility of determining that captured slaves would be labeled as war contraband, and in so doing they would be set free regardless of whether or not they were being used in the war effort. Additionally it authorized Lincoln to accept Blacks into the service; and then this crucial point was made, if they volunteered, their family (mother, wife, and children), would be set free. This was a landmark piece of legislation for two primary reasons: First, they were arming Blacks to kill Whites which was always viewed as a troublesome proposition as far back as the Revolutionary War. Second, they were acknowledging that Blacks were indeed human with families they cared about, a total contradiction to the principles of inferiority and the "three-fifths of a man compromise" as stipulated in the original draft of the Constitution (Quarles, 1987).

Lincoln was viewing these events as a direct challenge to his administration for the simple reason that his leadership on the war effort was being questioned. His previous responses insofar as dealing with the question of slavery was attempting to craft some type of arrangement whereby Blacks could be shipped out of the country. This in essence would be a deportation, and what crime had Blacks committed, they asked, to warrant such treatment; or would they be considered expatriated with a classical definition of "sending into exile or removing oneself from residence in one's native land, or to renounce one's allegiance to one's homeland" (American Heritage Dictionary)? None of these proposed solutions as their definitions showed would be suited to Lincoln's plan because acknowledging them as exiles with allegiance to America would be giving Blacks a status beyond what he wished them to have at that time. The other status would be one of emigrant, but it to had a classical definition of voluntary resettlement in another land (Ibid.).

There was absolutely nothing voluntary about Lincoln's plans for resettlement of Blacks in his out-of-sight, out-of-mind policy; because the delegation of free Blacks that visited him questioned his wisdom of making them leave their country of birth, for the only country they knew was the United States of America. Lincoln even approached the five border states that held slaves to craft an agreement to compensate them for freeing their slaves. These states did not secede and Lincoln wanted to ensure that their "property rights" were protected to keep them within the Union. Thus to demonstrate leadership Lincoln decided in the latter part of 1862 to issue the Emancipation Proclamation which would take effect on January 1, 1863. But the most historically inaccurate crucial clause in his edict which was reported to end slavery is that it did **NO** such thing at all because *it only freed slaves in the states which were in rebellion against the Union.*

Thus slavery in the border states of Missouri, Kentucky, West Virginia, Delaware, and Maryland remained untouched. If they so chose to hold slaves it was within their power to do so without interference from the federal government. Therefore Lincoln's philosophy of keeping the Union intact by freeing or not freeing the slaves became a reality. Interestingly though the slaves in Texas did not become aware of the edict until June 19, 1865. This is the date, "Juneteenth," that many Blacks today celebrate as the end of slavery because it also comes after the official end of the Civil War on April 9, 1865 when Lee surrendered to Grant at Appomattox. And "Juneteenth," with the funny sounding name, came a full two and one-half years after the Emancipation Proclamation was issued on January 1, 1863, with Texas a Confederate slave state impacted by the edict.

So much has been written and discussed about this time in our nation's history with very little, or anything at all, being stated or shown as a comparison to the feminist or women's rights movement. Further examination of the crucial dates and timelines, and the appendix, will show that the omission of facts, and the perpetuation of myths, contributes to our inability to accurately assess the significance of one movement when compared to the other. And when those who are in position of power and authority choose to perpetuate such nonsense as Lincoln freeing the slaves or rather ending slavery, and extolling him as the "Great Emancipator," then it does elevate one cause over another. The question then can be asked: What president does the women's movement have to champion their cause that would be of the stature of Lincoln. In the final analysis, even if all that was reported of him were true, our dilemma would remain the same in attempting to bring clarity and recognition to a nagging problem of historical gender inequity. But our task is made somewhat easier when we can demonstrate that the disparities are not insurmountable, and therefore the needs of one group does not necessarily have to be a priority over those of the other group.

Addressing myths will help each group to better understand the gravity of the challenges that lie before us. For example, it is incredible but true that a significant number of people still believe that Lincoln ended slavery, when in actuality it was the Thirteenth Amendment to the Constitution that accomplished that goal, which beforehand was articulated in the 1776 Declaration of Independence; nearly a full century after White Europeans declared life, liberty, and the pursuit of happiness to be a God-given virtue, but reserved only for themselves. The Civil War Amendments, and Post-Bellum policy and issues, will lead into our next chapter discussions. This will enable us to once again contrast truth with fiction, and bring into focus the difficulty that groups have in presenting their case for having their grievances heard.

Chapter Two – Endnotes

Bridges, Jeff (2000). "The Contender." Motion Picture. Millennium Studios. DreamWorks Distributors, CA

Fanon, Frantz (1963). *The Wretched Of The Earth*, Grove Press, Inc. NY.

Hine, Darlene Clark, William C. Hine, and Stanley Harrold (2009). *African Americans: A Concise History*, Third Edition. Prentice Hall Publishers, New Jersey.

hooks, bell (2000). *Feminist Theory: From Margin To Center,* 2nd Edition. South End Press, Cambridge, MA.

Matthews, Gerald E. (1995). A *Declaration Of Cultural Independence For Black Americans*, U.B. and U.S. Communications Systems, Hampton, VA.

Matthews, Gerald E. (2004). *Hegemony: America's Historical Link To International Racism.* Thomson Custom Publishers (Cengage), Mason, Ohio.

Matthews, Gerald E. (2007). *Evangelism Or Corruption: The Politics Of Christian Fundamentalism.* Thomson Custom Publishers (Cengage), Mason, Ohio.

National Urban League (2007). *The State Of Black America*, The Beckham Publishing Group, Silver Spring, MD.

Quarles, Benjamin (1987). *The Negro In The Making Of America*, 3rd Edition, McMillan Publishing Co., NY.

Roberts, Cokie (2005). *Founding Mothers: The Women Who Raised Our Nation*, Harper Collins Books, NY.

Smiley, Tavis (2006). *The Covenant*, Third World Press, Chicago, Illinois.

Stampp, Kenneth (1956). *The Peculiar Institution*, Vintage Books, NY.

Universal World Encyclopedia, Consolidated Book Publishers, Chicago, Illinois.

Websites:
http://womenshistory.about.com

http://www.1kwdpl.org

http://www.history.rochester.edu

http://www.wctu.org

http://www.womenshistory.com

CHAPTER THREE

Post-Bellum Historical and Contemporary Initiatives and Trends on Race and Gender

Section I: Trends In Abolition: An Overview

Heretofore I have not dedicated much time to the discussion of the Abolitionist

Movement other than to mention it within the previous chapter on Antebellum. Of

course the significance of the abolitionists requires more attention than a line, here and

there, particularly when there was a broad base collaborative coalition of like-minded

individuals who not only pushed for an end to slavery, but who also wanted Blacks to

have citizenship rights. The coalition, as previously mentioned, consisted of Black and

White activists with strong representation from feminists with a dual goal of women

suffrage. But the women, it seems, were perfectly willing to subordinate themselves to

the established leadership of the abolitionists such as William Lloyd Garrison. Historian

James Stewart asserts as much by offering this observation, "Within the Garrisonian wing

of the [abolitionist] movement, female abolitionists became leaders of the nation's first

independent feminist movement, instrumental in organizing the 1848 Seneca Falls

Convention [see timelines in previous chapter]" (website). There was however, a schism

within the movement itself, where Whites were often accused of racism, not unlike

today's Democratic Party where former President Bill Clinton had to, unjustly I might

add, defend himself against charges of racism leveled at him by Obama supporters, both

Black and White. The charges of racism in this context were used as a strategic ploy to gain a racial advantage over a strong adversary. In the contemporary sense, the initial

adversary to Obama was Senator Hillary Clinton.

Senator Clinton, before she became Madam Secretary, as a feminist herself, is

someone who has worked within the Civil Rights Movement's fight against racism in

America, therefore the historical analogy should be clear. For example, Stewart

continues by offering this similar view, "African American activists of the past often

complained …of the racist and patronizing behavior of White abolitionists. [Although]

Whites supported independently conducted crusades by African Americans to outlaw

segregation and improve education during the 1840's and 1850's. Especially after the

passage of the 1850 Fugitive Slave Law, White abolitionists also protected African

Americans who were threatened with capture as escapees from bondage, although Blacks

themselves largely managed the Underground Railroad" (Ibid.). The Abolitionist

Movement, with its well developed organizational structure, was mostly responsible for

alerting its allies and disseminating information on the mood of the nation and needs of

the group. For instance, Garrison, who was White, was the publisher of The Liberator

paper as was Elijah P. Lovejoy also a publisher, but who was killed by pro-slavers

because of his abolitionist publications. Then there was Frederick Douglass and Martin

Delaney, both Black abolitionists who published *The North Star*.

To be certain there were a number of publications that either supported the White

supremacist ideology, or created stereotypes of Blacks through faulty science; such was

the case of Charles Colcock Jones who wrote, *Suggestions on the Religious Instruction of*

the Negroes in the Southern States. This book was published by Presbyterians who were

conflicted on the question of slavery because they also supported a school in Troy, New

48

York which provided education for Black children and also was a meeting place for abolitionists.

Charles Jones publication offered a set of prescriptive suggestions on appropriate ministerial conduct for those pastoring to slaves, he advised:

a) missionaries to ignore the civil condition of slaves including squalor, beating, or ripping families apart -

b) missionaries were not to listen to any complaints against masters or overseers -

c) pastors were to preach against every vice and evil they even thought slaves had -

d) pastors were to advocate for the discharge of every duty, to work hard (put in the context of Nazism as they extolled the Jews they soon were to murder with a sign over the entrance to the Auschwitz concentration camp "albeit mach frei" or work will set you free) -

e) pastors were to support peace and order in the society -

f) pastors were to ensure that slaves would give respect and obedience to all those whom God in His providence has placed in authority over them -

g) religion, in short, should underwrite the status quo and therefore support the Southern Tradition (B. Quarles, 1987).

And there was Josiah Nott whose initial work in 1845 entitled *Two Lectures on the Natural History of the Caucasian and Negro Races* provided ridiculous foundations and explanations on the diseases coined by Samuel Cartwright as common to Blacks such as drapetomania, rascality (carelessness), and dyesthesia (a disease of inadequate breathing), and the first one listed defined as the insane desire to run away (J. Asim, 2007, pp. 50-54). Imagine a time in our history when people actually believed it to be insane for a Black person to attempt to escape from being enslaved. Now imagine a time when people actually believed Blacks to be inferior to Whites; and now imagine that time to be in the 21st century. These aforementioned diseases according to Nott were from the

49

science of "niggerology." Some contemporary publications are no different in spreading

the disease of hate and fear and can be purchased through any number of hate websites.

But papers and newsletters to counter this nonsense through modern day publications

and/or organizations such as the Southern Poverty Law Center, The Rainbow Coalition,

The International Feminist Journal of Politics, The NAACP, and The National Urban

League, to name a few, provide valuable educational and advocacy resource centers such

as did the Antebellum and Post-Bellum Liberator and North Star. As we move into the

Post-Bellum era, another very important instrument of the abolitionists was the one of

religion; but quite unlike the instruction provided by Chuck Jones, Black and White

pastors and priests, both men and women, displayed in Post-Bellum the nobility of their

calling by risking their prestige, and in some cases their life, by using the scripture to

uplift their congregations/society while the majority clamored to maintain the status quo.

Even today, the segregation and discriminatory practices of the past are still quite

evident; but mostly so on Sundays when Black and White Americans move in opposite

directions to worship in segregated churches, synagogues, mosques, and temples, and

Black unemployment remains consistently nearly twice that of Whites.

Section II: Examining Foundational Initiatives

As mentioned in the previous section there are organizations which provided the

foundation for the Abolitionist Movement. One such organization was the American

Anti-Slavery Society. It was formed in 1817 and included a diverse membership in

terms of race, religion, and gender. While the official end of slavery was in 1865 with

the passage of the Thirteenth Constitutional Amendment, the organization did not

disband until the 1870 passage of the Fifteenth Amendment to the Constitution that gave

Black men the right to vote. While women fought gallantly for the rights of men, the return of this noble gesture was a longtime coming with respect to women's equality. Asante and Mattson argues that, "When the final epic of the Black American people is written, the role of women in the struggle for equality, dignity, and honor will be seen as the centerpiece of the drama. [Furthermore they] were never content to watch the battles from the sidelines, women have placed themselves in the thick of every contest for human rights ever fought on American [and I might add foreign] soil" (1991, p. 69). Asante and Mattson adds this stirring tribute to women, "Open the pages of any book on the African American experience and the names of women leap forward with clarity and definition: Sojourner Truth, Charlotte Forten Grimke, Charity Still, Cornelia Loney, Ann Maria Weems, Leah Green, Frances Hilliard, Maria Jane Houston, Elizabeth Banks, Laura Lewis, Ellen Craft, Mary Shadd Cory, Desia Mills, Mary Cooper, Lydia Ann Johns, and thousands others who campaigned actively against slavery and oppression by their own individual acts of courage in preparing the way for others" (Ibid.).

This list of dynamic women certainly extends through the present modern day period, and includes the two women who occupy a chapter in this book. Former U.S. Senator Clinton and Governor Palin are feminist role models who have dared to pierce the proverbial glass ceiling, while doing the unthinkable, challenging men for the right to do so. For example it was in 1868 that Blacks, by the Fourteenth Amendment to the Constitution, were given full citizenship rights, due process of law, and equal protection of the laws of our nation, but sadly, yet today, women are fighting stereotypes and oppression which impede their inclusion of rights that men take for granted. For example, it would be almost unthinkable for a man to find it necessary to defend his right

51

to have dominion over his body along with our legendary protection of our means for full sexual fulfillment and to procreate, Viagra, etc.; however we have absolutely no hesitation at all dictating to women what they can and cannot do with their body organs that serve almost an identical purpose. Additionally, they must justify why they would desire to spend some time away from their children, and family, while pursuing a non-professional or professional career; or even working in a part-time job to care for their families (the pursuits are essentially the same), while men, on the other hand, it seems, have an expectation to be away from home as frequent as they choose.

These ridiculous double standards began hundreds of years ago, and many are imbedded in our antiquated belief system in which God traditionally has been the scapegoat for bigotry and injustice (*Evangelism or Corruption*, 2007). History teaches us that no matter what the religion, we always can find solace in certain passages that gives rise to a justification, in which doing harm to others can be excused, or even done so with impunity. No better example of this of course are the hundreds of years of slavery. However, after passage of the Civil War Amendments (13th, 14th, and 15th, see Chapter Six), and/or the Reconstruction Era, we, as a nation began attempts at the healing process of the disease of hate; but somewhere along the line, no matter what the ethnicity or religion, women were left behind.

And with singular respect to Black women, and the courage and challenges unique to them as they laid their portions of the building blocks for the future, Asante and Mattson offers this compelling case, "Women have contributed to every scene of the African American drama. From the very beginning when the slave ships left the shores of Africa, women demonstrated immense courage in the face of the most brutal and

52

callous rage. When they could no longer take the abuse, some threw their children to the sea; others leaped to the sharks themselves. On board the ships, women led in the comforting of the sick, the care for the dying, and the affection for the parentless. Most of all, they saw visions, gave hope, and dreamed dreams which kept people alive" (p. 69).

But it was also faith, however, that maintained the visions and stoked the fires of hope for the future. As an expression of faith, the American Black Church with its historical ties to the continent of Africa became, out of necessity, what could be characterized as the contemporary political church such as Trinity United in Chicago formerly pastored by the Reverend Dr. Jeremiah Wright. As I have previously reported in my other works, it is written in the Scriptures "that which is highly esteemed among men is an abomination in the sight of God" (Luke 16:15), and that the "improvement of man, and the situation in which man lives, does not come from outside man, i.e., through religious or political systems, but from within, where the Kingdom of God is" (Luke 17:21).

As servants of God's will, it is, at the very minimum, our obligation to ensure that His message of faith and deliverance is not co-opted for secular motives and gains. As noted by Eric Voehringer, "Gods actions are the reason for the message of the church" (1967, p. 18). With this being the case, we should realize and understand God's Word as written in Ezekiel 22:29 as a sign of our obedience. He says, "The people of the land have used oppression and exercised robbery, and have vexed the poor and needy: yea, they have oppressed the stranger wrongfully."

These uplifting words of wisdom are truly significant when measured in the context and backdrop of the immediate post slavery era known as the Reconstruction.

53

Certainly the moral and legal violations that occurred during slavery, and carried forward in post slavery America (Post-Bellum), are the very reason that the progressive Congress took strident actions to remedy the cancer of oppression and hate in America. Not only were the Civil War Amendments passed, but the Freedman's Bureau set landmark records in distributing food, opening schools, and educating thousands of former Black slaves, and Whites too. Also hospitals were established, and labor rights and fair wages were confirmed through a mediating agency quite similar to the 1935 National Labor Relations Board. Additionally, former slaves became members of state legislatures, and were active in drafting new state constitutions to confirm and ratify the Civil War Amendments. All of these landmark gains came about, in part, because there were those whose Judeo-Christian beliefs elevated them above the bias and baseness of White supremacy, but unfortunately did nothing to remedy gender disparity. "The numerous founding's of independent anti-slavery free churches" do confirm the former statement, but yields nothing to salvage the latter (J. Stewart).

Mahatma Gandhi, probably next to Jesus, was the holiest man to live, had this to say about race hatred and oppression, "In the secret [places] of my heart I am in perpetual quarrel with God that he should allow such things to go on" (in Matthews, *Journey Towards Nationalism*, p. 68). Similar types of sermons are preached every Sunday in many Black institutions of faith throughout America. One such church, as previously stated, is Trinity United in Chicago under the former pastorship of Reverend Dr. Jeremiah Wright, and a Mosque also in Chicago under the leadership of Minister Louis Farrakhan. A White minister in Chicago, Reverend Pfleger also is a devout opponent of any type of oppression. These three individuals, men of God, are more controversial today than they have been in the past, except maybe Minister Farrakhan, simply because there are those divisive elements in our society who have made their relationship to President Obama (The One), something negative. And to make matters worse, the President has repudiated these long term friendships and mentor-mentee relationships.

When these types of career decisions of denial occur, it does shed light on character, but more so, it speaks to the insidiousness of racism and misogyny when arrogance and ambition clouds decency, and good judgment is swayed by political agendas and convenient self indulgent allegiances. These denials in the recognition of friendship, and support, is remindful of Peter in the *New Testament* who denied knowing Jesus because of secular politics and fear. Peter in essence made a personal choice. However, no matter what the reason, party, or religion, "justice is indivisible," as Reverend Dr. Martin Luther King so eloquently stated. "Injustice anywhere, is a threat to justice everywhere." And Dr. King was consistent in his support for gay and lesbian rights, justice for women, as well as justice for Black Americans. What people have refused to understand about Reverend's Wright, Jackson, Pfleger, and Minister Farrakhan is that as men of God, such as King and Gandhi, they will not adjust their messages of justice to conform to political agendas, or the political season, or environment. And much to the chagrin of politicians, and some of their constituents and inner-circle advisors, these men of God will just not play ball. Indeed, this was the same response by the Pharisees in their indictment of Jesus – "Why won't he play ball??"

With respect to additional trends and initiatives, another institution must be examined which had, and continues to have, a significant bearing on progressive reform and legislation. The United States Supreme Court, particularly at the end of

Reconstruction, brought on by the Hayes Bargain (see Chapter Six), which removed the troops from the South, began deciding Post-Bellum cases by applying Four Basic Principles which worked in the interests of the Southern tradition of White Supremacy (B. Quarles). Because of the continued importance of these principles, I will examine them at length. First, according to Quarles, the Court decreed that the Civil War Amendments applied only to the actions that are taken by the states. And that the Amendments should not be interpreted to have any bearing at all on private parties or individuals. But if an individual, group or organization is acting on behalf of the state then the Amendments will apply.

The significance of this principle insofar as the Southern states were concerned, is that organizations such as the Ku Klux Klan (KKK) were free to carry out their campaign of fear and retribution against the former slaves. And many members of the Klan were also public officials, but frequently they conducted their reign of terror within the auspice of their official post, such as those who murdered Chaney, Goodman, and Schwerner in Mississippi during the Civil Rights Era. It was well known who the Klan members were/are, e.g., Senator Byrd, a democrat from Virginia was a well known Klansman until he repudiated his membership during the Civil Rights Era. There were many instances such as this, when a person/group filed suit for violation of their constitutional rights; if it could not be shown/proven that the state was responsible, the claim would not be upheld, even though everyone might be fully cognizant of the ties between the state, and/or group/person/organization in question.

The Second Principle is that if a "state law was not plainly discriminatory, the court would not attempt to ascertain whether it was being applied" uniformly to Black and White folks alike (Ibid.) This principle is designed to provide a jurist with wide latitude to rule against a claim of discrimination because the bar of proof is set so high. But not just in terms of Black and White, the same could be held true for male and female. The language of "plainly discriminatory" makes a mockery of justice in that it places the courts on the side of individuals with malice, and with the intent and purpose to maintain the status quo of "closed door" policies. In essence, it means that the state will provide opportunities to whomever they choose, whenever they choose, and that the 14th Amendment to the Constitution is only applicable as they see fit, thereby "pulling the teeth," so to speak, from the amendment. This made it necessary to adopt additional Civil Rights legislation, including Title IX that prevented discrimination of women in collegiate athletics in their ability to receive equal opportunity, e.g., scholarships on par with men. "Title IX of the Educational Amendments of 1972 is the landmark legislation that bans sex discrimination in schools, whether it be in academics or athletics. It states: 'No person in the U.S. shall, on the basis of sex, be excluded from participation in, or denied the benefits of, or be subjected to discrimination under any educational program or activity receiving federal aid.' In other words... the focus is on the necessity for women to have equal opportunities as men on a whole, not on an individual basis." [Say for example, to participate in wrestling or football is not the focus of Title IX.] (Title IX website.)

The Third Principle is one of "holding the state's police power paramount, and therefore more important than the rights given to the individual under the Fourteenth Amendment. The court obligingly found that state 'Jim Crow' laws (see endnotes) were a valid exercise of the power to protect the public health, safety, or morals, [and

57

therefore], of necessity, they had to be broad" (Ibid.). Here again the court was not only bending over backwards to protect its bigotry, it was demonstrating that it had no intention of complying with rulings that were designed to disrupt the "Southern Tradition." And who of course could complain, for after all the court was only protecting the citizens, albeit with draconian laws, with White women as much a target in the "Jim Crow Laws" as were Black men (see endnotes). Furthermore the Fourth Amendment on illegal search and seizure became less scrutinized by the court if the authorities could show "probable cause" in their detention, arrest, and/or entering a dwelling or automobile. As a matter-of-fact, in previous contemporary rulings, the court has denied some claims while upholding others who filed suit stating their rights were violated under the Fourth and Fourteenth Amendment. The Fourth Amendment "finds its roots in English legal doctrine …The house of everyone is to him as his castle and fortress, as well for his defense against injury and violence, and as for his repose" (http://en.wikipedia.org/wiki/Fourth Amendment).

A brief word on the history of the Fourth Amendment will help us to understand its contemporary application. "William Cuddihy in his dissertation entitled the '*The Fourth Amendment: Origins and Original Meaning'* claims there existed a colonial epidemic of general searches …up until the 1760s a man's house was even less of a legal castle in America than in England as the authorities possessed almost unlimited power and little oversight" (Ibid.). So under the protection of a limited general warrant, the English government ran roughshod over the colonies. Therefore, "Seeing the danger general warrants presented, the Virginia Declaration of Rights which explicitly forbid the use of general warrants. This prohibition became the precedent for the Fourth

58

Amendment" (Ibid.). The Fourth Amendment and its "Reasonable Expectation of Privacy" had two parts upheld in a 1967 *Katz v. United States* Supreme Court ruling. Justice Harland in a concurring opinion wrote, "…as the definition of a *search* for Fourth Amendment purposes: (1) governmental action must contravene an individual's actual, subject expectation of privacy; (2) and that expectation of privacy must be reasonable, in the sense that society in general would recognize it as such" (Ibid.).

To demonstrate how the Amendment has been applied, I will provide two examples, one in which the court denied an individual's claim under the Fourth Amendment, and another where their claim was upheld. First, under a "stop and frisk" police action (see again the Third Principle) "…in certain circumstances, authorities are permitted to conduct a *limitless warrantless* search on a level of suspicion less than probable cause. In *Terry v. Ohio* 392 U.S.1 (1968), the Supreme Court decided that when a policeman 'observes unusual conduct' that leads him to reasonably believe 'that criminal activity may be afoot' and that the suspicious person has a weapon and is presently dangerous to the policeman or others, he may conduct a 'pat-down search' (or 'frisk'), to determine whether the person is in fact carrying a weapon. To conduct a frisk, the policeman must be able to point to specific and articulable facts which, taken together with rational inferences from those facts, reasonably warrant his actions. A vague hunch will not do" (Ibid.).

This ruling places an enormous amount of power in the hands of the police, and we should be fully aware of the fact that "hunches" in many instances are all that some police officers have that will prompt them to stop Black or other minority citizens. It is this very "hunch principle" that has given rise to "Driving While Black" (see *Journey*

Towards Nationalism, Michael McMorris, Matthews, editor). The police have been exposed time and again as abusers of the power of "stop and frisk" and "seizures." For example, rulings upholding the Fourth Amendment were in 1914, 1920, 1939, 1949, and 1961. The Fourteenth Amendment came into play in the 1961 ruling.

The arguments and court cases are as follows: "The court adopted the exclusionary rule in *Weeks v. United States*, 232 U.S. 383 (1914), prior to which all evidence, no matter how seized, could be admitted in court. Additionally, in *Silverthorne Lumber Co. v. United States*, 251 U.S. 385 (1920) and *Nardone v. United States*, 308 U.S. 338 (1939), the court ruled that tips resulting from illegally obtained evidence are also inadmissible in trials *as fruit of the poisonous tree*. (The rule serves primarily to deter police officers from willfully violating a suspect's Fourth Amendment rights). The rationale behind the Exclusionary Rule is that if the police know evidence obtained in violation of the Fourth Amendment cannot be used to convict someone of a crime they will not violate it [but we do know otherwise]. In delivering the opinion of the court, Justice Frankfurter, in *Wolf v. Colorado*, 338 U.S. 25 (1949), rejected incorporation of the Fourth Amendment by way of the Fourteenth Amendment. Later, in *Mapp v. Ohio*, 367 U.S. 643 (1961), the Supreme Court explicitly overruled *Wolf* and made the Fourth Amendment (including the Exclusionary Rule) applicable in state proceedings as an essential part of criminal procedure" (Ibid.).

This leads us now to the Fourth Principle which is the one that had, and still has, far-reaching implications. It held that the "Court favored the White southerner in its ruling that there was a substantial difference between 'race discrimination' and 'race distinction,' the latter not being contrary to the Constitution" (Ibid.). Two major 19th

Century Post-Bellum rulings provide cogent examples of the perniciousness of this principle. The Civil Rights Act of 1875 which provided Blacks equal access to accommodations, hotels, etc., was struck down in 1883. Then there was the famous 1896 *Plessy v. Ferguson* ruling which affirmed separate but equal as universal law in America. Plessy sought redress to ride in the same railway cars as Whites. His claim was denied by the fourth principle of race discrimination v. race distinction. The law of separate but equal established American Apartheid which stood for 58 years (over two generations] until the Supreme Court overturned that ruling in *Brown v. Board of Education*, Topeka, Kansas.

The court ruled in Brown that separate was not equal, and that whatever White Americans received, Blacks and other minorities, including men and women, were entitled to exactly the same goods, services, and/or privilege(s). Unfortunately an incredible amount of damage had already been done by virtue of the length of time in which Apartheid was the law of the land. And unfortunately in many cases, particularly with our nation's schools, separate but equal still prevails. Our schools are more segregated today than they were at the ruling of *Brown*. Additionally, women in terms of pay, receive only approximately seventy seven cents ($.77) on the dollar of what men earn in today's job market. There is no equality in the schools, nor in the job market. These are two primary institutions which help to determine the value and worth of individuals in their ability to compete on a fair and level playing field. Thus the playing field is not fair – not is it level. And over the years only "lip service" has been given to remedying the disparity in gender equality. And the level of hate and its outcomes only intensifies.

Section III: Anti-Lynching Campaign and Jim Crow

At the turn of the twentieth-century a central figure emerged to spearhead another struggle against the increasing scourge of lynching, Ida B. Wells-Barnett. Ms. Barnett assumed the responsibility as editor of a Memphis, Tennessee newspaper – *The Free Speech* just prior to the *Plessy v. Ferguson* Supreme Court ruling in 1896. She was appalled by the brutality and frequency of lynchings of Blacks. Wells-Barnett "began to lead an energetic campaign" against it. It was 1895 in which she published her "…first pamphlet against lynching, *The Red Record*. Several additional pamphlets were written by Barnett and distributed widely in America and Europe" (Asante and Mattson, pp. 70-71).

As I reported in my *E Pluribus Unum: Justice, Liberty and Terror* text, one startling report on lynchings had this to say: "Lynchings were no longer unusual or shocking events that deviated from the norm [as shown in the latter part of the nineteenth-century and stretching beyond and throughout the twentieth-century]. Approximately 4,742 individuals were lynched between 1882 and 1968; of the victims, 3,445 or 73 percent were Black. [And] during the heyday of lynching, between 1889 and 1918, 3,224 individuals were lynched, of whom 2,522 or 78 percent were Black" (R. Perloff, 2001). Another report confirms the insidiousness of the problem by adding, "Lynching had become common in the South by the 1890s. Between 1889 and 1932, 3,745 people were lynched in the United States. An average of two to three people were lynched every week for thirty years. Most lynchings happened in the south, and Black men were usually the victims" (Hine, et al., 2009, p. 327). And one of the most fairly recent and well publicized case of lynching took place in the 1990s in Jasper, Texas when

James Byrd, a Black man was dragged to death, and his body hanged and brutalized by three members of a White hate group.

For the purpose of comparison please recall the data on the murder of young women in our nation as a result of misogyny. "An estimated 1.3 million women are victims of physical assault by an intimate partner each year ...and 86% of abuse victims are at the hands of a boyfriend. Females who are 20-24 years of age are at the greatest risk for intimate partner violence and on average, more than *three women are murdered by their husbands or boyfriends in this country every day*. In 2000, 1,247 women were killed by an intimate partner" while 440 men suffered the same fate. Therefore women are far more likely to be killed by a significant other than are men (*Diverse*, 2008, pp. 14-15). Hate and its companion of violence are common occurrences in our nation. And once again on the matter of race, the Southern Poverty Law Center, an anti racism and anti hate education and law firm founded by a White man Morris Dees reported that "...on the larger picture of racism in the United States, the center points to a 40% rise in hate groups in the last seven years [from 2000 to 2007] ...largely driven by anti-immigrant furor aimed at Latinos" (SPLC, "Klan Group Under Fire," Sept. 17, 2007).

Being Black in America means a loss of recognition and identity, as well as being a ready-made target, and I daresay for women their status is just as bleak. For some, the thinking is, the election of an African American president makes all of the problems of abuse and discrimination magically disappear. However the data does not bear out these assumptions, even though there may be a reason for optimism and hope. But as the old expression goes, "hope in one hand, and crap in the other and see which one fills up the quickest." It is the nature of the disease of hate, and its generational effects that creates a

63

sense of foreboding. For example we still see many automobiles driven by young and

middle age Whites with the Southern Battle Flag emblazoned on its bumper or window.

We still see the Swastika and Southern Battle Flag tattoos along with other symbols of

hate such as KKK and RAHOWA (Racial Holy War).

All of these occurrences of hate and violence have been in existence before and

during Obama's campaign and election as president. Interestingly it was another so

called liberal democratic president, at the turn of the twentieth-century, Woodrow

Wilson, who commented, "It was sad but true," after viewing the D.W. Griffith's

incendiary hate film, "The Birth of a Nation" which glorified the KKK at the expense of

Black men who were shown ravaging White women. Now we are at the turn of the 21st

Century, and the newly elected African American liberal democratic president refers to

himself as a "Mutt" while discussing with reporters his decision to possibly getting a

shelter dog for his two children as they move into the White House. "Unfortunately,

many of them [dogs] are mutts like me," he jokingly lamented. But it is not a joke, nor is

it humorous when for hundreds of years in this nation, Blacks have struggled against the

specter of being less than human as was written in the U.S. Constitution.

Obama's parents were of different race/ethnicity – mother White and father Black

Kenyan. Therefore he is biracial, not "mixed" as we call animals; and certainly "mutt" is

an inappropriate reference for anyone. His comments, the same as Wilson's, are

offensive and detrimental to the cause of erasing myths, lies, stereotypes and distorted

racial images that feed the racists' views of who Blacks are as a people. Unfortunately,

not much was made of the Obama comment, which is troubling in itself because it

demonstrates how people think, and the low-level in which Blacks are viewed, and

64

emboldens White bigots to compose and sing to the tune of "Puff the Magic Dragon," "Barack the Magic Negro," and believe it is not disparaging to Blacks. The notion of inferiority and superiority are lingering vestiges of hate with a long history of persons of so call good will saying and doing things that are injurious to others. And because these statements originate from persons who should know better, they carry more weight and authority than they do coming from a devout misogynist or White Supremacist. Hate laws on miscegenation were passed during the Jim Crow Era to protect the "sanctity" of White womanhood and the White race in general, so that there would not be a race of "mongrels," or mutts as one KKK leader stated at a hate rally in Mississippi.

Gandhi observed this same phenomena of arrogance and misspoken words among the upper class leadership of the Indian people. Inferiority from birth relegating one to the status of an "untouchable" was a problem he wanted to eradicate from the minds of the Indian people. Our challenge is the same, erasing the vestiges of Jim Crow from the minds of the people of all races, political ideologies, and gender. The following are actual examples of Jim Crow Laws that originated in the hearts and minds of White Supremacists. Please note that the targets were not only Blacks but also Whites who would dare have any type of relationship with Blacks, personal or professional. Black codes or Apartheid policies were given the name Jim Crow Laws. The name is believed to have originated from an antebellum minstrel show character popularized as Jim Crow. He was a character in a song and dance number written by Thomas Dartmouth who performed in the insulting black face. "These laws were passed into legislation by the Southern states as early as the late 1860s which exacerbated segregation, race discrimination, and the ideology of White supremacy in America. These laws were also soon adopted by many Northern states and their cities, such as Michigan, New York, Illinois, and Ohio and Western states such as Arizona, Utah, Oklahoma, Wyoming and Montana to name a few.

Examples of these laws are: (Please keep in mind the four principles of the Supreme Court which validated these laws.)

1. *Nurses.* No person or corporation shall require any White female nurse to nurse in wards or rooms in hospitals, either public or private, in which Negro men are placed.

2. *Toilet Facilities.* Every employer of White or Negro males shall provide for such White or Negro males reasonably accessible and *separate* toilet facilities.

3. *Intermarriage.* The marriage of a person of Caucasian blood with a Negro, Mongolian, Malay, or Hindu shall be null and void (to keep White blood pure to prevent the birth of mongrels or "Mutts").

4. *Cohabitation.* Any Negro man and White woman, or any White man and Negro woman who are not married to each other, who shall habitually live in and occupy in the 'night-time' the same room shall each be punished by imprisonment not exceeding twelve months, or by fine not exceeding five hundred dollars (and in some cases lynching was the response to such living arrangements, or interpersonal relationships. Banishment, ostracism and vile name calling/racial slurs all were order of the day, then and now).

5. *Education.* The schools for White children and the schools for Negro children shall be conducted *separately* (confirming American Apartheid, Separate but Equal still in existence today).

6. *Burial.* The officer in charge shall not bury, or allow to be buried, any colored persons upon ground set apart or used for the burial of White persons (a demonstration of the insidiousness of race hatred. Even in death the tradition of Apartheid had to be preserved and segregated cemeteries are still in existence throughout our nation).

7. *Restaurants.* All persons licensed to conduct a restaurant, shall serve either White people exclusively or colored people exclusively, and shall not sell to the two races within the same room or serve the two races anywhere under the same license (the most famous contemporary cases of restaurant segregation and discrimination were filed against Denny's food chain, and ultimately settled out of court).

8. *Parks.* It shall be unlawful for colored people to frequent any park owned or maintained by the city for the benefit, use and enjoyment of White persons …and unlawful for any White person to frequent any park owned or maintained by the city for the use and benefit of colored persons.

9. *Militia.* The White and colored militia shall be separately enrolled [segregated military through the 1940s], and shall never be compelled to serve in the same organization. No organization of colored troops shall be permitted where White troops are available, and while White troops are permitted to be organized, colored troops shall be under the command of White officers [master and slave].

10. *Transportation.* The utilities commission is empowered and directed to require the establishment of separate waiting rooms at all stations for the White and colored races.

11. *Teaching.* Any instructor who shall teach in any school, college or institution where members of the White and colored race are received and enrolled as pupils for instruction shall be deemed guilty of a misdemeanor, and upon conviction thereof, shall be fined in any sum not less than ten dollars no more than fifty dollars for each offense (created the necessity for the Historically Black Colleges and Universities – HBCU's. And contrary to popular myth, White students are admitted to these institutions and receive excellent education alongside Black students today).

12. *Theaters.* Every person operating any public hall, theater, opera house, motion picture show or any place of public entertainment or public assemblage which is attended by both White and colored persons, shall separate the White race and the colored race and shall set apart and designate certain seats therein to be occupied by White persons and a portion thereof, or certain seats therein, to be occupied by colored persons (www.nps.gov.Jim Crow Laws).

The Jim Crow Laws, as one can readily see, were designed to control every facet of the lives of those persons or citizens residing in the United States. They were so crafted to ensure that the separation of the races and gender were a display of inferiority and superiority. This terrible system of Apartheid underscores the unequal foundation of America's race and gender relations stemming from deprivation and slavery. But support for Blacks and others was to come from an unexpected source – the Communist Party. At the beginning of the Twentieth-Century, W.E.B. DuBois wrote of the Triple Consciousness that Blacks developed as a means of survival and securing a place for themselves in America. He effectively argued that it is "three significant aspects of their identity and personality: the impact of western/American culture, the idea of Black success, and the importance of Black struggle." He also further adds that "each person chooses to balance these powerful conflicting [psychological characteristics] in their own personal way" (http://racism.suite101).

It does not require much profundity of thought to conclude that DuBois was presenting a typology which could be used to explain the function of the coping mechanism of most any deprived group in American society. The only prerequisite being that the institutional decisions which define them and decide progress are, historically, outside their sphere of influence; and so much so, that the group in question must constantly look within themselves, and their group membership for acknowledgment of their value and self worth because they cannot take their equality and well-being for granted. Women, of course, are also depicted within this paradigm, due to the effect of double-standards, discrimination, and physical and psychological violence they have to endure. Therefore when an outside force presents itself with the capacity for caring about their long-term struggle, and provides a means where by grievances can be addressed, then that force or system will be embraced by the group that has seen itself locked out of the ability to secure justice and resources for progress. In the following chapter we will examine a few of these systems and methods for progress, and attempt to understand factors that gives rise to the socio-political changes through secondary data analysis.

Chapter Three – Endnotes

Asante, Molefi K. and Mark T. Mattson (1991). *Historical and Cultural Atlas of African Americans*, MacMillan Publishing Co., NY.

Dees, Morris (2007). "Klan Group Under Fire," Southern Poverty Law Center, Montgomery, Alabama.

Hine, Darlene Clark, William C. Hine, and Stanley Harrold (2009). *African Americans: A Concise History*, Prentice Hall Publisher, Third Edition, New Jersey.

Matthews, Gerald E. (2007). *Evangelism or Corruption: The Politics of Christian Fundamentalism.* Thomson Custom Publishers (Cengage), Mason, Ohio.

Matthews, Gerald E. (2002). *E Pluribus Unum: Justice, Liberty and Terror.* Thomson Custom Publishers (Cengage), Mason, Ohio.

Matthews, Gerald E., editor. *Journey Towards Nationalism: Implications of Race and Racism.* Thomson Custom Publishers (Cengage), Mason, Ohio.

McMorris, Michael and Barbara F. Turnage (2001). "Continuity 2000: A Realistic View of the Historical Relationship Between Black Americans and the Police," in *Journey Towards Nationalism: Implications of Race and Racism*, Gerald E. Matthews, editor (2001). Thomson Custom Publishers (Cengage), Mason, Ohio.

Quarles, Benjamin (1987). *The Negro In The Making Of America*, 3rd Edition, MacMillan Publishing Co., NY.

Stewart, James B. (1986). "Abolitionist Movement. The Readers Companion to American History" (see website).

Websites:

http://en.wikipedia.org/wiki/FourthAmendment

http://racism.suite101   (8-30-08)

http://www.nps.gov   Jim Crow Laws

CHAPTER FOUR

Political Strategies and the Effect
Of Community Organization

Section I: Issues, Theory and Conceptual Foundation

An age old adage states that as long as people can change, a community, state, nation and even the world can change. This philosophy is imbedded within the principled framework of community organization which can be traced to Saul Alinsky's Model of self help (see also Chapter Six); with a similar philosophy held by King Hammurabi of Babylon in antiquity who in 1750 B.C.E. (Before the Common Era) issued a Code of Justice which decreed that people help one another during times of hardship (G. Matthews, 2001, 2nd Edition, p. 131). As I reported in a previous text, a functional contemporary definition of the community organization model for self-help is taken from Sheafor, et.al. which epitomizes Alinsky's philosophy of community practice. It is described in the following manner: "Its purpose is to improve social functioning through a group experience and discussion with others who have or have had similar concerns or problems ...help groups usually depend on leaders indigenous to the group [regardless of gender or race] ...and this approach rests on the belief that an individual can be helped by those who have experiences with the type of problems that the target group is coping with, e.g. landlord/housing problems ...These programs are generally designed around five basic beliefs or assumptions:"

1) People have a desire to share their experiences.

2) People have strengths that can be used to accomplish challenging goals.

70

3) People are generally attracted to and feel most comfortable in small groups that are informed and lacks elitism. This group philosophy provides the foundation for the Democratic Party Caucus Model of primary voting in various states. They gained enormous popularity during the 2008 Democratic Primary in which Barack Obama surged ahead of Hillary Clinton in pledged delegates, giving him the nomination, and ultimately the Presidency.

4) People embrace most readily rules that are simple and guidance that is practical.

5) Humans have a basic desire to help others which is the antitheses of viewing people as "free market commodities," (B. Sheafor, 1997, p. 117).

Other earlier and equally potent examples of community-based and otherwise politically organized programs, from antiquity to present day, which have a foundation in the self-help model are:

1) "In 500 B.C.E., 'Philanthropy,' from the Greek word for acts of love for humanity, is institutionalized in the Greek city-states. Citizens are encouraged to donate money, which is used for the public good ['Spread the Wealth.' A phrase used in the 2008 presidential campaign in which the Republican Party candidates attempted to label Barack Obama a Socialist because he stated that he wanted to take money from those who are well-off to help those mired in poverty – Spreading the Wealth around became a catch-phrase symbolized by Joe Wurlzebacher, a.k.a., 'Joe the Plumber' who asked Obama about his tax policy. It led to Joe being investigated, by Obama operatives, and the firing of a high level Ohio public servant who was at the center of the controversy – see Chapter Six].

2) In 300 B.C.E. China, the Analects (Confucius writings), declared humans to be social beings bound to one another by Jen – a form of sympathy that is often expressed through helping those in need.

3) With the fall of the Roman Empire around 395 A.D., a Catholic Pope organizes programs to help poor people; the church replaces the state as the safety net (not unlike the manner in which churches/faith-based institutions operate today).

4) In 1795 the Speenhamland system is inaugurated. In the English district of Speenhamland, a poverty line is developed and some workers are made eligible for subsidization whenever their wages are below this amount. The amount is based on the price of bread and the worker's number of dependents. As prices increase or wages decline, the public treasury makes up the difference (once again this policy has marked similarities to 'Spreading the Wealth Around').

5) In 1819 Thomas Chalmers (Scottish preacher and mathematician) assumes responsibility for Glasgow's poor. He develops private philanthropies to help meet the economic needs of poor people and organizes a system of volunteers to meet individually and regularly with disadvantaged people to give them encouragement and training [political organization and jobs training program, community organization model].

6) In 1848 feminists throughout the United States convene at Seneca Falls, New York to declare the goal of equal rights for women and to establish the philosophy and objectives of the women's movement, including suffrage, equal opportunities in education and jobs, and legal rights.

7) In 1870 Social Darwinism (survival of the fittest gains prominence – adopted from biologist Charles Darwin's thesis, 'On the Origin of the Species: By Means of Natural

Selection,' 1839). The supposition by sociologist Herbert Spencer was that 'Survival of the Fittest' should apply to human society and that poverty was merely an aspect of natural selection [salves the conscience of the rich so that hoarding the wealth of a society is justified]. Helping poor people, it was conveniently believed, would make them lazy and non-industrious [sociology William Graham Sumner introduced this concept to the United States].

8) In 1835 the Reverend Joseph Tuckerman, a Unitarian minister who is influenced by the reports of Thomas Chalmer's work in Scotland, organizes the Boston Society for the prevention of Pauperism. This organization uses many of Chalmer's principles of individualized work with poor families including volunteer visitors, coordinated fundraising, and social action [community organization].

9) In 1909 the National Association for the Advancement of Colored People is founded. The forerunner is the Niagara Movement established to advocate for the protection of the legal and social rights of Blacks and other groups [Women suffragettes such as Jane Addams played a role in the organization of the NAACP].

10) In 1910 The National Urban League was founded [with a mission of service to the Black community in terms of jobs, entrepreneurship, and economic advancement].

11) In 1933 President Franklin D. Roosevelt proclaims a 'New Deal' for Americans and establishes major social welfare programs to combat poverty and unemployment brought on by the Great Depression which began in October 1929. [Macro-policy and community organization philosophies help to create programs, e.g.] the Civil Works Administration, the Federal Emergency Relief Administration (FERA), and later the Works Progress Administration (WPA). FERA initiated a federal grant program which

established public assistance offices in the states. The New Deal was based on the principles (theory) of 'Keynesian Economics,' using federal programs to address the economic collapse to 'Prime the Pump' as theorized by British economist John Maynard Keynes. [The severity of America's economic problems, beginning in the latter part of 2008, and the subsequent public works initiatives of the Obama administration are said to model the programs/projects begun by FDR in response to the Great Depression beginning with the stock market crash of 1929; but despite FDR's best efforts the depression dragged on until it was ended by the inducement of materials and labor (manufacturing and services) brought on by the Second World War.]

12) In 1957 the U.S. Civil Rights Act of 1957 (P.L. 85-315) is passed.

13) In 1964 President Lyndon B. Johnson (LBJ) launches the 'Great Society' programs with legislation including the Economic Opportunity Act of 1964 (P.L. 88-452), and the Civil Rights Act of 1964 (P.L. 88-352), the resulting programs include the Job Corps, model cities, Operation Head Start, Volunteers in Service to America (VISTA), the Neighborhood Youth Corps, and the Community Action Program [community organization and political activism became the foundation for the Association of Community Organizations for Reform Now (ACORN) (see following section on organizations)].

14) In 1965 more Great Society programs and organizations are enacted [from community organization efforts] and implemented including Medicare, Medicaid, the Older Americans Act of 1965 (P.L. 89-73), and the Elementary and Secondary Education Act of 1965 (P.L. 89-10). The U.S. Department of Housing and Urban Development (HUD) is established [with a mission of assisting low and moderate income Americans to

achieve the 'American Dream' of homeownership – FANNIE MAE and FREDDIE MAC quazi public mortgage lending institutions which overextended credit using questionable policies was held responsible for the spark that lit the economic meltdown beginning in 2008].

15) In 1968 the Kerner Commission (National Advisors Commission on Civil Disorders) issued its report, blaming White racism and limited opportunities for Black people [no such mechanism developed for women] as major causes of the strife and [rebellions] in urban ghettos [the work of community organizations using principles and theory of Social Action became incredibly useful to establish self-determination, political advocacy, and economic progress. The 25th anniversary of the Kerner Commission reaffirmed its 1968 conclusions on the intractable nature of racism].

16) In 1975 personal social services, work training, housing and community development, juvenile justice, and delinquency programs became laws. The amendment to the Social Security Act of 1933 known as Title XX (P.L. 93-647) becomes the major source of funds for personal social services. Each state is reimbursed by the federal government for helping individuals to achieve economic self-support and independence, preventing and remedying neglect and abuse, and reducing and preventing improper institutional care.

17) In 1980 the U.S. Department of Health and Human Services is established when the Department of Health Education and Welfare is divided. The U.S. Department of Education is established as an independent cabinet-level department during President Jimmy Carter's democratic administration.

18) In 1982 the Job Training Partnership Act (P.L. 97-300) and the Emergency Job Bill (P.L. 97-404) are enacted. This legislation replaces many CETA [Comprehensive Employment and Training Act first enacted in 1974 (P.L. 93-203) for job opportunities and education for disadvantaged people], public service job training programs, and seeks to encourage state governments and private industry to train needy people for suitable employment.

19) The Family and Medical Leave Act of 1993 (P.L. 103-3) becomes law, requiring larger U.S. companies to permit employees job-protected unpaid leave to care for family members.

20) In 1995 the U.S. National Voter Registration Act goes into effect giving U.S. citizens easier access to registering to vote while applying for government services [this precipitated the increase in ACORN activities with community organizers such as Barack Obama working in large urban areas such as Chicago to elect liberal or philosophically progressive candidates to public office. His meteoric rise in politics to state and national office and then the presidency is indirectly, however some would argue directly, related to the activities of ACORN, see also Chapter Six].

21) On August 16, 1996, President Bill Clinton signed the Personal Responsibility and Work Opportunity Act. This legislation released the federal government from the obligation of administering the public assistance program Aid to Families of Dependent Children (AFDC), thus 'changing welfare as we know it' (President Bill Clinton). The program would now be called the Temporary Assistance to Needy Families (TANF)." This effectively changed the public assistance program of the last 50 years enacted under President Franklin Delano Roosevelt's administration in 1935 as part of the New Deal

(Leslie Montgomery, Final Paper, BSW Program, Ferris State University). (These 21 programs are adopted from the Social Work Dictionary, 3rd Edition, edited by Robert L. Barker, published by the NASW Press, 1995).

Section II: Socio-Political Models of Interventionist Thought

As we examine the historical and contemporary programmatic efforts for positive consequential planning paradigms, we must be cognizant of the environment in which the model is to be replicated. For example during the Civil Rights Movement, Dr. Martin Luther King, Jr. studied the non-violent tactics of Mahatma Gandhi and found this faith-based model to be a workable strategy in the southern states. But as he turned the SCLC's (Southern Christian Leadership Conference) attention to the northern cities, such as Chicago and New York, he discovered a resistance to his methods from both White and Black Americans (Hampton, *Eyes On The Prize*). Indeed the competing interests of other organizations which also had well-defined missions similar to the SCLC seemed to be far more effective in recruitment and achieving their objectives. For instance, the Black panthers and the Nation of Islam (commonly referred to as the Black Muslims) had a message of "militancy" which was far more appealing to urban Blacks than the one espoused by Dr. King.

Even the Student Non-Violent Coordinating Committee (SNCC) underwent an organizational *transformation* (we will deal with this term later) as they went from a social action model of passive resistance under the leadership of John Lewis (now a long-term U.S. Congressman from Atlanta, Georgia) to a more openly confrontational structure with the late Stokely Carmichael, a.k.a., Kwame Ture, and then later H. Rap Brown at the helm. Their message of "Black Power" which was first used by the late New York Congressman Adam Clayton Powell (also a minister), and "Burn Baby Burn" in response to the rebellions was a tenor of resistance that overshadowed Dr. King in the North. It should also be noted that during this era leading up to the present, the role of women was traditionally behind the scene support, except for a few exceptions such as Fannie Lou Hamer, Marian Wright Edelman, Marian Lofton, and Angela Davis. Even when Rosa Parks took the bold step of refusing to surrender her seat to a White man, her place in history will be forever solidified with this one act of courage, but relatively few reports speak of her longtime involvement in civil rights, and that she was no stranger to civil disobedience.

Had the social action organizational machinery been put to use as forcefully in promoting justice for women, as it had, and is being used to advocate for racial justice, then the incidences of misogyny and crimes against women may have by now declined, at least to the degree that shelters would be a thing of the past, and their wages would be on par with men.

There are at least five models, among others, that we might examine which can provide some utility towards our understanding the issues of double standards, discrimination, and women hatred. They are the Power-Politics Model, Social Planning, Locality Development Model, the Rational and Natural Systems Models. Each of these models fall under the rubric of community organization, a term which by now should be familiar to the reader due to all of the buzz it received during the 2008 Presidential election. Subsequently, before he was President, Barack Obama spent a number of years working as a community organizer on Chicago's south side, helping low-income Blacks, and poor people in general, gain a better standard of living, upgrading their quality of life, and demonstrating how to access the powerful political machinery to enable them to have a voice so that their grievances could be heard, and addressed. Defining each of these models will be a prelude to our recognizing how they might fit in the electoral process in the political world of "isms," meaning populism, federalism, and the two most dreaded ones in American society, socialism and communism. Each of these concepts will be dealt with to the degree that there exists some shared relevance to the American democratic process, and/or the reality of connectedness upon which our society is structured.

The following definitions are adopted from Sheafor, and they also appear in my *Journey Towards Nationalism* text (see endnotes):

1) The Rational Model - "Assumes [sometimes in error] that the people making decisions are in agreement about the organization's goals and are committed to those goals. However, incompetence and hidden agendas, as well as behavioral problems, can contribute to goal displacement." [To keep us on the right track, we need only to examine the two major political parties and the dissatisfaction within the ranks to the candidate selection process, and the grueling primaries leading up to the conventions prior to the election for president. Factored in this of course is also the astronomical amount of money that candidates must raise to just be competitive with their rivals. For example Obama had initially signed an agreement that he would accept federal funds and thereby his spending for the campaign would be capped. He actually opted out of the agreement and ended up raising more money than any candidate has raised in history. His three-quarters of a billion dollars ($750,000,000) exceeded the amounts raised by both George W. Bush and John Kerry combined in the 2004 presidential race.

The term "buying the election" has gained prominence as the advertisement wars have increased. Furthermore, the primaries, particularly within the Democratic party, appears to be flawed because of the caucuses and the allocation of delegates in 2008, which left a number of voters extremely upset in their belief that Senator Clinton was treated very shabbily by the party. And the hypocrisy of disenfranchisement became

79

applicable in 2008, thus negating the Democratic Party's argument for the "stolen" election in 2000 in which a tally of votes in Florida were not counted and/or were arbitrarily given to George W. Bush. A number of lawsuits were filed, and thousands of people believed the election was "stolen" by Bush. When we fast-forward to 2008, the same bad-taste is in the mouth of thousands of voters because of Michigan and Florida votes were arbitrarily split thus favoring Obama (see Chapter Five). Certainly the leadership of the party was called into question.]

2) The Natural System Model – "Views an organization as a *system* made up of a multitude of individuals" but it does not specify diversity as desirable for the group composition. When following a model, the model itself should be specific, (around potential polarizing ideals/concepts) so as not to provide any unnecessary and/or unpopular "wiggle room" for its application. If care in the design is not taken, then discrimination within the ranks of those targets for "change" may be the resulting outcome. And discrimination by those liberal/progressive persons of good will or those of one's own group, is more maddening than when it comes from those who are identified as the traditional adversary.

Such is the case with feminists who have made strident personal attacks against Senator Hillary Clinton and Governor Sarah Palin (see Chapter Six), and/or Black Americans working against reactionaries such as Supreme Court Justice Clarence Thomas, former U.S. Congressman from Oklahoma, J.C. Watts, and media radio huckster Armstrong Williams; and the so-called Black conservatives of Project Twenty-One (21), that defended radio and T.V. political analyst, Bill Bennet's remarks when he declared "that if you wanted to reduce crime …if that were your sole purpose, you could abort every Black baby in this country, and your crime rate would go down." He conceded that

80

aborting all Black babies "would be an impossible, ridiculous, and morally reprehensible thing to do," then he also added, "but the crime rate would go down." These statements by Bennet are indefensible by anyone, let alone by Blacks themselves. They are stereotypically derogatory and racist with overtures supporting genocide. This is a common problem faced by minorities and women, so the best place to begin is within the group itself. Thus, so you see, Obama's "mutt" comment is far from being helpful to the cause of proactively dealing with the baggage of harmful speech.

Now if we might return to the completion of the Natural Systems Model, it underscores my previous comments on the intractable nature of intra-group division and societal discrimination and stereotypes. It maintains that "roles, subsystems or [coalitions], and formal and informal processes striving to function and survive in a wider social environment [and] efforts to change such an organization or systems should emphasize the clarification of goals and objectives, improving communication, recognizing and addressing the social and emotional needs of personnel, morale building, and the like." The emphasis on balancing the achievement of goals while maintaining a certain level of functioning order prevents the degeneration to disorder, and even unmanageable chaos, which revolutions were made of in times past.

In other words, those with grievances should take precautionary measures not to "rock the boat." So with the cameras rolling on Mary 31, 2008 at the Democratic Rules and Bylaws Committee meeting, the Democratic Party showed signs of fracturing in its zeal to place Barack Obama at the head of the Democratic Party ticket over his primary rival Hillary Clinton. While Hillary ended the campaign with more popular votes than did Obama, the Rules Committee exercised its authority by reapportioning votes in both

81

Florida and Michigan which factored heavily in his victory. These loose interpretations

of the rules led to heated exchanges between the Clinton campaign and the committee

which in this scenario represented the power and status quo as well as being pro-Obama,

instead of being a neutral mediator.

I have selected three comments which were telling about the process, and which I

believe will shed additional light on our thesis. One Obama supporter stated "…there is

no such thing as a legitimate election where one of the candidates wasn't even on the

ballot, and there is no such thing as a legitimate election where the rules are changed to

benefit one of the contestants after the fact," and a Clinton supporter argued, "We sat

back in 2000 and allowed Bush to steal the election by our not insisting that all the votes

were counted. Over the past eight years we have paid a huge price for our not standing

up for democracy, and insisting that the votes be counted. Obama is now attempting to

emulate Bush in 2008. We are sorry Barack. We have learnt our lesson from 2000.

Americans are going to insist that the democratic process not be undermined by

politicians like yourself and Bush who have contempt for democratic values. Americans

are going to insist that the votes are counted." And this final statement crystallizes the

rationale for the decisions by the committee. It was short and to the point, "If Hillary is

the nominee she will lose the election." Of course if that were the main goal of the

democrats regardless of fairness or the resulting long term harm to the party, the goal was

achieved by the election of President Obama. But is it not interesting that when

presented with the choice between a Black man, and a White female, even for the

presidency, the Black man was chosen as the more viable candidate.

82

However the fracturing of the party was evident in that a significant number of democrats chose to leave, but of course these numbers were probably balanced by the new voters brought in, largely due to the efforts of ACORN which I will discuss very shortly. But Black Americans have seen, for generations, the voting process stacked against them, and rules enacted or changed to lock Blacks out of the ballot (see Chapter Five). It was Fannie Lou Hamer who made the famous remark of being "sick and tired of being sick and tired" with respect to deprivation and discrimination. Ms. Hamer was the granddaughter of slaves, and in "1962, when she was 44 years old, voting rights volunteers came to her town and held a voter registration meeting. Fannie was surprised to learn that Blacks actually had a constitutional right to vote" (http://www.7biblio.org).

As a result of that meeting Fannie decided to become a volunteer to encourage others to vote. These activities resulted in her being thrown off the sharecropping farm in which she had worked for years, but in conditions akin to slavery; she also received death threats and was shot at because of her voting right activities. "Hamer co-founded the Mississippi Freedom Democratic Party (MFDP). In 1964, [this is crucial] the MDFP challenged the all-White Mississippi delegation to the Democratic National Convention. Hamer spoke in from of the Credentials Committee in a televised proceeding that reached millions of viewers [sound familiar?]. She told the committee how Blacks in many states across the country were prevented from voting through illegal tests, taxes and intimidation. As a result of her speech, two delegates of the MFDP were given speaking rights at the convention and the other members were seated as honorable guests" (Ibid.).

Hamer, a dynamic Black woman, the granddaughter of slaves, armed with nothing but a powerful conviction of justice and right, almost single-handedly changed an illegal

83

repressive Southern tradition that had been, for years, fully sanctioned by Northern state delegates, and the Democratic Party Credentials Committee (Ibid.). This is the same party that in 2008 was being asked to decide on yet another challenge on behalf of a group that has withstood many discriminatory policies and actions. The contemporary dilemma for the party however, was that this case was being brought forward by a White female, and the ruling as such, potentially would go against the interests of an African American male.

After years of discrimination, and being victimized by violence and murder, for the first time ever, an African American was poised to be nominated for Presidency of the United States of America. Ironically it was a scant fifty-four years (54) earlier in "1954" that the Supreme Court had ruled that "separate but equal," i.e., American Apartheid was unconstitutional. There is no denying the weighty historical significance of the possibility of the first Black/African American president that loomed over the Democratic Party, and drove the direction in which the party ultimately ended with its goal achieved. While some might consider it fate, and others yield to the belief that hard work creates the opportunities which become your reality. The principles need not be mutually exclusive; but when the planning efforts proceed as determined, and the results after years of hard work are finally reached, certainly for many people, they understandably conclude there must be some element of Divine Intervention. And from a theological, if not a Black Perspective, it is no coincidence that one of Obama's nicknames is "The One."

This is essentially what Hillary was up against: the power elite, buoyed by the expectation of the masses/rank and file membership, including 99% Black support, betrayals and defections, an economic collapse, and a terrible Bush administration with an approval rating just above the cockroach. It is not surprising that all of these events occurring at the same time, particularly when given Obama's good fortune as he won the Illinois state senate seat, and then the U.S. Senate by way of competition default, the belief of Divine Intervention becomes a more viable rationale for some than coincidence or happenstance. To put it yet another way, for those who hold religious beliefs, it does become a matter of Divine Intervention, while the Secular realm may interpret those events as a "Perfect Storm" which swept Obama into the Presidency.

3) Power Politics Model – According to Sheafor, "In this model the organization [the system] is viewed as essentially a political arena in which various individuals, departments, unity, and other subsystems compete for power, resources, and personal advantage …to change such an organization, one needs access to persons in positions of influence over the organization and must be able to persuade those within the organization that a specific change is in their self-interest" (Ibid.). To this end, president Obama owes a debt of gratitude to those who came before him, and challenged the intractable, if not racist and sexist, nature of the Democratic Party. It is a process in which the Republican Party is now embarking because of the vice-presidential candidacy of Governor Sarah Palin. Indeed, because of Barack Obama, the Democrats are much further ahead than the Republicans in sorting out race issues. But with respect to the idea of gender, and a woman at the top of the party's ticket, both parties have a long road to travel; not as long as it once was, but still quite far.

Certainly on the democratic side, heroes and sheroes such as Reverends Jesse Jackson and Al Sharpton, and Shirley Chisolm, and Geraldine Ferraro, each challenged

85

the rules and stereotypes, and moved the party forward, as did Fannie Lou Hamer. The party had to discover that its self-interest was tied to the interest of justice and progressive decency by permitting all Americans to pursue, unimpeded, their constitutional rights of citizenship. This is a well-traveled road with pot-holes strewn along the way. The Democratic Party has hit quite a few, and one can only wonder whether the Republicans are smart enough to have been taking note of the Democratic party experiences. The external barriers to progress are significant enough on their own, therefore neither party needs additional reactionaries from within its boundaries to continue to muck up the works, so to speak.

4) Locality Development - In speaking of external forces, we can draw upon the conceptual language contained within the larger encompassing macro model of Locality Development. In terms of community development, "it presupposes that the community consists of people who share a sense of belonging to their locality and can, therefore, reach a consensus on the nature of community problems, and what should be done about them. It emphasizes broad citizen participation, sharing of ideas, democratic decision-making, cooperative problem solving, and self-help" [also commonly referred to as self-determination or empowerment] (Ibid.). It is within this model, coupled with the following Social Planning Model, that Saul Alinsky gained prominence as a strategic tactician community organizer.

5) Social Planning Model – With Social Planning the focus is on specific social problems, e.g., crime, inadequate housing, lack of health care, and the response of the human services delivery system to these problems. It recognizes the complex legal, economic,

and political factors that must be addressed in solving a major community problem (Ibid.).

Reaching a consensus requires knowledge of the art of negotiation and compromise, without which, we cannot achieve mutually agreed upon goals, which is the essence of consensus building. Once the goals have been determined, we can move to the next stage of articulating them to the resource holders. This is why the notion of "change" has such a powerful and romantic appeal to those who have been discouraged by the current state of affairs, and/or disillusioned by powerbrokers, and have lost faith in ever achieving the American Dream. Articulate and charismatic messengers can reach and inspire those persons who have wanted more than they are currently receiving from our institutions and political leadership. Harnessing this accompanying pent-up anger and frustration of the masses becomes a major challenge and necessary goal of the community organizer/charismatic leader. However building trust and confidence is as important as having the ability to motivate people to not only want change, but are willing to invest time and effort to achieve the change that is desired.

Section III: the Message of Change As An Ideological "ism"

Embracing the methods and models of community organization/development within the framework of social planning will determine how adept the organizer might be in putting together a team of indigenous leadership, which are those who the disenfranchised and/or the dissatisfied will view as sharing their values and beliefs. These individuals will articulate the message of change to the extent that others will come to believe that change is possible, and that their lives or circumstance will be made better by "The Change You Can Believe In." When there is such widespread dissatisfaction with the government, the message of change is an easy sell. Indeed, logically speaking, why would one wish for change if there is general satisfaction

87

with the direction in which the nation is heading. This is the major reason why second presidential terms are granted, and why first term presidents are not voted to serve a second. A commonality of interests, and motivating individuals to take direct action has been hallmarks of ACORN (Association of Community Organizations for Reform Now) since its inception in 1970.

ACORN's goal, or better put, its mission is, "to unite welfare recipients with needy working people around issues such as school lunches, unemployment, Vietnam veteran's rights, and emergency room care. The organization expanded to organize farmers for confronting environmental issues concerning sulfur emissions" (http://en.wikapedia.org). The organization has a history of coalescing with lower stratum persons to help provide them with the necessary support and tools to give them access to the halls of power. ACORN utilizes the principles of community organization, and embraces both traditional and non-traditional methods of bringing attention to their client's issues, and needs, such as placing announcements in print and electronic media sources, picketing, marching, demonstrating at places where their adversary lives, works, and/or worship. All of these methods are in their arsenal of community intervention.

And confrontation, in ACORN's view, is a good thing. While most persons will tend to shy away from open warfare, so to speak, ACORN seeks out the unusual places to meet, and will visit homes, churches, schools, and/or civic centers for organizational strategy sessions. They will pull together unlikely partners such as the homeless, union members, rural and urban dwellers the poor, and the wealthy. What ACORN looks for is a common thread with which they can bind these persons together, and the message of change in the 2008 political cycle resonated with equal strength in Hollywood, in the farm and rural areas of mostly White states, poor communities, and with the working class, and across racial lines. As Obama said in his 2004 Democratic Convention speech – there are no red states, there are no blue states, we are the United States of America. This message was operationalized in the 2008 campaign, and ACORN played a central role in reaching out to diverse and low income persons to bring them into Obama's "big tent" of one America.

This strategy was also found to be useful in the Communist efforts to organize workers and common Americans, both professional and non-professional, across racial and gender lines, at the turn of the 20th Century, up through the Civil Rights Era. Prominent and well known actors, educators, and authors gravitated to the Communist/Socialist banner where Lenin, Marx, and Mao Tse Tung speeches were quoted and memorialized. Most everyone in the counter culture movement had on their bookshelf a copy of the little red book entitled *Quotations From Chairman Mao Tse Tung*. My copy tends to move from shelf to shelf depending upon where I last used it as a reference. The Communist and/or Socialist ideology gained a foothold in America because of worker dissatisfaction and disillusionment with America's two party capitalistic system. The Communist Party provided these persons with a viable alternative to exercise their right to protest and assembly as acts of defiance in the American government. Senator Joseph McCarthy (McCarthyism) held the famous Congressional Hearings on Communism in America, and turned them into a witch hunt spectacle where careers were ruined, people were blacklisted, and even criminal charges were brought against others all because of American fear of the ideologically detrimental "ism" of Communism and its near philosophical twin of Socialism.

Further examination of the definitions will enable us to better understand the major difference(s) between the two "isms," and how they may have come into prominence within

America. Let us first explore the theory of Communism and just why it is an anathema to American society. The reason could be imbedded in its definition that states that it is a "doctrine that advocates the overthrow of capitalism by the revolution of the proletariat (the class of industrial wage earners who must earn their living by selling their labor)" (American Heritage Dictionary). Even when Communism today appears to be on the wane, the threat is still very real in the minds of millions of Americans including those who have the power to set policy and wage war. It is an "economic system that is characterized by *collective ownership* of property with the organization of labor for the *common advantage* of all members. It is also a system of government in which the state *controls the economy*, and a single party holds power while claiming to work towards a social order in which all goods are equally shared" (Ibid.).

However there is a reality of both that we must address which is the collapse and reemergence of Communism, and the concomitant cyclical crises associated with capitalism. The low to middle income workers in both "isms" find themselves squeezed financially; with the hate and suspicion of our international neighbors growing, militias on the ready, monetary policies change, while wage equity for women gets pushed further on the back burner, and the ideological debate continues. While one leader claims more government intervention and control to be the answer, yet another calls for aggressive tax cuts and less government control. Reagonism is espoused, and FDR (Franklin Delano Roosevelt) is vilified. The question must be asked, where does this debate take us? Are our solutions found in debate or action? The bottom line is that the free expression of the former, leads to the latter. This is the primary reason why our constitutional democracy has been argued to be superior to any form of government on our planet. But we often lose sight of the fact that it is *our* system, unique to *our* history and circumstance; as other forms of government are best suited to the countries in which we often do business. We should be able to debate and negotiate, then reach a consensus without either

entity feeling threatened by the other. In this regard, debate is a good thing.

For Socialism, it rests on "various theories or systems of social organization in which the

means of producing and distributing goods [which] are collectively owned, or by a centralized

government that often plans and controls the economy." It is considered the "stage in Marxist-

Leninist Theory [to be] the intermediate between capitalism and communism in which collective

ownership of the economy under the dictatorship of the proletariat has not been successfully

achieved" (Ibid.). Oftentimes socialism is referred to as Marxism or Marxist ideology. The

rationale for this conceptual switch rests in the fact that Karl Marx, collaborating with his friend

and colleague Frederich Engels, wrote a seminal text on communism and socialism entitled *The

Communist Manifesto* (1848). And then Leninism is recognized as the "Theory and practice of a

proletarian revolution" (Ibid.). This was founded with the Russian Bolshevik Revolution in

1917, and its leader Vladimir Ilich Lenin who was also the first head of the USSR (Union of

Socialist Soviet Republic). The Bolsheviks established by Lenin replaced the autocratic Czarist

(TSAR) system of government. Bolshevik(s) is defined as a "member of the left wing majority

group of the Russian Social Democratic Worker's Party that adopted Lenin's theses on party

organization (1903). [They] seized power in November 1917, and were considered 'radical'

insofar as Russian politics and government is concerned" (Ibid.).

Placing the two ideologies together demonstrates the appeal they have for certain

groups in America, which have struggled against a repressive democratic capitalist system, and

where their labor has been exploited either through slavery or low wages. In America,

capitalism is an economic system in which the means of production and distribution are privately

or corporately owned and developed. It is proportionate to the accumulation and reinvestment of profits gained in a free market. After reading this definition, in contrast to the other two, the language suggests that communism and socialism just may be more appealing than capitalism by assessing terms such a collective ownership, common advantage, planning and controlling the economy, power for the proletariat, and finally, left wing social democrats (see the above underlined phrases). Also the definition of a Bolshevik as a left wing radical does bring to mind our classification of a feminist, and a progressive leftist within the Democratic Party such as Obama is reputed to be by those who make a living labeling others.

Historically speaking, communism and socialism roots run deep in America. For example Hanes Walton Jr. and Marion Orr writing in the *Souls Journal* had this to say, "African American voters and political activists have supported Socialist Communist and Worker party ticket's throughout the country, especially in the industrial states and urban areas of the northeast and mid-west" (p. 19). And the rationale for this support was given as, "Black candidates and voters have come together to send a message to the community and the major parties that wage, job, and employment discrimination impacted the Black community as much as the lack of civil rights. Many of these independent political activities on the left called for progressive policies and programs" (p. 19).

With respect to specific turn of the Twentieth Century events and the dramatic rise of the Communist party, and the tenuous relationship between Black and White workers, including the nuance of gender as it relates to race relations, Mark Solomon chronicles the following in his text, *The Cry Was Unity: Communists and African Americans, 1917-1938.* "While the Communist Party is now viewed in the literature as the single most important ally of African Americans during the 1930s, especially within the labor movement, we know relatively little about how the relationship between left-leaning African Americans and Communists developed

92

...Those who only know about the relationship between Communists and African Americans in the 1930s might assume that the Party was always in the forefront in terms of the 'race' question. In the early thirties, the Communist led International Labor Defense (ILD) defended nine African American males sentenced to death on charges of raping two White women in the Scottsboro case. The ILD defended the boys by taking the battle against Jim Crow into the court of public opinion" (*The Black Scholar Book Reviews*, p. 45).

What is interesting in Solomon's work is that he accepted the unpopular view that Blacks had the ability to organize revolts and demonstrations on a large scale by reaching the Black masses with shared grievances on an international scale. The late great historian Harold Cruse also spoke of the same dynamic of political organization for the purpose of rebellion against injustice. In Cruse's work, *Rebellion or Revolution*, he also argued from the perspective that Black militancy rose above the initial violent outbursts associated with riots, into more patterned planned revolts commonly associated with revolutions (1968). Of course Americans have traditionally been very leery of Black militancy, no matter what the provocation may be, Black rebellions, and sometimes violent revolts have created a sense of foreboding within the population. On each occasion in which these events have occurred, they have created a backlash of police force and power, and policies that challenge Black constitutional rights to have grievances, let alone to actually act on them.

However Communists pressed forward in their strategies against the American government, on behalf of Blacks, to seek redress of grievances. Bates' discussion of Solomon's work adds the following, "Their [meaning Communists] militant approach raised questions about appropriate strategies for challenging racial inequities in a justice system embedded in a racist social context, winning massive numbers of sympathizers for the Party among Black Americans.

93

During the Popular Front period – roughly between 1935 and 1939 – the Communist party was noted for its steadfast support of the Black freedom struggle. Particularly in the Congress for Industrial Organization (CIO), Communist organizers [using the principles and strategies of community organization/social planning] crusaded for an equal place for Black workers in labor unions and industries. But the Communist Party's progressive position on race was the outcome of at least two decades of trial and error as the Party tried to woo Black Americans into its fold" (Bates on Mark Solomon, 2002, p. 45).

A few well known Black Americans who were members of the Party had some successes in addressing grievances, such as A. Philip Randolph of the Sleeping Car Porters Union, the prolific scholar William Edward Burghardt (W.E.B.) DuBois who co-founded the NAACP, who at one time was a party member, but became disillusioned with its philosophy and methods as they related to Blacks, and therefore he resigned his membership. There was also the Black female scholar and political activist, Angela Davis who rose within the ranks of the Party, and was prosecuted, in part, for her Party membership. In Harold Cruse's pivotal work, *The Crisis of the Negro Intellectual*, he discusses in great detail the role of the Communist Party during the Harlem Renaissance Period circa 1920's – 1930's which saw a heightened awareness in Black culture, e.g., art, music, literature, and the theatre. Therefore Socialism/Communism ideologies were thought to be instrumental in the rejuvenation of Black pride, and many artists of that time were active party members.

It is ironic though that the two major European proponents of the working class Socialist political ideology, were also self proclaimed racists, as was shown in their letters to each other where they spoke with disdain about Blacks. Also Marx spoke with disfavor of Jews when in 1847, "he was calling most other socialist thinkers in Europe 'dirty Jews of Negro Blood'."

After wearing out his welcome in Paris and France he and Engels received a more cordial

reception in England where the Communist League had tentacles reaching from

Germany, and we know what eventually happened there (Randall, 1964). But recalling

the contemporary challenges of the organizational phenomena that swept Obama into

office, was devoid of any racist philosophies, even though there were distinct gender

differences in terms of class and race, these of course were overshadowed by the dual

message of "hope and change." And those of low-income status were seen to be the

primary beneficiaries of this phenomena, regardless of geographic region or race (see photo).

Library of Congress, Prints and Photographs Division FSA-OWI Collection

The Southern Face of Rural Poverty the Challenge for President Barack Obama

Section IV: Voting Outcomes and Data Analysis

Even to the casual observers it was thought that the southern states of the "Old

Confederacy" would deliver their 163 Electoral College votes to McCain (see Table 1 below),

and then it would be just a matter for McCain to win the same swing states, such as Ohio as did

George W. Bush, and the Presidency would be his in 2008. However, even given the southern

culture and tradition in which loyalty to the south is as strong as ever, and that, many southerners

will defend their southern roots until the day they die, it is their close knit family pride and

community ties which provides a fertile ground for organizational efforts in times of despair. No

matter whether the effort is targeted at Black or White citizens, it is the number and percentage

of Black voters that made the difference in many of these Southern states

(http://blackcommentator.com).

But in the four Southern states of Alabama, Arkansas, Louisiana, and Mississippi,

Obama's percentage of the White vote was lower than the vote total than John Kerry received in

the 2004 Presidential election polling less than George W. Bush. Table 1 shows that these four

states have nearly the higher percentage of Black voters save Arkansas at sixteen percent (*JET*,

2009, p. 10). Additionally, as reported by *JET*, "Of the 24.8 million Blacks eligible to vote, 16.6

million (or 66.8 percent) actually voted, smashing the previous record of 58.5 percent in 1964"

(Ibid.).

But throughout tough times, it remains a fact that many racial problems are still very

visible to this day; and the celebration of southern antebellum holidays, along with schools

named after former slave owners and confederate officers, is part of what comprises the

troubling Southern tradition (L. M. Henline). On November 4, 2008, as the data shows, the

Obama organizational machine with its strategy of reaching into the southern states that had

previously, for years, voted Republican, showed the wisdom of that decision.

TABLE 1
Black Population of States of the Old Confederacy and Electors

State	Black Population	Black Population %	Electors
Alabama	1,168,998	26.3%	9
Arkansas	427,162	16.0%	6
Florida	2,471,730	15.5%	27
Georgia	2,393,425	29.2%	15
Louisiana	1,489,317	32.9%	9
Mississippi	1,041,708	35.6%	6
North Carolina	1,776,283	22.1%	15
South Carolina	1,200,901	29.9%	8
Tennessee	963,349	16.8%	11
Texas	2,493,057	12.0%	34
Virginia	1,441,207	20.4%	13
			163

For example, Obama won North Carolina with its fifteen electoral votes, Florida with

twenty-seven, and Virginia's thirteen, by gaining overwhelming Black support in three southern

states that in 2004 had been won by George W. Bush (see again Table 1). Additionally Obama

enjoyed a decided advantage among age groups (see Table 2). And among gender the data tells

an equally compelling story in that men overall were almost equally divided between Obama

TABLE 2

Age	18-29	30-44	45-64
Obama	66%	52%	50%
McCain	32%	46%	49%

TABLE 3

	Male	Female
Obama	49%	56%
McCain	48%	43%

and McCain. However, it was the disparity among female voters that showed women were not inclined to vote for a ticket on the sole basis of gender, 56% for Obama and 43% for McCain (see Table 3), where the Sarah Palin effect appears to have less of an impact than previously thought; probably due to the negative media blitz that she received in the last month or so of the 2008 campaign (see Chapter Six) (http://www.cnn.com). But another interesting finding was that while Obama's advantage among women over McCain was significant, "he lost the White women vote by over seven points," which could be attributed to Sarah (http://wikianswers.com). Also the matter of race, Table 4 clearly shows a race dichotomy which can be explained, in part, by the fact that Blacks generally vote overwhelmingly for Democrats, more so than Republicans. It also can be stated, however, that even to the most casual observer, Black Americans were probably energized more than any other group in America for the 2008 election because of the prospect of the first African American president.

TABLE 4

	Whites	Blacks
Obama	43%	95%
McCain	55%	5%

This election contagion did carry over to other group/individuals nationally as well as internationally. What was surprising though, and probably what really helped tip the election in Obama's favor was that 41% of White males voted for Obama "making him the first Democrat since Jimmy Carter [in 1976] to take more than 38% in this category." Additionally, Hispanics voted 66% for Obama, and 31% for McCain which was determined to be the "best ever result for a Democrat." Once again the division along racial lines is quite astounding, which needless to say, should put to rest any suggestion that race is no longer a factor in America insofar as politics is concerned. Further evidence of this fact is provided by *JET* which reports that John McCain received the smallest percentage of Black votes of any Republican candidate in history (Op. Cit., p. 10). And here is where ACORN comes into play in the media photo opportunities of ACORN field workers. The visual images we received were of ACORN workers, many of whom were Black, reaching out to mostly low income persons, and those we saw were also predominantly Black.

There was another race related issue that was reported, and designed to reflect poorly on Obama; it was the registration process characterized as being unlawful by some in the press, and ACORN, at the center of the controversy, was being investigated in some states because of their voter registration practices. But Obama as a former ACORN field worker/community organizer in Chicago had absolutely nothing to explain or apologize for insofar as ACORN is concerned because their history was founded on correcting the history of disenfranchisement experienced by Blacks and others. As recounted in the *Soul Journal* by Omar Ali:

> "*By the turn of the 20th Century, virtually every southern state legislature had amended its constitution to disenfranchise Black Americans. Literacy tests, poll taxes, White primaries, grandfather clauses, [unjustified criminal convictions (see Chapter Five)], and other measures used to disqualify Black voters from participating in elections produced a dramatic fall in voter registration ...the <u>Mississippi Plan</u> of amending state constitutions with the explicit purpose of disenfranchising Black voters, which the state's Democratic legislature [the irony of the Democratic party] launched in 1890 was implemented in South Carolina in 1895, Louisiana in 1898, North Carolina in 1900, Virginia and Alabama in 1901, and in Georgia by 1907 [states of the Confederacy]. For all intents and purposes, the southern Black electorate had been eviscerated with the opening of the 20th Century; the electoral arena all but closed to Black independents. The brutal takeover by Democrats of the two remaining independent political strongholds in the South, Wilmington, North Carolina (1898) and Grimes County, Texas (1901), signaled the end of Black <u>populism</u>. In both places Black independents and their White allies were elected to office, and in both places Black Americans were murdered as part of a campaign to terrorize them into submission as the Democrats reasserted their authority ...The demise of Black populism followed ...and it took the Civil Rights Movement to dismantle Jim Crow ...While voting rights have been guaranteed by the federal government since 1965 [easing barriers to the ballot], and despite the fact that*

99

thousands of African Americans now hold elected office [at some of the highest level of government including the presidency], and notwithstanding the growth of a visible Black middle class, most Blacks remain intractably poor and politically dependent on the Democratic Party ...The voices of Black populists from the late 19th Century continue to reverberate ...Leading and intersecting these trends, are Black independents ...such as the former Black independent for president Dr. Lenora Fulani who was the first Black presidential candidate ever to be on the ballot in all 50 states ...building strategies that have translated into political power, namely fusion ...FUSION is a tactic used since the late 19th Century ...publicly championing structural political reform issues ...FUSION is allowing for new kinds of coalitions that challenge bipartisan politesse" (pp. 13-15).

The challenges of bipartisanship gave rise to different third parties such as the Reform Party, Socialist Party and Green Party. Also well known third party candidates such as Ross Perot and Ralph Nader used the message of reform, and also argued the point that Blacks should support their candidates and not continue to permit the Black vote to be taken for granted. The interesting fact is that reform brought about the Civil War Amendments, and the Civil Rights Movement. The message of hope and change has been at the foundation of each pivotal gain for the disenfranchised, along with candidates considered as *Populists*. It is important to note that there are marked similarities between Populism and a political term we used earlier in discussing Russian politics that factored into its revolutionary reform which is "Bolshevik" (left wing social democrat fighting for the rights of the proletariat/disenfranchised working class). Populism, according to the Heritage Dictionary, "is a political philosophy supporting the rights and power of the people in their struggle against the elite." Organizational efforts around this principle is at the foundation of community organization and has served as the impetus for ACORN. In the 2008 political cycle ACORN was largely responsible for registering hundreds of thousands of new voters, "seventy one percent of whom voted Democrat compared to only twenty nine percent for McCain. In 2004 John Kerry managed fifty three percent of new voters," a significant number to be sure, but pales in comparison to those who voted for

Obama (http://wikianswers.com). But disenfranchisement still represents a blot on our democratic process, and therefore we will address it in the following chapter, with its implications on race and gender.

Chapter Four – Endnotes

Ali, Omar H. (2005). "Independent Black Voices from the Late 19th Century," in *Souls*, Vol. 7, No. 2, Spring 2005. Columbia University, NY.

Barker, Robert (1995). *Social Work Dictionary,* 3rd Edition, Published by the NASW Press.

Bates, Beth T. (2002). Review of Mark Solomon's, *The Cry Was Unity: Communists and African Americans*, the University of Mississippi Press, 1998, in *The Black Scholar, Journal of Black Studies and Research*, Oakland, CA.

Chappell, Kevin (2-16-09). "Blacks Key to Obama Victory, Report Finds," in *JET*, Vol. 115, No. 5., Boulder, CO.

Cruse, Harold (1968). *Rebellion Or Revolution*, William Morrow and Co., NY.

Henline, L.M. (2000). *Southern Culture and Tradition* (see userquest website).

Matthews, Gerald E. (2001). "The Principles of Advocacy: Issues, Concepts, and Case Examples" in *Journey Towards Nationalism*, 2nd Edition, G. Matthews, editor. Thomson Custom Publishers (Cengage), Mason, Ohio.

Montgomery, Leslie (1998). "Final Paper," BSW Program, Ferris State University, Big Rapids, MI.

Randall, Francis B. (1964). "Introduction" to *Communist Manifesto*, (1848). Simon and Schuster, NY. pp 20-22.

Sheafor, Bradford, Charles Rittorejsi, and Gloria A. Horejsi (1991). *Techniques and Guidelines For Social Work Practice*, 4th Edition. Allyn and Bacon Publishers, Boston, Mass.

Walton, Hanes, Jr. and Marion Orr (2005). "African American Independent Politics on the Left: Voter Turnout for Socialist Candidate Frank Crosswaith in Harlem and New York," in *Souls: A Critical Journal of Black Politics, Culture, and Society*, Vol. 7, No. 2, Spring 2005. Columbia University, NY.

Websites:

http://blackcommentator.com

http://en.wikipedia.org

http://www.cnn.com

http://www.ibiblio.org

CHAPTER FIVE

The Historical Damning Effect of Disenfranchisement:
And Its Effect On The Electoral Process (Revised)

Section I: Electoral Overview and the Irregularities of Disenfranchisement

The purpose of this discussion is to shed light on the electoral process from the perspective of those whom the literature refers to as the disenfranchised or disfranchised American. In this regard it is important that we concentrate on the most salient aspects of the procedures that factor in the debate. The major questions that should be asked are: First, were the election processes fair? Second, what are the major factors in the system that contributes to the debate insofar as Americans in general and Black Americans specifically, are concerned? Third, are there events in the electoral process which operate singly or in tandem with other contributing factors? Fourth, are the outcomes of elections a true representation of the wishes of the American people in the spirit and intent of the U.S. Constitution? Fifth, how might historical antecedents be used as a blueprint for behavioral adjustments for both the White and Black populations?

To examine these questions we must first understand them in the context of the historical traditions that brought about the debate, grievances, and the adjudication of constitutional issues in a partisan/neutral manner. The eventual certification of contested votes or the prerequisite registrations have historically precipitated multiple legal challenges and have been viewed by most as more than snapshots of events in the course of time. Also these events are really on a historical continuum; and they serve as guiding beacons for the outcomes we witness today, and the concomitant criticisms.

For example, to put it another way, the circumstances of the modern day American Indian in terms of the quality of health care, and employment factors are due to the reservation mentality of years past. We are fully aware of the fact that the reservation is a white European creation, so too are ghettos and barrios. These geographic entities were created for containment purposes for those who are characterized as different and/or inferior. They were also created for the exercise of political power, race/ethnic and gender separation, and control. But every now and then a new paradigm is needed to explain phenomena for which the traditional thinking has led or leads to an inadequate response. Such is the case with school shootings and violence against women.

It was previously thought that the majority of our intervention efforts should be in the community where the containment process is complete, i.e., reservations, ghettos, and barrios. It is in these locations where police patrols and fixed barriers are commonplace. Those with wealth have long absconded from the cities and are now residing in our nation's suburbs and rural districts. It has been their belief that they had left the problems of social inadequacies behind. But we are now witnessing the confusion and uncertainty of what to do next when our basic freedom and bedrock of our republic, voting, is compromised. The political promises of economic comfort and opportunities are just two issues at stake when it is believed that our voting rights have been impaired. But much more than this, is the harm that is done to the established values guaranteed in our Constitutional Bill of Rights, and to all of the amendments in their totality which are the embodiment of who we are as Americans. After each voting irregularity episode there is a lot of finger pointing, but no clear solutions have been advanced. A new paradigm is required because the majority group traditions of one person, one vote has been breached; and lingering attitudes on causal relationships are difficult to change which percolated to the surface in the years 2000, 2004, and 2008.

Returning now to our original problem on the electoral process, and the first question regarding the issue of fairness, the *Los Angeles Times* had this to say, "Elections throughout the country are under-financed, badly managed, ill-equipped and poorly staffed. Election workers are temporaries; pay is a pittance, training is brief, and voting systems are obsolete. In Miami-Dade county Florida alone [for the 2000 election] 9,000 votes were discarded" (*The Orlando Sentinel*, 12-17-00, p. G1). Thus disenfranchisement becomes a reality because we are now realizing a situation that is the result of more than an occasional error here and there.

While presidential campaigns are rapidly becoming billion dollar business ventures, for example, Obama spent three quarters of a billion dollars in his 2008 presidential campaign, one would think with that amount of money being raised and spent, the mechanisms which are used to record the votes would be the state-of-the art technology. Unfortunately such is not the case. The same *Los Angeles Times* reported that, "New York City voters use metal lever-action machines so old they are no longer made and each with 27,000 parts. Similar machines in Louisiana are vulnerable to rigging with pliers, or a screwdriver, or cigarette lighter, and [even] a Q-tip can be used to alter the intentions of the voter" (Ibid.). In the recent past, ample evidence has been provided which shows that these problems are more prevalent in minority communities.

Additionally, in Texas, they have a system in place that is colloquially called "vote whores" whose purpose are to do favors for people in return for their absentee ballots. While they prefer to be called canvassers or consultants, the label "vote Whores" has stuck because they simply purchase ballots, and some even go so far as to steal them from mailboxes which compounds the problem by escalating a misdemeanor into a felony (Ibid.). Therefore should we not wonder how Bush beat Ann Richards in the 1994 Texas gubernatorial race, and then was reelected in 1998; or why he carried Texas so handily in the 2000 presidential election, and once again in 2004, and in 2008 nothing was stated or occurred that would make such practices transparent and obsolete. And then the many accounts of irregularities in Florida have become almost legendary. Historically these aforementioned corrupt practices have evolved and flourished under the scrutiny of election officials whose job it is to ensure a fair and open process. Apparently the so-called transparency factor which supposedly America prides itself on in our voting system is not as crystal clear as some would have us believe. Rather it is more prone to optical illusions, and cheap slight-of-hand carnival tricks, i.e., the candidate for whom you thought you cast your vote for is not the one that received your vote. All of this is accomplished by calculated design that is intended to disenfranchise a group in a particular locale or district. And who better to serve as a target than the group who has historically experienced disenfranchisement. Therefore, with this group, any complaints of impropriety would be met with skepticism; and the traditional mindset of White supremacy and male dominance, and the concomitant oppressive practices would be legitimized by defensive tactics and support.

On further reflection we must also consider the psyche and background of the person who has aspired or conspired to become the most powerful individual in the world – the President of the United States. Has he earned the right to be called Mr. President, or soon, Madam President? While I will continue to advance this discussion to address these major points, it is interesting to note that for many who make character a major argument in campaigns, will often be less than forthright in bringing many of their shortcomings to light. Character, it would seem, should be an important requisite for the job.

In 2000 the majority of American voters cast their ballots for Vice President Al Gore, and likewise, the majority of Democrats during the 2008 primary cast their votes for Senator Hillary Clinton. Therefore, what they each have in common is that while they received a majority of votes, they both lost their elections. If a person would not hesitate to win at any cost, and thus use the disenfranchising tactics that I spoke of earlier and in previous chapters, what then is our obligation to them as "pseudo-victors." As an example, some say George W. Bush was the architect of his father's 1988 presidential strategy that used a Black man, a felon named Willie Horton, in his political ad to provoke a racial backlash against his father's opponent, Michael Dukakis. I have already established that race was used against President Clinton as he supported his wife's candidacy in 2008. Also keep in mind a similar charge was made by the Clinton supporters against the Obama campaign which aided in him receiving a technical win as opposed to an outright victory, in the primary of 2008. And the data that is most revealing which gives me reason to pause is that 16% of all adults surveyed in 2000 stated that they would not accept "Bushie" (nickname his wife gave him) as president, 30% of Gore's supporters stated the same; and 1% of his (Bushie's) own supporters would not accept him as president.

And while 1% does not sound like much, keep in mind that 50,456,169 people voted for him which was 539,947 votes less than the 50,996,116 that voted for Vice President Gore. And 1% of Bushie's total is 50,456 people. These are his own supporters that will not accept him as president, enough to populate a small city, which is a lot of folks when viewed in this context; particularly when they may influence another person's vote in the future. For example there is substantial evidence that Bush and his inner circle were less than candid with the people about the war in Iraq. Also in the month of March (2001), he broke a campaign promise about clean air legislation and the pollutant carbon dioxide which will not be part of his legislative agenda.

And Obama himself broke a campaign promise that he would not receive campaign funds beyond that allowed under the federal guidelines. The federal funding is provided to maintain an even playing field where one candidate does not receive a financial advantage over another. This also guards against the appearance that one candidate is attempting to "buy" the election with ads and marketing gimmicks designed to overwhelm their opponent with spending. It is commonly understood that money in America can purchase almost anything including the Presidency of the United States. If we are not to acknowledge the basic truism of the power of money, then we all must do a reality check of why we established federal guidelines in the first place. The reversal by Bush was said to have caught many members of his own party off guard, and embarrassed his Environmental Secretary, Christine Whitman (CNN, March 9, 2000). Breaking campaign promises do tend to catch people by surprise. No doubt this will not come as a revelation to anyone reading this text.

Additionally in 2000 and to date, the majority of Americans disagreed with Bush's tax proposals, and are not too crazy about the Obama plans either. Bush eliminated the Office of Race Relations from the White House, a move, of course, which some of his supporters applauded. But the controversy surrounding his Faith-Based Initiative with his core constituency has not helped his political image, however, Obama has established his own faith-based program. These were events that Bush's fragile coalition could ill-afford, particularly when the majority of Americans did not support him in the first place. But Obama appears to be getting a pass for developing the exact same religious agenda. Many European leaders criticized Bush's environmental positions, and they question whether he was up to the job (*Associated Press*); and Obama with less experience has not been scrutinized in like fashion. Bush also went on record to try and convince Americans that a little more arsenic in our drinking water will not be injurious to our health which was a ridiculous assertion; but Obama also has nonsensical statements to account for that has contributed to his image as arrogant, and his self-proclaimed personal trait of being egotistical.

In the closing matter of George W. Bush and the comparison with the 2008 Obama campaign, it is one thing to have a 53% job approval rating, but yet a far other problem to have 47% of the American public state that they would not accept you as their president. Even President Clinton, with all of his so-called moral issues, in December 2000 had a job approval rating of 66%, the highest it had been since after impeachment and acquittal by the U.S. Senate. It appeared that the closer "Bushie" got to the presidency, the more the American public embraced Clinton (*USA Today*, 12-18-2000, p. 8A). And the closer Bush got to the end of his second term the more the public embraced Obama which makes his 2004 re-election all the more puzzling. Finally an article by journalist Richard Benedetto concluded that for "Bushie" to "Rebuild public confidence most [of those surveyed] said [electoral] reforms are needed to make the mechanics of the voting and vote-counting systems more fair." But the question of voter fraud still lingers in the question of the registration processes that led to federal investigations in subsequent years.

Section II: Critical Thinking and Fact Based Knowledge

In this section I will explore the dual concepts of Critical Thinking and Chaos Theory. They were purposefully selected as a means to provide conceptual clarity to the complex problem of disenfranchisement and its historical foundation. Critical thinking is defined as that thinking which involves the capacity to distinguish beliefs from knowledge, and fact from judgment. According to one source "Someone skilled in critical thinking [and fact based knowledge] is able to analyze, criticize, and advocate ideas... [and furthermore] when a critical thinker makes a judgmental conclusion that is based in whole, or in part on a personal belief, s/he should understand the extent to which the belief has influenced his/her judgment" (Steffen W. Schmidt, Mark C. Shelley II, Barbara A. Bardes, [1989]. *An Introduction To Critical Thinking In American Politics: American Government and Politics Today*, West Publishing Co., St. Paul, MN, p. 2).

It is the last sentence in the above paragraph which best characterizes much of the logic, or rather illogic that has guided the political process, insofar as Black Americans, women, and other ethnic minorities are concerned. But in this treatise I will continue to demonstrate that White supremacy and misogyny transcends even the most tension provoking boundaries of Black-White and male-female relationships due to mistrust, violence, and fear which are essential ingredients for it to thrive; and thus it may even have a pejorative effect on its potential political allies. That is to say that there are other ethnic minorities, and a fraction of the poor, who, for their own ignorance and selfish reasons have traditionally aligned themselves against Black and female interests and equality.

For example, the intercultural and class alliances which are formed as a protest against affirmative action are often themselves victimized when the spirit of justice is compromised and manipulated by reactionaries. It is commonly understood that White females are the greatest beneficiaries of Affirmative Action and Title IX. (Title IX is that section which stipulates that there should be parity in the funding of both female and male athletic programs. Historically women athletics have been under funded and undervalued which placed them at a disadvantage to fully participate.) But many of them are taught that Affirmative Action is a Black initiative that provides preferential treatment. And they embrace this myth often at the expense of their own future progress. Unfortunately it is also their daughters who will experience negative effects and discrimination at the hands of men who they have helped to eliminate their remedy for justice in the job market and elsewhere.

Also in analyzing elections from a Chaos Theory and systems perspective, with the juxtaposition of the principles of Critical Thinking, will help us to further determine if there is true randomness in the nature of events. On the other hand, if there were a contrived set of circumstances set in motion by over-zealous loyal supporters, then the extent of partisanship will help us to analyze those visible conflicts of interest.

While Chaos Theory presupposes a condition which is subject to some in-deterministic factor(s), it also posits that some of these factors have clear parameters with historical antecedents that were, at the same time, subject to human manipulation (Ralph Anderson and Irk Carter [1990]. *Human Behavior in the Social Environment: A Systems Approach*, 4th Edition, Aldine Detroiter, NY). The founders of our nation recognized that there was a potential for electoral irregularities in terms of power and control issues of the wealthy which is, in large part, why they made constitutional provisions for the separation of the branches of government, as well as differential terms of office in the House and Senate.

Furthermore, their distrust of a too powerful government led them to add the constitutional Tenth Amendment which is commonly known as "States Rights." It is this amendment that served as the philosophical and political basis for the eleven state secession and the resulting Civil War. A number of historical events can be traced to show the interplay of the logical and illogical aspects of critical thinking, and the White supremacists, and/or the misogynist's roles in a Chaos Theory paradigm.

No one can doubt the greatness of our Constitution, and the years of thoughtful labor it took for its creation. But as already mentioned elsewhere in this treatise, the founders were faced

112

with the dilemma of slavery, and extending citizenship rights with the franchise guaranteed by the Constitution to those they had enslaved and oppressed. By relegating Blacks to a subhuman status in the Constitution (three-fifths of a person, Article I, Section 2, Clause3), they demonstrated the illogical side of fact-based knowledge, and critical thinking, as they are applied within a White supremacist and political framework. And similar arguments can be used, in part, as we examine the value of woman hatred in America.

Another example is the 1816 Presidential Election of James Monroe in which he received virtually no political opposition (see Appendix). And by the time of his 1820 re-election, his victory was so overwhelming that they dubbed this time period the "Era of Good Feeling." According to an encyclopedic source, this period signaled a *transformation* in American life in terms of its internal and external political development (Inter-American Copyright Union, Processing and Books, Inc., Chicago, IL, 1968, p. 5150). Internally there was the Missouri Compromise of 1820 which was hailed as a legislative victory by the abolitionists. It prohibited the expansion of slavery into newly acquired U.S. territories.

Then externally there was the Monroe Doctrine that served as the basic philosophy of American foreign policy until the Second World War. This Doctrine gave "official sanction to an isolationistic attitude toward the rest of the world indicating [our] growing preoccupation with the development of [our] vast continental domain" (p. 5151). Of course this development, to a great extent, depended upon the sweated labor and pain of some four million American slaves who never realized the "Era of Good Feeling" as they were a disenfranchised group by Constitutional Law. The following discussion on this part of America's history is important for our understanding of its significance to our contemporary electoral dilemma:

> *The 'Era of Good Feeling' [did finally come to an end] with the presidential election of 1824 when despite the existence of only one political party, the intra-party quarrels*

113

manifested themselves in four candidacies, those of John Quincy Adams, Henry Clay, William H. Crawford, and Andrew Jackson. Since none of these men gained a majority of electoral votes, the decision was thrown into the House of Representatives for the first time since the election of Thomas Jefferson in 1800. There Clay, who had received the fewest number of votes, threw his support to Adams, with the result that the two other candidates were defeated. Jackson's supporters immediately advanced the unsubstantiated charge of a 'corrupt bargain' between Adams and Clay, particularly after Clay was named Secretary of State; and in 1827 Jackson revived the accusation to defeat Adams' bid for reelection and to gain the presidency for himself. [This should serve as a precedent lesson for subsequent presidential elections given the backdoor manner in which George W. Bush attained the 2000 presidency, and the manner in which Obama emerged victorious in the Democratic 2008 primary.] Thus, Adams [as did George W. Bush] began his administration with a great deal of personal opposition; and to compound his difficulties he proposed a program of nationalistic legislation [which at the time was highly controversial] of road and canal building, and the Tariff of 1828 (Encyclopedia, Op.Cit.).

The Adam's Tariff plan is a tax scheme which should sound familiar due to "Bushie's" legislative agenda of an unnecessary tax cut plan primarily for the wealthy, which Obama pledged to overturn. Adam's tax plan was characterized by the Jackson supporters as the "Tariff of Abomination." It was seen as too high, and untimely, which is a chillingly familiar reminder of the 2000, 2004, and 2008 election campaigns where taxes, political/legal ethics, and disenfranchisement were of central focus. Interestingly in the elections of 1800 when Jefferson took the oath of office on March 4, 1801, which was then inaugural day, he too was concerned with stability and unity in the nation. "He was aware that his speech would be published and widely read, [and therefore] he called upon America's founding ideals. He spoke of his election reflecting 'the Voice of the Nation, the Will of the Law,' and the Rules of the Constitution. He[also] appealed to 'common efforts for the common good'" (Delio M. Rios, Newhouse News Service, 12-17-2000).

It must be pointed out, in keeping with the thesis of this treatise, that Jefferson himself was a slave-owner; and as one of the architects of the Constitution, he helped guarantee that slavery and disenfranchisement would be institutionalized as the "common good." The "common efforts" of course included maintaining the status quo of superiority and inferiority, which added to the flux of illogical speech and actions that set the traditions of White supremacy and disenfranchisement in motion. Inevitably, there had to be chaos, albeit well thought out, even illogical, but planned just the same. There was no randomness to the events, past or present. As the "states rights" proponent Jefferson was once quoted as saying, "If there is a God, we are going to pay for this," i.e., the incongruence on which independence was won, the language of the Constitution, its compromises, its high moral tone, and slavery itself.

Section III: Civil War Amendments and Jim Crow Laws

As previously mentioned there are three post "Civil War Constitutional Amendments," the 13th, 14th, and 15th. They were adopted in succession as legal remedies to correct the injustices of slavery. Enslavement, like misogyny, carries with it the automatic stigma of "nobodyness," and as far as America was concerned this was a cultural tradition that was not going to pass easily into oblivion. History has demonstrated that it was easier to pass laws and adopt Constitutional Amendments to address the problem of slavery, than it has been to dismantle the institutional barriers it has created. And because America's primary institution is the ballot box, it has been the most vigorously protected freedom in the nation. Dialogue at the local, state, and federal levels of government have taken place between, and during political campaigns since America's inception to sort out ideologies related to the franchise.

While the abolition of slavery, the 13th Amendment, did not change attitudes regarding the inferiority status of Black Americans, the 14th Amendment was necessary to provide citizenship and equal protection of the law because the attitudes of the White population were resistant to change. The 15th Amendment which guaranteed the right to vote was incomplete because it only extended the franchise to men; and it was not until a half a century later that the

115

voting rights of women were fully guaranteed by the 19th Amendment to the Constitution, and then the Daughters of the Confederacy attempted to deny Black women the benefit of this amendment. But in between that time span, 1870 to 1920, Black Americans were subjected to some of the most brutal and criminal acts imagined while trying to take full advantage of their newly granted Constitutional rights.

The restrictive Black Codes that replaced the slave codes were instituted post-bellum, 1865-66. The Black Codes prevented the newly freed slaves from free access to America's institutions and became known as Jim Crow Laws after the abolition of slavery (13th Constitutional Amendment) in 1865. There were three primary mechanisms adopted by the White supremacists to ensure their "superior" voting status. The Poll Tax, the Literacy Test, and Grandfather Clause were the result of a lot of time and energy spent in state legislatures developing laws for repressive purposes to demonstrate a kind of fact-based knowledge on the Black Americans inability to participate in the political process.

The sweeping effect of the Jim Crow Laws covered every movement and every act, both in the public and private sectors, for which Blacks could, by Constitutional right, legally engage in, but were prohibited to do so by Jim Crow. Thus, Jim Crow ordinances superseded the Constitution's Fourteenth Amendment, thereby rendering the Fifteenth amendment weak and ineffective, with the result of calling into question the validity of the Thirteenth Amendment. As an example the South Carolina Code stipulated that in the making of contracts "persons of color shall be known as servants and those with whom they contract shall be known as masters" (Benjamin Quarles, 1987, p. 154).

Interestingly enough, legal and political challenges to Jim Crow were blocked by the Tenth Amendment (States Rights); and this bizarre twist of fate resting in the illogical

116

conclusions of White supremacy as fact-based knowledge was upheld by the post antebellum Supreme Courts. As we have witnessed in the 2000 and 2004 elections, it is indeed extremely important as to who is elected president, if for no other reason than their ability to appoint Supreme Court Justices who will serve long after the president who appointed them is out of office. "Bushie" was "selected" president by a Supreme Court that was largely comprised of appointees made by his papa, (George Sr.), and the darling of the Republican Party, Ronald Reagan.

These issues were cogently addressed by Justice Stephen Breyer who argued the following: Although the selection of the President is of fundamental national importance, but his importance is political, not legal. And "this court" should resist the temptation unnecessarily to resolve tangential legal disputes, where doing so threatens to determine the outcome of the election. Justice Breyer further contrasted the 2000 election with the Hayes v. Tilden election in 1896. He contended that the court members becoming partisan undermined the nation's respect for the court.

To further press the point on the Supreme Court's decision in Bush v. Gore, various critics have maintained that the need to decide the case was far less compelling than it has been in other cases in which the other branches of the state or federal governments had failed to properly redress wrongs (Tony Sutin, ed., Appalachian School of Law, April 2001). It was Justice Breyer again who countered the late Chief Justice Rehnquist's rationale that the Presidential election was a compelling reason for the court to hear the case. Breyer stated that "no preeminent legal concern, or practical concern related to legal questions, required the court to hear the case, let alone to issue a stay that stopped Florida's recount process in its tracks" (Ibid.).

117

And the court being divided down ideological, and some would say, political lines in their 5-4 decision is evidence enough that Justice Breyer was correct in his assertions. Indeed, this was a repeat of the only other three cases of this type in American history, i.e., Thomas Jefferson in 1800 v. John Adams an incumbent who was denied a second term; John Quincy Adams in 1824 v. Andrew Jackson; and Rutherford B. Hayes v. Samuel Tilden in 1876. In each instance the values of the country of course prevailed by the political deals that were cut which left their mark in American history, while undermining Black progress under federalism or state's rights.

I hope by now it is very clear that we are engaged in an analysis of fact based knowledge of events that have predictable conclusions, particularly for disenfranchised Americans. It does not take much stretch of the imagination to assert that very little has changed since 1787, in the way of attitudes and law to rectify White supremacy, and its long-standing companion, disenfranchisement. While voting rights and election laws have been passed by many progressive minded and decent people of diverse backgrounds, these laws are still subject to interpretation and challenge by reactionary forces, Black as well as White. It is common to these folks to maintain an obtuse tradition of States Rights and Constitutionality even at the expense of our American Democracy.

For example, under Chief Justice Salmon P. Chase (1864-1873), we have learned that the Supreme Court's rulings reflected a preservation of the prior courts attitude towards "legal localism," or States Right (http://gi.grollier.com/presidents/es/side/const.html). Also federal law instituted to correct or provide a remedy for a local issue was not viewed as an appropriate solution. Even the Civil Rights Act of 1875 was deemed unconstitutional eight years later by the Supreme Court, at that time, because it was said to interfere with local authority and police

118

responsibilities for upholding the law. The laws that were being called into question were Jim Crow which prohibited Blacks from exercising their citizenship rights and equal protection of the law (14th Amendment), in terms of access to courts, accommodations, and the franchise.

After the *Plessy v. Ferguson* ruling in 1896, where the Supreme Court took a firmer stand on keeping Blacks in "their place," by affirming that separate was equal (American Apartheid), the issue of the ballot box also became closed to Blacks in the south, and open only on a limited basis in the north. The primary areas in the north where Blacks were able to exercise a semblance of voting rights were in the large urban areas where their numbers could be useful to White political machine politics, say for example in Chicago. But Blacks knew that any challenge to the "machine" might be dealt with by violence to themselves and their family. Therefore the corruption of gangs, political cronyism, neighborhood deterioration, and rampant discrimination flourished, in the early 1900s (20th Century), as it still does in this early part of the 21st Century.

And, too, historically the degradation that Blacks experienced by being called to segregated military service, and forced into sub-standard conditions and job assignments; then serving and dying for their country, but unable to freely vote as a right of citizenship, is beyond comprehension. But this is commonplace in America. It was, and still remains, tradition; and the recent events in Florida, Ohio, and Michigan are an indication that in the 21st Century we are not far removed from these disparaging, unconstitutional conditions. The same premise upon which the Twenty Sixth (XXVI) Amendment to the Constitution was based, as adopted in 1971, which lowered the voting age to 18 years is the same premise that Black Americans expects from the nation. But often it takes community organizers, and organizations such as ACORN to help those who have been locked out of the political process. The war in Vietnam was graphically

119

shown on television for everyone in the nation and world to see. What they witnessed were young Americans, some barely out of high school, not old enough yet to legally buy beer, were dying on the field of battle in unprecedented numbers

For most Americans it was appalling that these same young people were not permitted to vote, and therefore unable to have a say in the election of those political leaders who were making policy decisions on a war which was increasingly becoming unpopular nationwide. To many Americans this disenfranchisement was unconscionable. How unfortunate it is, that so many Americans have fought and died on the home front to secure the franchise for Blacks; and then for there to be constant resistance to a barrier free electoral process where every vote counts is also unconscionable. Indeed a significant number of people believed that the Vietnam War was utter chaos. But war in general is chaotic, even though a considerable amount of strategy and planning goes into its prosecution.

This is all the more reason why those who have experienced the weight of oppression and battle should also have the power of an unencumbered vote. When Rutherford G. Hayes, for example, took the oath of office after he too was "selected" for the presidency; he knew that the deal he cut with Congress that secured the defeat of Samuel Tilden, would ultimately lead to the destruction of the hopes for justice held by millions of Black Americans. The "Hayes Bargain" (1877), was intended for one purpose only which was to relegate Blacks to their antebellum status of chattel, with no citizenship rights regardless of the provisions contained in the Civil War Amendments.

It was also the voting irregularities in the southern states of Louisiana, South Carolina, and of course Florida which were central to the special circumstances that brought Hayes to the Presidency. His selection was similar to Bushie's, 123 year later, with both of their ascension to

120

office marked by the loss of a majority popular votes. Other similarities are also worth mentioning, in addition to the fact that Florida once again played a pivotal role in both the 2000 and 2008 elections, along with Michigan in the latter year. This could indicate that these voting irregularities are endemic to our electoral process (see endnotes, "More Primaries"). The Hayes selection ushered in Jim Crow in full force, with all of its negative and dire consequences for Blacks, in terms of restrictions, exclusions and violence.

The advent of the Black Codes in a Jim Crow society was a calculated effort to return Black Americans to antebellum chattel status. And with Bushie and Obama being the most recent beneficiaries of disenfranchisement problems, they of course have no real incentive to investigate and prohibit their reoccurrence. Therefore it is safe to say that they, like Hayes, have benefitted from a significant amount of barriers to progress and justice.

Section IV: Felon Disenfranchisement

In researching this portion of the text, it occurred to me, as I examined the Constitution, that it is devoid of language that speaks directly to the voting rights of incarcerated persons. The Constitution is silent on the nation's or individual state's responsibility in allowing or disallowing a convicted person their right to the ballot. Of course there are many different circumstances and all types of criminal behavior that must be considered by the government and its agents of law enforcement.

However it is worth evaluating whether or not the law enforcement community's job is made easier by denying a convict, or an ex-felon the right to vote. But there must be some legitimate reason, aside from additional punishment, that denial of one's voting rights is never stated as part of the formal sentencing procedure. It is sort of an understood section of a state's statute that upon conviction, zap, there goes your constitutional voting rights. An estimated four

121

to five million Americans, disproportionately Black and Brown, have lost the vote because they have committed felonies.

According to Jonathan Tilave of the Newhouse News Service, "The impact of felon disenfranchisement is uneven across the country, because the rules vary state by state." For example, Maine, Massachusetts, Utah and Vermont do not disenfranchise any of their incarcerated criminals, but in Alabama a pardon is the only means for a felon to regain their voting rights (August 2000). It is critically important to point out that the Sentencing Project based in Washington, D.C. reported in a 1998 study, that estimates given at that time had 3.9 million Americans under felony disenfranchisement, and 1.4 million of them were Black. Additionally, and of equal importance, research found that when they examined close U.S. Senate elections since 1978, the "felon vote could have reversed Republican victories in Virginia, Texas, Georgia, Kentucky, Florida, and Wyoming."

It should be noted also that five of these states are part of the old confederacy, steeped in the tradition of apartheid. Also, two of these states, Texas, and Florida are the home states of the Bush regimes which are historically noted for their repressive policies against minorities. Also in Michigan, only the 45,000 felons held in prisons or elsewhere, including home confinement cannot vote; and 54% of the inmates are Black. If those who cannot vote, could vote, the American electorate would be less White, and the fortunes of Democrats, who tend to win minority voters by significant and sometimes overwhelming margins, would be more secure than they are now (Ibid.). And women candidates might do much better on the progressive side. Furthermore, Michigan and Florida were central to Obama's victory in the 2008 primary; at best, an interesting coincidence given each state's voting/legal challenges in the past.

When we add to this mix an observation made by an Alabama democratic party operative we get a very disturbing picture of American apartheid. He stated the following: "In Alabama, we have 105,000 Black men who are ineligible to vote because of felony convictions. If I had just 20,000 of them, that could have turned around several close statewide races in the 1998 general election where Democratic candidates lost by less than 10,000 votes" (Ibid.). The disparity in the incarceration rates and sentencing procedures between Black and White folks is well documented. Political mischief and schemes are an ever present part of American tradition which was again confirmed in the 2008 election cycle, Democratic primaries included.

The following table, graphically demonstrates this dynamic. Please observe the incredible differences between the percentage of adult's disenfranchised category, and the percentage of Black men who are disenfranchised in each state. Laws of disenfranchisement have an impact on the number of those who cannot vote. And states that disenfranchise felons for life have a greater number of those who cannot vote than other states. The United States totals are equally depressing, i.e., overall there are 2% of adults disenfranchised, and there are an astounding 13.1% of Black men who are not permitted to vote by law.

To add further clarity to these twenty-three state data, it is important to point out that one of the states with the highest percentage of disenfranchised for life is Florida at 5.9% with 31.2% Black men denied the right to vote. Interestingly enough, Texas is also among the states with the highest number of total disenfranchised persons at 4.5% with 20.8% of Black men officially denied the franchise. These data, coupled with the incarceration rates of Black men at about 50% of the total prison population nationwide, demonstrates that we must consider these events when put in a historical context. They simply are too compelling to be purely happenstance; nor

123

TABLE 1

States with over 10% disenfranchisement rates for Black men	Percentage of adults disenfranchised	Percentage of Black men who are disenfranchised
Alabama	7.5	31.5
Arizona	2.3	12.1
Connecticut	1.7	14.8
Delaware	3.7	20.0
Florida	5.9	31.2
Georgia	2.5	10.5
Iowa	2.0	26.5
Maryland	3.6	15.4
Minnesota	1.6	17.8
Mississippi	7.4	28.6
Missouri	1.5	11.3
Nebraska	1.0	10.2
Nevada	1.4	10.0
New Jersey	2.3	17.7
New Mexico	4.0	24.1
Oklahoma	1.5	12.3
Rhode Island	1.8	18.3
Tennessee	2.4	14.5
Texas	4.5	20.8
Virginia	5.3	25.0
Washington	3.7	24.0
Wisconsin	1.3	18.2
Wyoming	4.1	27.7

Source: Census Bureau. Current population survey data by Steven A. Camarota, Center for Immigration Studies. The Sentencing Project. (Newhouse News Service, 8-2000).

should there be disenfranchisement in the 21st Century as occurred in Michigan and Florida.

This is another major reason that the differential sentencing policies for crack and powder cocaine were ruled grossly unjust. It is believed that a greater percentage of Blacks use the less costly "crack" form of cocaine rather than the expensive powder form, and that the reverse is true for Whites. Despite legal wrangling, a Black man using crack in our society is still more apt to receive a felony conviction, while a White man is more likely to be offered a plea bargain to a misdemeanor. The Congressional Black Caucus attempted to address this inequity with a "fairness in sentencing" proposal to the Clinton administration, but the Republican controlled Congress, at that time, rejected their efforts, and political pressure continues to effect the judicial decisions.

These sentencing practices are occurring all over the United States. In those states with felony disenfranchisement, the Black men, some as young as 18 years of age, who are given prison sentences for crack possession will lose their voting rights for life; while a White drug abuser of powder cocaine in the same state can continue to vote. It is the stereotype of the crack user as a low income, violent inner city/ghetto resident; and powder cocaine as the drug of preference by the upscale or middle class person, educated and with some political influence that the rationale for the unequal sentencing structure is and was biased. While it is generally understood that drugs are the scourge of our society, the unequal sentencing and disenfranchisement tells us that historically it is the Black perpetrator who is the menace and should be feared. (Note: Still today the debate continues on the medicinal effects of legalizing marijuana, with some referring to it as a selfish act by drug users cloaked in effective clinical practice. Decades ago the Surgeon General pronounced that smoking is hazardous to one's health. Has this medical decision changed?) (See Jim Webb Endnotes.)

Section V: The Voting Rights Act and The Debate on the Need For ACORN

A "Bill of Rights" was not included in the original Constitution; and in regards to the principle that all American citizens should have equal rights and opportunities assured by society, the Constitution itself was devoid of specific language or mechanisms for attainment of these principles. According to one historical discussion, the framing of the Constitution and the talk of its revisions even then had steadily grown. Alexander Hamilton, a nemesis of Thomas Jefferson, had been dissatisfied with the Articles of Confederation from the very start. While the "Articles" had been written and ratified in 1781 during Britain's occupation of the "colonies," the fledgling government that was being conceptualized by the framers indicated that they were more concerned with individual state protection and responsibilities than instituting a powerful central government. Of course Hamilton and his crew did not agree with that philosophy.

But the inclusion of judicial power and authority, the rule of law for both citizenry and government protection, as well as the separation of government to achieve a balance of power were the concepts that precipitated support and approval of the original Constitution. Although there were several aborted attempts to amend the Articles of Confederation, those involved in the Constitutional Convention in 1787 all agreed that a new document was necessary; and too, there were still compelling and conflicting interests to be resolved between small and large states.

One major question of course, as previously stated, was the sticking point of Congressional representation and slavery (Grolier website, Op.Cit.). The Compromise of 1787 resolved that issue by imposing a twenty year time frame for the continued importation of slaves, and establishing the three-fifths of a man principle (Article I, Section 2) from which our nation has yet to overcome its serious divisive effects. And Article II, Section 1 of the Constitution that gave us the Electoral College has been a point of consternation, for instance in the 2000

126

Presidential race. Bushie receiving 271 electoral votes to Gore's 266 does not reflect the majority will of the people. The battle in Florida was over its 25 electoral votes, but the issue of power between the central government and states' rights are underscored below.

Two central issues of federalism are, first, providing the federal government with sufficient power to enforce its will, and second, imposing a limit on the concept of popular democracy. The latter is defined by the concept of rule by the majority while at the same time protecting the principles of social equality, and the respect for individual rights. The notion of federalism of course has been at the center of the debate by scholars for well over two hundred years. The Federalist Papers written by Alexander Hamilton in collaboration with James Madison and John Jay (his crew) were originally a series of letters that he sent to the *New York Press*, and then subsequently published as *The Federalist*. In *The Federalist* he pushed for the ratification of the Constitution, and it was his interpretation that provided the foundation for much of the activity of our current government policies on finance and social welfare (The New College Encyclopedia).

The collection of the eighty-five Federalist essays (1787-88) which were published in two volumes in 1788 provided support for a strong national government and was the basis for our two party system. But it was the Federalist Chief Justice John Marshall who set many lasting precedents in constitutional interpretation. In *Marbury v. Madison* (1803) he established the Supreme Court's right to rule on the constitutionality of Congressional legislation interpreted as "Judicial Review." He also repeatedly opposed the doctrine of state's rights and his rulings strengthened federal prerogatives (Ibid., p. 558). Interestingly it was in the *Marbury v. Madison* ruling in which the court held that the Constitution did not empower the court to issue "writs of mandamus," and the section of the Judiciary Act of 1789 that granted such power was declared unconstitutional.

Mandamus is a legal writ that is issued by a superior court which orders a public official or body or a lower court to perform a specified duty. For example a state supreme court ordering a trial court to change its opinion on the validity of ballot recounts, or ordering the Secretary of State to reverse their decision on recounts and certification of an election. Even though the Florida Supreme Court overruled a trial court as an exercise in State's Rights, it too was overruled by the United States Supreme Court which was a contrary position to State's Rights. This ruling would have been applauded by the first Chief Justice John Marshall, who established this precedent, but much to the chagrin of the third president of the United States, Thomas Jefferson. Ironically his two-term presidency (1801-1809) (see Appendix), expanded through part of the tenure of Chief Justice John Marshall (1801-1835).

Although Jefferson had bitter disputes with Alexander Hamilton over centralism; he was elected to his first term as President by the House of Representatives (73 to 65 electoral votes) after Hamilton supported him to block the election of Aaron Burr. Jefferson easily won reelection in 1804, but Hamilton was subsequently challenged to a duel by Aaron Burr, the sitting Vice President, who shot and killed Hamilton on July 11, 1804. A fitting precedent; learning to settle disputes with gun violence (thirteen years after passage of the Bill of Rights 1791, including the 2nd Amendment – gun rights).

While it was Jefferson who supported individual liberties and recommended the elimination of slavery in the western territories; the schisms that we have today over State's Rights versus the rights of the individual, and the role of the federal government (Congress, Administration, and the Supreme Court) are not without a great amount of historical drama, consternation, and conflict. This dynamic made the Civil War an inevitable consequence, and gives rise to our current inability to sort these problems out in a just and concluding fashion.

The pervasiveness of this dilemma, and alliances that preceded the Civil War can be understood yet in another way. Napoleon Bonaparte and the French people could not rationalize the purpose and onset of the French Revolution (1789-99) while at the same time pursuing the course of slavery in the West Indies, particularly in Haiti. Then after losing Haiti in its war for independence from slavery and oppression, Napoleon figured that he would cut his losses in the Western Hemisphere altogether, and thus sell all the territory owned by France in the West Indies and America to the United States. The Louisiana Purchase (1803), as it was called, doubled the size of the United States; and because it was accomplished under the administration of President Thomas Jefferson it created other major concerns for The Federalists, i.e., Alexander Hamilton, Aaron Burr, et al.

First, the acquisition failed to please The Federalists of New England – the northern states, many of whom were fanatical in their fear of an increase in the numbers of slave states; thereby, secondly fearing a tilt in the balance of Congressional power resulting in the growth of leadership of the Virginia contingent led by Jefferson. And because Hamilton refused to go along with a scheme that would have made Burr governor of New York to thwart the power and influence of the southerners, he paid for this decision with his life (Ibid.). The ideological differences in the two parties became increasingly distinct and hardened in the ensuing decades prior to the onset of the Civil War (April 12, 1861).

France and England, once bitter enemies vying for the control of the colonies and Western Hemisphere were united in their refusal to recognize the Confederate States of America as a separate power. Even though each country had a common history and shared a destiny

129

woven by Revolution, Civil Strife, Government, and Ethnicity, they also created many of their own troubles by institutionalizing the practice of Slavery.

But unfortunately as previously described, the extraordinary events surrounding exclusionary politics and rhetoric that gave racist attitudes, beliefs, and actions their foundation in America, are little understood by the vast majority of Americans. It was noted in 1968 by the National Advisory Commission on Civil Disorders that "most Americans know little of the origins of the racial schism separating our White and Black citizens. And few appreciate how central the problem of Black oppression has been to our social policy" (Bantam Books, NY, 1968). The purpose of the previous discussion then is to provide the reader with a sense of the historical connections, and continuum of events that have led to the need for legislation and judicial action to correct past injustices.

And moreover, the question of whether or not to uphold the Constitutional guarantees insofar as Black Americans are concerned is an issue for all Americans to grapple with no matter what the political ideology or belief system. The oldest American civil rights organization, the NAACP has established that a vote in a Black American majority precinct in Florida was three times more likely not to be counted than a vote in a majority White precinct in Florida (K. Mfume letter, 3-2001). With these irregularities in question, is it not hypocritical then for the Supreme Court to argue in its decision in *Bush v. Gore* (Dec. 12, 2000), that "the state may not, by later arbitrary and disparate treatment, value one person's vote over that of another," and then rule that a recount should be discontinued; or for the Democratic Party, for that matter, to disallow duly cast votes to one candidate by giving half of those votes to another. Such was the case in the Michigan and Florida 2008 primaries.

For legislation, time and timing are critical factors which is a major reason that women's rights are always behind race and male issues. The Civil Rights Act of 1964 contained a voting section that ultimately required additional legislation for its passage. It appears that one Constitutional Amendment (the 15th) was not sufficient to guarantee Black Americans this basic right that others take for granted. It is interesting that a similar provision was not enacted for women whose voting rights lagged 50 years behind Black males. Also, the Twenty Fourth Amendment to the Constitution adopted in 1964, Sections one and two further guaranteed the right to vote and empowered Congress to enforce the Amendment by appropriate legislation.

But due to continued White resistance to Black participation in the franchise, particularly in the south, another voting rights initiative was needed. In March 1965, Martin Luther King, Jr. led a march from Selma to Montgomery, Alabama, to dramatize the voting issue. Immediately after the march, President Johnson sent a voting rights bill to Congress, and it was quickly passed with his signature on August 6, 1965 a year later the Supreme Court responded by declaring poll taxes unconstitutional in state elections (B. Quarles, p. 314).

The Voting Rights Act authorized the U.S. attorney general to send federal examiners to register Black voters under certain circumstances, much like the processes that took place during the Reconstruction Era. The act also suspended all literacy tests, and poll taxes, instituted during Jim Crow. And Section 5 was designed to prevent states and other government entities with a history of voting discrimination from continuing to devise new ways to discriminate after the abolishment of prior discriminatory practices. Bear in mind that this act came eighty-seven years after Reconstruction that saw a period of open defiance of the Fifteenth Amendment by White supremacists.

To highlight this blatant disregard for Constitutional authority, Grolier presents the following, "A display of racist ingenuity was a source of pride to South Carolina's infamous Senator 'Pitchfork' Ben Tillman, who led one of the bloodiest campaigns against Black enfranchisement. Said Tillman: "We have done our level best. We have 'scratched our heads' to find out how we could eliminate every last one of them. We stuffed ballot boxes. We shot them. We are not ashamed of it" (Multimedia Encyclopedia, 2001).

This tradition was carried out throughout the south under the banner of protecting White superiority. The Ku Klux Klan, and the White Citizens Council were two of the most notorious proponents of that belief system. And Sheriff Jim Clark of Dallas County, Selma, Alabama was the embodiment of evil perpetrated against Blacks. His blocking of the courthouse to prevent Blacks from registering to vote was broadcast by the media worldwide. So, too, were the violent repressive actions of Sheriff "Bull" Conner. It was he who turned high-powered water hoses on children, and used dogs to attack marchers engaged in peaceful demonstrations in exercising their First Amendment Constitutional rights. These actions by law enforcement officials was done with the total sanction of the local and state governments.

Much to the displeasure of these officials and groups, The Voting Rights Law had an immediate impact. By the end of 1965, a quarter of a million new Black voters had been registered and a full one third were registered by federal examiners. And registrations by ACORN is an extension of these activities, past and present.

Quarles also adds the following as further evidence of the effectiveness of the Act. He tells us that during the four months after its passage more than 175,000 southern Blacks were registered; and more than 50% of those newly registered were directly due to the efforts of the Southern Christian Leadership Conference (SCLC – Dr. King's organization). Other Black groups that became politically active during that tumultuous period in America's history was Lowndes County Freedom Organization, developed following a plea by the late Stokely Carmichael, a.k.a., Kwamé Touré; and the Mississippi Freedom party, whose best known figure was Fannie Lou Hamer who was instrumental in opening the Southern Democratic Party to Black activists and new delegates (discussed in Chapter Two).

Other significant events that followed according to Quarles were, "In the two years after passage of The Voting Rights Act the Black registration in Mississippi, the state with the largest black population, and one of the worst records of racial bias, went from 6.7 to 59.8 percent [and to 70.8 percent by 1986], and in Alabama from 19.3 to 51.6 percent. In this span the number of Black office-holders rose to over 200, more than double the previous high. In Macon County, Alabama, Lucius D. Amerson became the first Black sheriff since Reconstruction. In Arkansas, Black votes helped Winthrop Rockefeller win the governor's chair." And in Selma, the site of some of the most bitter and violent actions against Black voting rights, the recently registered Black Americans brought about the defeat of the notorious Sheriff Clark for re-election (Ibid. pp. 314-15).

The Voting Rights Act was readopted and strengthened in 1970, then again in 1975, and 1982. But in 1993 the tide shifted ominously when the Republican stacked Supreme Court, the same one that gave Bushie the Presidency in 2000, on the last day of its term delivered a dire message to the advocates of voting rights. The Court decided in the case of Shaw v. Reno that White voters could challenge what they considered any bizarre shape of a majority/Black Congressional district in North Carolina – even though oddly shaped districts have long been tolerated in nonracial cases. Nonracial in this regard refers to the tradition and status quo of maintaining White dominance at the polls.

According to Grolier, "the [court's] decision was narrow, legally speaking, but devastating in its implications. White voters and judges have seized upon Shaw as an invitation to question the propriety of all race-conscious districting, on every level of government. Suddenly, the Voting Rights Act and its mandate to create equal opportunity at the ballot box [was faced with] the most serious challenge since 1965" (Ibid.).

Of course in the state of Florida, during the 2000 election, the problem of voting rights could have been resolved had the U.S. Supreme Court held to the basic constitutional principle that "every vote should count." Ironically this same principle should have prevailed in the 2008 Democratic Primary in which Florida and Michigan voters were disenfranchised. Had they ruled that the citizens of Florida were entitled to have their voices heard at the ballot box, no matter how long it took to recount the votes, as we do in run offs and overseas ballots, the dilemma of disenfranchisement could have been a lasting legacy of a different kind for America, as opposed to reinforcing the status quo which reoccurred in 2008 with Michigan added to the dilemma.

Section VI: Race Conscious Districting

According to Grolier, a 1973 Supreme Court ruling in *White v. Regester*, was pivotal in which at-large election schemes were deemed unconstitutional when such election plans "diluted minority voting strength," and required the creation of minority districts to offset the imbalance created by the at-large scheme (Ibid., p. 4). But soon thereafter, while the forces for progress were having success in demonstrating voter disenfranchisement, the Supreme Court in 1980 in another ruling, the *City of Mobile v. Bolden*, decided that the challengers to at-large election schemes must now show intent as well; and that the systems "had a racially discriminatory purpose" (p. 4). The challengers soon found that proving "intent" is not only difficult, it is almost next to impossible which was the intent of the Court in the first place with its repressive ruling.

But as fortune would have it, and much to the ire of then President Ronald Reagan, and his forces, the Voting Rights Act came up for renewal in 1982. Due to citizen pressure, Congress which still at that time had a democrat majority, amended Section 2 of the Act which before was not specific regarding districting plans that diluted votes. Specifically Section 2 is a nationwide provision that prohibits the use of voting laws, practices or procedures that discriminate in either purpose or effect on the basis of race, color, or membership in a minority language group. The language groups covered are Native Americans, Asian Americans, Alaska Natives, and persons of Spanish heritage (pp. 20-21). The Voting Rights Act amended in 1975 and 1992 required that political jurisdictions with language minority groups must provide bi-lingual voting assistance (p. 21).

Unfortunately since the Shaw ruling, the Supreme Court has continued to chip away at voting rights which is no wonder there is a quagmire or log jam in the voting registration process during each major election cycle. The 9th Court handed down two additional pejorative decisions at the end of the Court's 1994 term. In *Holder v. Hall*, the Justices upset an ACLU (American Civil Liberties Union) lower court victory by upholding the single commissioner form of government in Bleckley County, Georgia – despite solid proof of minority vote dilution. Incredibly the Court even noted that the "District Judge stated that, having run for public office himself, he 'wouldn't run if he were Black in Bleckley County'."

On the very same day, this Court, in true form, ruled against minorities in a Florida redistricting case. In *Johnson v. DeGrandy*, the Court rejected a Section 2 challenge, despite continuing discrimination and White bloc voting on the grounds that the number of

135

predominantly minority districts was in their language, "roughly proportional" to minorities share in the population. Is it any wonder that this same tired Court ruled that the 2000 Florida presidential vote was legally certified?

And more troubling than the Johnson Decision was the position staked out by two of the Court's most reactionary Justices, Thomas and Scalia. They argued that Section 2 applied only to vote denial, and not to vote dilution. This position was in stark contradiction to established precedent and the legislative history of The Voting Rights Act. Thus further entrenching their pro positions on disenfranchisement which was the salient factor in their future votes against Florida recounts. But three times in his dissent, Justice Stevens called their view "radical." (See next section on "Strict Constructionalists.") (See subject endnotes #16 on redistricting.)

Additionally, and what is crucial to our historical analysis, Grolier adds the following on the implications of the Thomas and Scalia arguments. He states, "Against this backdrop . . . the challenges to majority and Black Congressional districts created in Georgia and Louisiana after a 1990 reapportionment, and since Shaw was based on the Fourteenth Amendment, not on the Voting Rights Act, Congress will not be able to step in and repair the damage as it was able to do with the Bolden disaster of 1982 [recall the Supreme Court ruling of demonstrating intent]. This time, the Court will have the final word, and if it continues on its present course the result could be catastrophic" (Ibid.).

To date the redistricting plans that have come before the Court may give them additional opportunity to further destroy Black Voting Rights; such as their butchery of *Bush v. Gore*. Section 5, it seems, was totally ignored by the Court when they ruled in favor of Bushie and then Florida Secretary of State, Katherine Harris. This section was designed to prevent states and other governmental entities with a history of voting discrimination from continuing to devise new ways to discriminate after the abolishment of prior discriminatory practices (Ibid.).

Incredibly with Florida's history of past discriminatory practices and voting irregularities, it is this reactionary Court that refuses to acknowledge what other Americans have long since realized, it is that the Supreme Court cannot be counted on as a vehicle to address long-standing racial grievances. Certainly this was not the intent of the Civil War Amendments, nor is it a fitting tribute to the thousands of Americans who have suffered and died for the sake of justice. Clarence Thomas especially should be ashamed of himself.

For instance in regards to the Shaw decision, Thomas and the others who voted for the plaintiff knew full well that since 1901 not a single Black American had been elected to congress from North Carolina. The new districts were designed to include everyone equally in the democratic process. Whites still enjoy more than their fair share of representation. While Blacks constitute 22 percent of North Carolina's population, only 2 of 12 districts – 17 percent are predominantly Black. In addition the 12th North Carolina congressional district is less segregated, at 57 percent Black and 43 percent White, than any congressional district previously drawn in the state. To call it segregated, while calling a district with the numbers reversed integrated, defies logic. But the Obama victory here in 2008 was indeed quite remarkable.

Justice White wrote in his dissent in Shaw, "A regularly shaped district can just as effectively effectuate racially discriminatory gerrymandering as an odd-shaped one. By focusing on looks rather than impact, the majority immediately casts attention in the wrong direction; toward superficialities of shape and size, rather than toward the political realities of district composition." **Additionally Justice Stevens in his dissent wrote, "If it is permissible to draw boundaries to provide adequate representation for rural voters, for union members, for**

Hasidic Jews, for Polish Americans, or for Republicans, it necessarily follows that it is permissible to do the same thing for members of the very minority group whose history in the United States gave birth to the Equal Protection Clause, a contrary conclusion could only be described as perverse" (Grolier, Op.Cit., p. 6).

What is extremely unfortunate is that there are two Shaw copycat suits. One is *Miller v. Johnson* which targets Georgia's 11th District, and the other is *Louisiana v. Hays* which is also unique. Louisiana's population is 30 percent Black, yet it was not until 1990 that the first Black American since Reconstruction was elected by the state's first predominantly minority district. And two years later, after the Congressional reapportionment, a second predominantly minority district was created which resulted in the election of another Black representative (Ibid., p. 8). While the resolution of these suits might still be pending, one thing is certain, and that is the Justices who ruled in favor of Bush and Shaw are determined to, in the words of Julian Bond, "turn the Civil Rights clock back to a sundial" (B. Quarles, p. 349).

While the Supreme Court's determination as to whether or not race was a factor in drawing the majority Black districts in Georgia, Florida, and Texas, the same 5-4 vote which prevailed in Bush v. Gore, are the same Justices who voted 5-4 to invalidate the districts of the previously mentioned states. And unfortunately the Supreme Court's ideological persuasion has not changed with the addition of two Bush appointees. However the addition of conservative Chief Justice John Roberts as a replacement for William Rehnquist, and Associate Justice Samuel Alito to replace swing voter Sandra O'Connor, confirms the Bush reactionary legacy on the courts. David A. Yalof puts it this way, "Stated simply, George W. Bush may have done more to *transform* [see Chapter Seven] the constitutional landscape in a conservative direction than any president in the past century, including Ronald Reagan and Richard Nixon. To be sure, this incredible story would not have been possible without a Republican-controlled Senate in place during half of his presidency. Bush won nearly every battle he waged to get extremely conservative judges and justices confirmed" (website, Vol 8, No. 3).

But with the Democrat advantage in Congress, and the White House, the judicial advantage in appointments naturally will change. Interestingly though, the redistricting challenges were not upheld by the court which permitted the tactic of drawing congressional districts that would favor Black voters, thus increasing representation in keeping with the Fourteenth Constitutional Amendment, and the 1965 Voting Rights Act. Additional good news was provided by the court ruling in favor of the redistricting plans in Alabama, Georgia, New Jersey, and North Carolina is that it opened the door for other such plans to counter Republican efforts at disenfranchising Black voters in states such as Texas and Florida.

To demonstrate the severity of the problem that redistricting and the Voting Rights Act are intended to address, is shown by the Black representatives in Congress, particularly from the aforementioned states, as well as all of the remaining states. In the 111th Congress, seated as of January 2008, there are forty-three Black representatives, thirteen of which are women in the House out of 435 members; and one Black U.S. Senator out of one hundred members. While there have been small gains made in the House of Representatives by Blacks since the Reconstruction Era, the Senate remains mostly an all White, mostly male institution. In the mid-Twentieth Century, one Black man has served, Edward Brooks of Massachusetts (1967-1979), in the latter part of the Twentieth Century, a Black woman served, Carol Moseley Braun (1993-1998), then Barack Obama (2006-2008), both from Illinois; and recently, a controversial, if not a contentious Senate appointment from Illinois took place. Governor Rod Blagojevich, under a cloud of suspicion for the common practice which no politician will admit to, of quid pro quo (this-for-that) of filling Obama's Senate seat, eventually appointed Roland Burris, who at first the Senate Democrats refused to seat. Eventually they came to their senses, and seated him making Burris once again the lone Black member of the U.S. Senate.

Even with this paucity of Black representation, districting that favors one group over another is constantly under debate. The Congressional Black Caucus (CBC) founded in 1969 with a mission of advocacy and representation of Black issues has met the districting challenges since its inception. But like the CBC, the justices realized to invalidate the drawing of the districts and finding them unconstitutional on the grounds of the 14th Amendment would have been a tragedy. The Black plaintiffs in the case argue that the boundaries were drawn along political lines as opposed to racial lines so that this Supreme Court will not rule in their usual manner, i.e., against Black justice and equality which the original intent of the 14th Amendment was adopted to correct. **While this court is extremely reactionary in their majority opinions where race is concerned; but in this instance, this ruling was the correct decision.**

For further justification on this point The Voting Rights Act addresses the abuses of power by states, institutions, or persons by determining that no person acting under "Color of Law" shall determine whether any individual is qualified under state law or laws to vote in any election. They shall not apply any standard, practice, or procedure different from the standards, practices, or procedures applied under such law(s) to other individual(s) within the same county, parish (Louisiana), or similar political subdivision who have been found by the state officials to be qualified to vote.

Clearly this language of the Act can and should have been applied to Florida's Secretary of State Katherine Harris, who under the Color of Law, certified Bush the winner in Florida; not unlike, for example, Sheriffs Clark and Connor in 1964 Alabama. She clearly had a conflict-of-interest by not only being an active operative in Bushie's Florida campaign, but also a close family friend to him and Bushie's brother, the Governor of the state. *The "Color of Law" specifically defined is the appearance or semblance without the substance, of a legal right.*

The term usually implies a misuse of power made possible because the wrong doer is clothed with the authority of state. Thus, state action is synonymous with "Color of Law" in the context of federal civil rights statutes or criminal law (Black's Law Dictionary). The state of Florida situation exactly, and Thomas, O'Connor, Rehnquist, Kennedy, and Scalia knew that to be the case, as did the justices in the Reconstruction Era.

Part B of Section 2 of The Voting Rights Act continues by stating that no person acting under the "Color of Law" shall deny the right of any individual to vote in any election because of an error or omission on any record or paper relating to any application, registration, or other act requisite to voting, if such error or omission is not material in determining whether such individual is qualified under state law to vote in such election. And part C refers to the practice of requiring a literacy test which too is prohibited (Jerry Goldman, 1996-2001. *The OYEZ Project, Northwestern University Website*).

These provisions certainly can be applied to the undisputed practices of requesting identification to establish proof of one's eligibility to vote as was done in Florida, and is now being adopted elsewhere. It is believed that this occurred because Blacks were voting at record numbers. It was a discouraging disenfranchisement tactic, as well as the antiquated equipment that was used in many of the inner city districts; certainly older than most equipment used elsewhere.

Is it not extremely interesting that when laws begin to work for, rather than against, Blacks and other minorities to correct past injustices, these laws are seen as a threat and unconstitutional? It is this similar thinking that ushered in the oxymoron concept of "Reverse

Discrimination." Clearly the intent of the Civil War Amendments was to acknowledge race as a

factor which had to be considered in future remedies. Grolier says it best in his Reaffirmation

Requiem for The Voting Rights Act. He argues the following:

> *"In a perfect world, remedial race-conscious districting would not be necessary. We would all prefer to live in the color-blind society hypothesized by Justice O'Connor in Shaw, but that simply is not reality. To claim otherwise willfully disregards the fact that race has always mattered in this society. Up until the middle of the last century Blacks were locked out of the political process [same as this new century in Florida] and rendered second-class citizens solely because of their color. While literacy tests and poll taxes may have passed into history, but at-large election schemes, racial polarization and bloc voting remain facts of life. And race-based problems requires race-based solutions"* (p. 9)

This last sentence bears repeating a second time, **"Race-based problems requires race-**

based solutions." The logic of this is so clear that any opposition to it must surely be the work

of strict constructionalist Supreme Court Justices.

And in the matter of the negative controversy surrounding the drawing of districts that

cater only to a voting bloc of Blacks is to suggest that this practice is without precedent in the

American political scheme of things. This is an unsubstantiated claim as shown by Grolier who

argues that:

> *"Predominantly minority districts that are oddly shaped - often reflecting the irregularities of city boundaries - are in keeping with, not divergent from, tradition. Historically, the courts have approved all kinds of districts that were drawn in odd shapes for partisan reasons. Thus, to call predominantly minority districts 'apartheid,' as the Supreme Court did in Shaw, while accepting without question districts drawn to accommodate, say, Irish or Polish Americans, is to apply a discriminatory double standard in redistricting"* (p. 10).

Indeed this is not only a double standard it reeks with bigotry. It is a common

disingenuous ploy of bigots to use their own past bigoted practices as an objectionable problem, and then claim injury in that they are being victimized by "reverse discrimination." And what is more ludicrous is that they are successful in making this case in the courts, with the end result of perpetuating the very system in which the remedy was initially intended to correct! But past Supreme Court decisions recognized this ridiculous strategy for what it really is, an illogical and somewhat desperate argument designed to protect the tradition of repressive privilege and power as noted by a Senate subcommittee in the Reagan Era, "calling minority-controlled districts the cause of, rather than a response to, racial polarization, is like saying that it is the doctor's thermometer which causes high fever" (p. 4).

Grolier concludes by cogently stating that the Voting Rights act is arguably the single most successful civil rights law ever enacted "[But] partly due to this record of success is a growing chorus of claims that the law has outlived its usefulness, and that race-conscious voting remedies are anachronistic." However as the events in Florida, Ohio, and Michigan have shown, the 2000, 2004 and 2008 elections were marred with all sorts of voting irregularities which is strong evidence that the Voting Rights Act as a remedy is needed now more than ever.

While we have experienced improvement in access to the franchise, it is still abundantly clear that had it not been for gross disfranchisement in Florida, Bushie just may very well still be an ineffective governor of one of America's largest states, but his refusal to move ahead on improving race relations (refusing to sign a hate crimes bill, and refusal to support Affirmative Action), then ignoring the environment, and pressing forward on a war in Iraq killing thousands at home and abroad helped put him in disfavor with the population. And with him at our nation's helm, equal representation for minorities and women was a distant dream; but with a peculiar irony of sorts, if not for him being such a terrible president, the likelihood of American's voting in unprecedented numbers for a Black man/African American to be president probably would never have occurred. An assumption held by some listeners calling in to a conservative radio show, is that Bush so wrecked the image of the presidency, that even a Black man was seen as a viable alternative to anyone that the Republicans would put up as a challenger to the Democrats. And as a final insult to Blacks and progress, he blatantly stated during the campaign that his selection of judges for the federal bench would be "Strict Constructionalists" of the Constitution.

Richard Nixon also made the same comment when he was asked about his judicial appointments. It was Vice President Gore who enlightened the nation as to what the phrase "Strict Constructionalist" actually means. To reemphasize, Joan Biskupic of *USA Today* argues the following, "Taken with the nomination of Ashcroft, Bushie's actions seem to indicate a return to the Reagan era when judges often were screened for a conservative ideology." And Sheldon Goldman, a political science professor at the University of Massachusetts-Amherst had this to say, "It appears that [Bushie gave] the judiciary to the right wing of the Republican Party." It is Tom Jipping of the conservative Free Congress Foundation who offers a damaging blow to the forces for justice when he said "He hoped that Ashcroft would take the lead in picking judges during Bushie's administration, the coup d' etat for justice" (Ibid.).

Indeed it was Ashcroft who schemed and lied to block the federal judgeship appointment of Ronnie White who was a Clinton nominee that happened to be Black. Ashcroft went so far as to label Judge White as "Pro-criminal." Under Bushie the person who had a leading role in the judicial selection process was Lee Liberman Otis. He served in the Justice Department in the Reagan administration, and was an assistant White House counsel in Bushie's papa's term as President. Otis is the founder of the conservative Federalist Society and protégé of the far right Supreme Court Justice Antonia Scalia. He had long been associated with the ideological right which is more than enough to make all progressive minded people shudder with nervous

trepidation. And with this line-up of judicial reactionaries working in the top jobs in our nation,

there is no wonder that our worst fears regarding the Supreme Court, and other federal judicial

appointments were realized (J. Biskupic, March 27, 2001. pp. 1-3). See update in Endnote.

Section VII: Justification for Educational Role In Defeating Bigotry

The ambivalence that America has towards Voting Rights, Affirmative Action, and Equal

Opportunity Laws, is a reflection of the deep division of the nation in the matter of race and

gender rights. The contemporary debates, judicial decisions, and political compromises are not

unlike those that took place between the founders of our nation, such as the Compromise of

1787. Indeed as I have argued throughout this work, it was that compromise which, in large part,

made the contentious intrigue of race policies, i.e., fear and mistrust what they are today.

If the nation is serious about embracing diversity, then it must have policies that reflect

the mood of the nation. And for the courts, judges, and elected officials to deny this realism is a

denial of the changing political landscape of our society. Remember that Vice President Gore

demonstrated leadership by running strongly on the issue of Affirmative Action, and the majority

of Americans agreed with him. Unfortunately it was not an issue in the 2004 and 2008 debates;

and the Supreme Count continues to chip away at it in terms of their rulings on school

enrollment and employment opportunities. The latter of which is predictable given the fact that

experience has been rendered inconsequential owing to the Obama phenomenon and the so-

called post-racial America (see Chapter Seven).

Progressive realism is a function of possessing true fact-based knowledge. It is also a

function of learned beliefs, and most of all, it is a function of fairness and justice. Our nation

prides itself on having a moral compass; but it is useless without the tools to direct its focus. We

145

have spoken at length in terms of political and judicial remedies; and providing historical antecedents that must be considered for any future programs to realize effective results. Education not only provides the students of progressive change with functional tools, it also instructs us on how they should be applied.

Unfortunately there are still some factions within the academy who criticize the tools for justice, and will feed a student's instincts to follow the American tradition of repressive behavior. It is difficult to change a child's mind who has been taught a bigoted predatory belief system; but that then becomes the challenge of the university. These children soon become adults, and the cycle repeats itself. Feeding a predator with bigotry and hate is a recipe for social destruction. However, critical thinking and fact-based knowledge can do wonders in opening the eyes of the teacher as well as the student.

In keeping with the historical theme of this treatise, Thomas Jefferson who is one of the most quotable presidents once commented that "The process of education has been the basis of hope for the endurance of our democracy" (L. Keith Yohn, 3-5-01, *The University Record,* Vol. 56, No. 23. The University of Michigan, p. 12).

Educationally speaking, in a fact-based knowledge paradigm, it becomes the discretion of the individual teacher to discern and disseminate the type of information which is most relevant for their individual discipline(s). However, I have yet to see a course entitled "How To Be An Ultra-conservative Formed in the Likes of Mark Levin, Ann Coulter, Sean Hannity, Rush Limbaugh, and Bill O'Reilly, to Name a Few." But some students are learning these behavioral patterns and belief systems somewhere, and their home is not the entire answer. At times, for some teachers, it becomes expedient to circumvent various belief systems when they become evident in a classroom. For example, it emerged in the matter of the 2008 presidential campaign, and the Democratic primary in which disenfranchisement was a consequence of disobedience. Of course the Constitution gives no person, organization, or entity wiggle room to deny any person their right to fully participate in the franchise. In the matter of the states of Michigan and Florida, voting became a classic 10th Amendment states rights issue, which even the aforementioned named persons will probably agree.

I maintain that it is not in the best interest of education, or the academy, for professors to shy away from the important challenge of positively shaping a young mind when their racist and/or misogynist beliefs become known. In moving towards this philosophy certainly there are risks, and in our litigious society, some students may even charge that they have been unfairly treated when their grade reflects their rigid shallow thinking and meandering in the illogical precepts of bigotry, and trying to pawn them off as individual rights or scholarly assertions.

According to Yohn, "The court has held that like judges, teachers should not punish or reward people on the basis of inadmissible factors, e.g., race, religion, gender, or political ideology; but teachers like judges, must daily decide which arguments are relevant, which computations are correct, which analogies are good or bad, and when it is time to stop writing or talking. Grades must be given by teachers in the classroom. And to this end teachers, like judges, must direct the content of speech" (Ibid., p. 13 *Stettle v. Dickson County School Board,* 53 + 3d 152, 155-56-6th Cir. 1995). This ruling also concludes with the assertion that "Teachers must be given broad discretion to give grades and conduct class discussion based on the content of speech" (Ibid.).

Along with the above statement Robert Hutchins who is an Associate Director of the Ford Foundation gave the following testimony before the United States House of Representatives Select Committee. He commented that a university is a place that is established and will function for the benefit of society, provided that it remains a center of independent thought. And precisely because it is a center of independent thought and criticism, which is created in the interest of the progress of society, it is the one reason we know that every totalitarian government will fail is that no totalitarian government is prepared to face the consequences of creating open universities; or for that matter, a free enterprise system.

Education is a kind of continuing dialogue, and a dialogue assumes, in the nature of the case, different points of view. A university, then, is a kind of continuing Socratic conversation on the highest level for the very best people you can think of, that you can bring together about the most important questions, and the thing that you must do to the utmost possible limits is to guarantee those men and women the freedom to think and to express themselves on a plane worthy of the academy (Hutchins, Op. Cit., p. 13). This is the major reason why I felt compelled to write this text. Although it may be perceived as an anti Obama critique bordering on sacrilege by some, because it contains arguments which are less than favorable to "The One." "Perceptions" of anti-Black dialogue are generally not viewed with much favor within the academy, which is unfortunate, given our mandate for free and open inquiry. But if we criticize George W. Bush on issues of hypocrisy and going beyond constitutional boundaries, then Obama should receive the same treatment for his actions. It should be made clear that the ethnicity/race of the president is *not* under scrutiny, but rather it is his policies which are the focus of concern.

As bigotry abounds in the American university and academy, the vigilant protection of constitutional freedoms is nowhere more vital than in the community of American schools (Ibid.). Academic disputes consistently comes before the bar, and the legal authority for judicial decisions are those which have been presented by attorneys arguing both sides of the issue. What is unfortunate is that a case law precedent is often set by a ruling or set of rulings by jurists

148

who have a preconceived notion of the facts based on tradition, illogical assertions, and of course bigotry. Examples are the 1875 Civil Rights and 1896 Plessy v. Ferguson rulings by the Supreme Court; both had a bearing on segregation which impacted our educational institutions.

A contemporary example is that a federal judge in Detroit ruled that the Affirmative Action policy at the University of Michigan's Law School is unconstitutional (NPR, 3-6-01). But what is also equally important to note is that another judge in 2000 ruled that the undergraduate program's affirmative action policy is constitutional. While the negative ruling on Affirmative Action has since been stayed, we must accept the fact that there will be continued assaults on progressive policies that are remedies for injustice.

These are three separate and different rulings made on a policy at the same university. Logic would have it that someone is incorrect in their interpretation of the Constitution, but who or which one is correct becomes the question to consider. Certainly the answer to this question is more complex than laying the outcome at the doorstep of the attorneys who argued the case.

The judge that held for affirmative action has an interpretation that is in keeping with the intent of the 14th and 15th Amendments; no matter how unpopular the remedy is for the problem. While the other judge is interested in using the language of bigotry such as "preferential treatment," and denying the existence of *a longstanding racial problem* that requires a race-based solution. One has to wonder what exactly he was studying in his constitutional law class; which Obama also taught at the University of Chicago. But it was mostly his undergraduate studies, coupled with a family belief system, politics, and tradition, that planted the seed for his rulings many years ago, which leads one to wonder about Barack Obama defunding HBCUs (see endnotes). Indeed, Clarence Thomas, Ward Connerly, Juan Williams, Armstrong Williams and other anti-Affirmation Action Black Americans have all stated a Bushlike desire to end the

149

much-needed policy. Christopher Caldwell, a senior editor at the ultra-right wing journal and literary home of William Kristol, The Weekly Standard, had this to say: "Affirmative Action has been a revolution in American rights and in our idea of citizenship. To judge from 'almost' all polls and referendums over the past few decades, it is reliably unpopular. [However, judges like Sonia Sotomayor] prop it up" (Time, 6-8-07, p. 32). These data are reflective of views on Affirmative Action when couched in the myth of preferences. But Obama, like most politicians, is a habitual poll watcher which quite possibly contributes to his approach-avoidance behavior on Affirmative Action.

I assert that if more time is taken with liberal arts challenges to the status quo it may make a difference in the type of rulings that continue to come out of certain courts; or the need for a ruling may evaporate if true education is allowed to take root. However there are also many other variables that factor in the decision(s) such as political cronyism, ideologies, co-optation, and fear of judicial suicide to name a few that makes us question how we might secure justice in the face of so much powerful opposition.

The question of these illogical rulings beg further analyses in an educational context, especially when we turn to the uttering's of politicians such as Bushie who has referred to Affirmative Action as affirmative access – how sad! He has made the term "compassionate conservatism" a household word, but what exactly does it mean. He borrowed the term from a professor at a Texas university who wrote a book with the same title. Thanks to Bushie though he proceeded to demonstrate that the phrase was really an oxymoron. For instance, Byrd, the man who was dragged to death in Texas while Bushie was governor was the victim of a hate crime. His family went to Bushie to request that he sign a Hate Crime's Bill – his answer was an emphatic "No!" A similar criticism can be made about Obama who refused to attend two forums

150

on race soon after Hurricane Katrina, and to defund HBCUs, interestingly enough, in direct contrast to Bush policy (see endnotes).

So much for the compassionate part of the phrase with respect to both politicians. Unfortunately there are still students at the University of Texas and elsewhere who are "benefiting" from reactionary professors' "Knowledge" on social issues. Of course the First Amendment to the Constitution does not tolerate laws that cast a pale of orthodoxy over the classroom. But as in the model of medical practice, the motto of "first do no harm," is a truly significant statement; and one that many educators could benefit from by fully embracing the meaning of its message.

In the matter of voting rights, a previous membership recruitment drive letter distributed by the NAACP, its then President Kweisi Mfume had this to say: "My heart is troubled. You know as well as I do that much of the bloody and heroic history of the Civil Rights Movement has been built on the struggle for the vote... To receive reports that racially driven purges of voter rolls, selective distribution of updated voting technology, poorly designed ballots, and even police roadblocks prevented even more Blacks from voting is troubling... It is also troubling that a vote in a Black majority precinct was three times more likely not to be counted than a vote in a majority White precinct in Florida, and that Black voters in Georgia and Illinois faced equal or greater odds of being disqualified."

And finally, given the sheer mass of the evidence we gathered of clear violations of the 15th Amendment and the Voting Rights Act of 1965, the Justice Department under then ultra conservative Attorney General John Ashcroft had refused to launch a full-scale investigation (March 2001). This is the state of America's race problem and disenfranchisement in the 21st Century. The Founders would be proud. Ashcroft's stewardship of the office of Attorney

151

General, in the Bush administration, was unlike the responsible role demonstrated by Attorney General Katzenbach under President Lyndon B. Johnson. Katzenbach had to deal with the likes of racist Sheriff Jim Clark in the 1960s, while over a generation later the officeholder was in league with the forces that President LBJ and Katzenbach fought so hard to defeat, and his successors under the Bush administration were no better. And Obama's Attorney General appointee, Eric Holder, began his tenure with controversial decisions on medical marijuana and Guantanamo Bay detainees (see Endnotes, Jim Webb). Holder also remarked that the United States is a "nation of cowards" insofar as the issue of race is concerned. It was argued that this comment was "needlessly" divisive to some and "refreshingly candid" to others (M. Isikoff, 2009). This is the crux of the long-term history of race and its splintering effects between groups.

And registering and participating in the franchise, indeed, is also the result of a historically significant massive demonstration movement; and at its core is education. It is an effective intervention process that requires a three stage approach: 1) An aggressive community based campaign such as the one sponsored by ACORN and the NAACP. Their purpose is to inform people of their rights under the Constitution and other legal remedies. They are also designed to inform people of the threats to their rights, and provide concrete examples of the nature of that threat, 2) Educating for recruitment of new members, and solidifying the base of current members, 3) Moving aggressively in the classroom means challenging longstanding assumptions, stereotypes and ineffective dialogue which is said to be a scholarly exercise simply because one happens to be in a place where scholarly exercises supposedly occur.

Again as Yohn so eloquently states, "The vigilant protection of constitutional freedoms is nowhere more vital than in the community of American schools" (Op.Cit., March 2001). The challenge then is clear, our historical goal has been identified, the struggle for justice and freedom must continue, for the "Essence of constitutionality is that government must be confined by the Rule of Law" (Grolier). And finally in the eloquent words of Justice Stevens, we find the most powerful truism of any election. He asserts that "While we may never know with complete certainty the identity of the winner of the 2000 Presidential Election, the identity of the loser is perfectly clear. It is the Nation's confidence in the judge as an impartial guardian of the rule of law" (William G. Ross, Cumberland School of Law, Sanford University, 2000, p. 4). Justice Stevens's words are equally applicable to 2004, and 2008, and to any future issues which will provide a rationale for disenfranchising any American citizen. Thus the historical intent of this chapter was to make very clear why the Democratic Party's actions in Florida and Michigan in 2008 were so objectionable.

"At its August 25, 2007 meeting the Democratic National Committee's Rules and Bylaws Committee found the Florida Democratic Party plan in non compliance, and voted to penalize Florida Democrats 100% of their delegates to the national convention if they did not come up with a plan within 30 days that complies with the timing requirement. However, Florida Democrats stood firm. On September 23, 2007 Florida Democratic party Chairwoman, Karen Thurman announced the Party would participate in the January 29th primary. On October 4, 2007, U.S. Senator Bill Nelson and Congressman Alcee Hastings filed suit against Howard Dean and the DNC in the U.S. District Court, Northern District of Florida. The Rules and Bylaws Committee voted to penalize Michigan Democrats 100 percent of their delegates at its meeting on December 1, 2007, while rejecting penalties for Iowa, New Hampshire and South Carolina" (http://www.gwa.edu). After the selection of Barack Obama in 2008 to represent the Democratic Party, and his eventual election to the presidency, all sins with respect to disenfranchisement

153

were forgiving. The Democratic Party came together as if nothing major or of any consequence had occurred. However another serious precedent had been established, which is, a person's vote could be taken and/or manipulated at the whim of a powerful majority or body of persons at will. This is not how our Constitution is intended to work. The marginalization of the Florida and Michigan voters based on their disenfranchisement by the DNC is an illustration of the continued problems experienced by Hillary and Sarah as discussed in more detail in the following chapter.

Chapter Five – Endnotes

Anderson, Ralph and Irl Carter (1990). *Human Behavior in the Social Environment: A Systems Approach.* 4th Edition. Aldine DeGruyter, New York.

Articles of Confederation (1781). Continental Congress.

Caldwell, Christopher (2009). "The Limits of Empathy," in *Time*, June 8th, p. 32.

Camarota, Steven A. (8-2000). Census Bureau. Center for Immigration Studies.

CNN (March 8, 2000).

CNN (March 9, 2000)

College Encyclopedia (1968). Inter American Copyright Union, Processing Books, Inc. p. 5150.

Congresswoman Corrine Brown, Florida's 3rd District.

Constitutional Convention of 1787. Continental Congress.

Goldman, Jerry (1996). "The OYEZ Project." Northwestern University Website.

Grolier Multimedia Encyclopedia (May 1995). "Reaffirmation or Requiem for The Voting Rights Act." ACLU.

Hamilton, Alexander, James Madison and John Jay (1787-88). "The Federalist Papers." The New York Press.

Isikoff, Michael (2009). "A Race Case? Duck and Cover," in *Newsweek*, March, 16th, p. 10.

Los Angeles Times Newspaper.

Miami Dade Newspaper (3-2001).

National Advisory Commission On Civil Disorders (1968). Bantam Books. New York.

Newsweek (April 6, 2009). Medical Marijuana Fight: Up in Smoke?

New York Daily News, December 24, 2000.

Orlando Sentinel Newspaper, December 17, 2000.

Quarles, Benjamin (1987). *The Negro in the Making of America.* 3rd Edition. MacMillan Publishing Co., New York.

Schmidt, Steffen W., Mark C. Shelley II, and Barbara A. Bardes (1989). *An Introduction to Critical Thinking in American Politics: American Government and Politics Today*. West Publishing Co., St. Paul, MN.

Tilave, Jonathan (August 13, 2000). Newhouse News Service.

Twenty Fourth Amendment to the Constitution.

United States Constitution.

USA Today, December 12, 2000.

USA Today, December 18, 2000.

Webb, Jim (2009). "Our Prisons," in *Parade*, March 29. [With respect to medical marijuana has the Surgeon General's Office changed its mind that smoking is hazardous to your health. If it still is, then the notion of medical marijuana is an oxymoron at best, or hypocritical at worse.] U.S. Senator Jim Webb (D, VA) states, "Justice statistics show that 47.5% of all the drug arrests in our country in 2007 were for marijuana offenses" (p. 5). And non-violent offenders for drug use should not be serving time in our crowded jails and prisons. Particularly with the racial disparities of Blacks who comprise 12% of the U.S. population "accounted for 37% of those arrested on drug charges, 59% of those convicted, and 74% of all drug offenders sentenced to prison" (Ibid.).

Wise, Tim (2000). Independent News Media.

Yohn, Keith L. (March 5, 2001). The University Record, Vol. 56, No. 23, p. 12.

Websites:

http://en.wikipedia.org

http://knowledgerush.com

http://www.highbeam.com

http://www.house.gov

http://www.kansascity.com

HBCU Note: Historically Black Colleges and Universities (HBCUs) have had $85,000,000 cut from their Budget by the Obama Administration. Even President Bush had supported these 101 institutions. "Shame on President Obama for cutting funds to HBCUs, and shame on Obama for continuing to make an example out of us while allowing others to run amok…I do not believe that Blacks should be (penalized) because our president looks like us" (Nsenga K. Burton, 5-13-09, website, see also The Mo'Keely Report Website).

Non-Attendance at Race Forums: President Obama, much like his predecessor, George W. Bush, who boycotted Durban I, refused to attend the second international conference on race held in Durban, South Africa, April 20-24, 2009. A number of comments made on his non-attendance, three of which are: "Blacks get nothing from Obama's White House except permission to worship him as the ultimate role model" (G. Ford, 4-15-09); and "Barack Obama knows full well that he risks nothing by disrespecting Black Americans at will" (Ibid.). Then actor-activist Danny Glover added, "[The Durban Conference] should be a moment for the U. S. to rejoin the global struggle against racism, the struggle that the Bush administration so arrogantly abandoned (4-8-09, *The Nation*).

CHAPTER SIX

Defining Stereotypes: The Prelude to Misogyny Targets Sarah Palin and Hillary Clinton

Section I: Overview

As the previous chapter was more focused on the issue of disenfranchisement with all of its attending problems and challenges, this chapter will build on that theme by taking a personal introspective analysis on gender differences and misogyny. By this I mean, contrasting the targets of the most recent high profile demonstrations of socio-political angst toward women, Governor Sarah Palin, and former U.S. Senator and now U.S. Secretary of State Hillary Clinton. To be sure, as expected, this political treatise will give rise to defensive posturing by those in disagreement with its merits and assumptions; but heretofore the scientific methodology was strategically laid in anticipation of the criticism that my work will engender.

But such is the case when an unpopular subject is broached, and popular individuals' behaviors are called into question. Certainly the so-called liberals of the progressive movement do not, and probably will not accept a characterization that places them in a similar mindset and behavioral mode as those who for years they have howled their displeasure at/for bigotry, divisiveness, and race and class discrimination. For years they, or better put, we have resisted negative epithets and stereotypes with an admirable passion that bespeaks of a genuine concern for others and compassion of the human quality that Gandhi, King, Malcolm, Mother Teresa, Eleanor Roosevelt, Harriet Tubman, and Ida B. Wells-Barnett displayed. Then along came Hillary Clinton and Sarah Palin with the audacity to challenge "The One's" meteoric rise to national prominence and ultimately the Presidency.

Herein lies the nature of the problem, the rub against established tradition, is the role of women, and the sacrifices that we as a society are willing to make to ensure that there is a level playing field for all citizens. For after all, this is Affirmative Action in operation. A person may say what they choose with respect to the principle of equal opportunity, but if we are to practice it, then each person, no matter what their station in life should actually believe they have a legitimate chance to rise unencumbered to any level they seek. But once again, there lies our constitutional paradox with human forces at work which creates an atmosphere of negativity and differential impediment(s) for their advancement in violation of the 14th Amendment. Then, too, human nature provides us with neatly packaged defense mechanisms to protect us from behavioral guilt, and we are also able to receive subjective support for our actions, and the wheels of unfair adversity will spin, and those responsible will feel vindicated in their actions. There is no societal indignation, and the rumor mills owing to double standards and discrimination are free to operate at will.

All of these factors may operate in tandem or separately, what difference does it really make though when the end result is that a person or group will suffer from the oppressive acts of others. There is nothing coincidental or happenstance about discrimination, and oppression. These are not nebulous actions that are destined to mystify all who are observing them or create groundless actions for their victims because they are simply classified as acts of nature. In this respect the dynamic that is most compelling about the Hillary and Sarah phenomenon is that ideologically speaking they

159

are polar distances apart; yet they are both feminists in their own right, and have suffered from the same oppressive mechanisms put in place by each political party and their supporters to keep women in "their place." And any aspirations beyond that place is proscribed by internal and external powers, men and women alike who determine the worth and value, not of her fitness or readiness to serve, but of her ability to serve based on personal traits and attributes.

As we shall soon see these assessments became personal in nature; and degenerated into vicious attacks designed to lower their value as a person(s), and their self-esteem as women that have no right to an office for which they do not look the part in the eyes of their attackers. It does take a person of strong will and character to withstand these personal attacks and demonstrations of double standards masquerading as legitimate exercises in the vetting process. In discussing this issue of victimization and abuse of power in our nation targeted at Hillary and Sarah, bell hooks describes it this way, "As long as the United States is an imperialist, capitalist, patriarchal society, no large female majority can enter the existing ranks of the powerful. The feminist movement is not advanced if women who can never be among those who rule and exercise domination and control are encouraged to focus on these forms of power and sees themselves as victims. The forms of power that these women should exercise are those that will enable them to resist exploitation and oppression, and free them to work at transforming [an important term we will revisit in Chapter Seven] society so that political and economic structures will exist that benefit women and men equally" (p. 94) (underline mine).

Section II: Sarah Palin

On numerous occasions Governor Palin spoke of the harm that can be done to the feminist movement if women were to "whine" (sic) about the unfair and disparate treatment they receive compared to that afforded men; and Senator Clinton agreed with her when even on occasion she has been known to complain about the advantage men have over women. And Sarah herself has spoken out about the unfair treatment that she received during the 2008 political cycle. But of course to complain and point out this disparity is not the same as bemoaning why it exists in the first place. In writing about Sarah Palin, Joe Hilley describes leadership qualities that she has in terms of principles which may "seem counterintuitive [in] running against the traditional formula for political success, i.e., that your weakness can be your greatest strength; also sacrificing your personal ambition can unlock the path to your destiny, and removing boundaries between your public and private life can insulate you from personal attack" (2008, pp. 28-29) (underline mine). It must be pointed out that Sarah speaks of success not failure, while placing an emphasis on strength not weakness. But the true measure of her strength, courage and character is that Sarah believes in putting aside one's personal ambition to "unlock the path to your destiny" (Ibid.).

Sarah's faith helps to define who she is much to the chagrin of the legion of detractors who have on numerous occasions attempted to place a restrictive barrier around her personality by making her the brunt of jokes, cynicism of her education and credentials, and lack of sincerity with respect to her language, speech and plain folksy demeanor which they have attempted to pierce with misogynist barbs. One individual that typifies these attacks prides himself on his political knowledge and insight when in actuality Jack Cafferty of CNN is an overbearing, self indulgent egotist who wears his

161

ability for sarcasm as if it were a journalistic badge of honor. The few minutes of public exposure that CNN allows him to have each day sort of sums up their respect, or lack thereof, for his analyses. So how does he use his few minutes of exposure? He interjects personal barbs directed at his target's character, motivation, and personality while rarely taking issue with true ideological differences. As a muckraker he uses his website as a gossip column where non-scientific surveys are conducted to reinforce his negative view of women in powerful positions. His diatribe and running dialogue against Governor Palin was matched only by his treatment of then U.S. Senator Hillary Clinton. If what he does is recognized as journalism, then that profession is in more trouble than it is thought to be; for example, it was the Katie Couric interview of Sarah which drew his harshest criticism. Who was it that said, "Patriotism is the last refuge of scoundrels!"?

Of course he was not alone in his strident remarks of Sarah's answers; however it was he who admonished anchor Wolf Blitzer for attempting to place the interview in perspective given the performance of other politicians from time-to-time. It was Cafferty who stated that Sarah's performance was the worse display of intellect and knowledge he had ever seen in a politician. He made a point in his arrogance of attempting to demonstrate that she was ill-prepared to be a candidate for Vice-President, by attacking her personally, as if to say that she had no business even being a governor even though she was duly elected by the citizens of Alaska; and was at the time of being selected as McCain's running-mate enjoying over an eighty-percent approval rating. In his few minutes before the CNN cameras I dare say that his ratings have never come close to Sarah's. But yet he pushed demagoguery to new heights, as he wanted to be certain that his viewers would be left with a certain fear of Sarah, should McCain win the Presidency.

162

And Sarah's only problem in the Couric interview was attempting to convince a skeptical journalistic community, that she, too, deserved the same respect that the Democratic candidates received, in particular, her counterpart Joe Biden whose notorious conduct and comments went mostly ignored by the press.

But before we go much further, let's take a few moments to analyze the Palin-Couric interview. Now keep in mind that this is the same Katie Couric that has been assailed by members of her own profession as being ill-prepared and lacking of skills and depth of knowledge to take on the responsibility of being an evening news anchor. Of course this is a coveted position for electronic-TV journalism, but after subtracting the advertisements and commercial breaks, a thirty minute newscast is about twenty minutes in duration; while a one-hour show with a question and answer format may be a total of 30-40 minutes at best.

For this time, and off camera preparation, Couric gets paid the big bucks, and no doubt, there is a hefty amount of jealousy by certain colleagues, a few of whom probably wrote her off as being un-prepared for the job. Now with the Palin interview, Couric's stock went up because she managed to provide other media/print journalists with fuel to further assail Governor Palin, as if the Tina Fey Saturday Night Live TV Show impersonations were not enough. Fey received many accolades and a boost in her career by doing ridiculous impressions of Governor Palin. It is sad, but true, how some people can benefit at the misery and expense of others. And the exploitation becomes more despicable when it comes from a member of your own group. To Sarah's credit she handled the insults with class.

Below are a few questions and answers that we will examine prior to contrasting Sarah's issues with those of Joe Biden.

Question from Couric: "You recently said three times that you would never, 'second guess' Israel if that country decided to attack Iran. Why not?"

Palin: "We shouldn't second guess Israel's security efforts because we cannot ever afford to send a message that we would allow a second Holocaust, for one. Israel has got to have the opportunity and the ability to protect itself. They are our closest ally in the Mid-east. We need them. They need us. And we shouldn't second guess their efforts" (sic).

This was an excellent answer which was ignored: then on further pressing by Couric, Governor Palin begins to speak of good guys v. bad guys, with a history of making provocative advances, or using threatening language to challenge Israel's security, or even right to exist. Of course this issue is complex, dating as far back as antiquity, then up to and beyond the 1948 establishment of Israel, and its war between the Arab nations in which the disputed occupied lands for years were, and have been, a source of consternation in the Middle East (see my text *E Pluribus Unum*). Governor Palin's well thought out answers only articulated this complexity in which no previous administration, since 1949, has had an answer that resolves the problem.

If the media has a desire to be fair and honest, why then don't they converse openly about Israel's possession of atomic weapons, and where and how they secured them; and why are the Arab nations under such scrutiny when it is they who are living under the threat of nuclear annihilation. What is unconscionable, in my humble opinion, is the hypocrisy of the questions; and Couric embracing the media's hands-off approach

164

to Obama on similar issues, particularly when he was not challenged on the consequences of his "without pre-conditions" statement with respect to talking to so-called "Rogue States" such as Iran, North Korea, and Cuba. Couric knew full well that a double-standard was in play as it pertained to Sarah, but she ignored it, and went right ahead with her "cross-examination," not interview of Sarah's position on these issues. Couric herself had been subjected to this kind of scrutiny; she understood how it feels, and she had no regard for fairness, only for scoring points to elevate her own image as a "competent" journalist. This was after low ratings and negative stories which had plagued her as she labored under the microscope at CBS for a few years. Another woman, Katie Couric, exploiting Sarah to add to the Tina Fey column of self-promotion. At least Fey was honest in her artistic role at Saturday Night Live. The others had no such excuse (Ibid.). However evidence of the exploitation factor is that Fey's and Couric's stars have dimmed since Palin has left the national scene and no longer represents a threat to Obama; which may at anytime, change, in the near future, as politics are subject to bend without a moment's notice.

It is a cruel irony that the same people who passed judgment on Couric, are themselves, self-proclaimed guilty participants of soft-pedaling the questions on Bush with respect to Iraq's possession of weapons of mass destruction. They vowed that they would not again be asleep at the switch when it comes to fulfilling their obligation of public trust and disclosure. But it soon became quite evident that Sarah was the new object of their intense investigation, while they once again neglected to question, with similar intensity, their favorite sons, Obama and Biden. Please keep in mind that they were questioning Sarah as if she was at the top of the ticket, and to John McCain's credit,

165

he remained steadfast in his defense and support for Sarah, even after their loss in the election. Then again it was Sarah's responsibility to provide the face for the future of the Republican Party, and unfortunately she was up against the same odds that Couric, and Hillary had to contend with, and which women have fought against for generations. And to reiterate the thesis of this text, in America, Race Trumps Gender as far as equal rights for women are concerned.

The second Couric question focused on the financial problems that materialized just before the 2008 elections: "If the bailout doesn't pass, do you think there's a risk of another Great Depression.

Palin: "Unfortunately, that is the road that America may find itself on. Not necessarily this, as it has been proposed, has to pass or we're going to find ourselves in another Great Depression. But, there has got to be action – bipartisan effort – Congress not pointing fingers at one another, but finding the solution to this, taking action, and being serious about the reforms on Wall Street that are needed" (sic). Even with this very prophetic response, Sarah was accused in the first instance of using the word Holocaust, and the images that it injures, and then accused again for mentioning the Great Depression. But in the context in which the questions were asked, both usages by Sarah were appropriate. It is illogical to comprehend how any rational person, operating without a hidden agenda, could find fault with Governor Palin's answers to this, or the first question. Certainly, the Holocaust is always in the back of everyone's mind that speaks of Israel's right to exist. The threat to its sovereignty can be shown in the same manner in which the United States, with a preemptive attack, provided a threat to Iraq's sovereignty. Its government has been radically altered with tens of thousands of Iraqis killed. Such could be the fate, if not worse, for Israel.

And in regards to the Great Depression, Sarah has been vindicated by others who have applied the term the "Great Depression," to the economic problems and financial collapse of various institutions of our nation. She knows far more about it than Joe Biden which we will discuss soon. Furthermore, as a sitting Governor, she has the responsibility for managing a budget, and making administrative/executive decisions, that far exceeded the expertise of the three men involved in the 2008 campaign. Certainly in placing service ahead of personal ambition, she has held the belief that "Government should be about making life better for the people it was created to serve, not about lining the pockets of friends." Interestingly she was the only non-millionaire of the four central figures in the 2008 campaign. (Note: I wonder what it is about our government that makes multi-millionaires of our federal elected officials, might it be the influence of lobbyists?) But Sarah eschewed cronyism, and unethical practices by policymakers. The multibillion dollar oil and gas industry which fell under her purview is a glaring example of her courage, and managerial expertise, with the *Alaskan citizens* benefiting from the decisions that she has made. She spoke of efficiency in government, and bipartisanship, long before she was asked to join the Republican ticket. It was for these very reasons, as well as her strength in character, which provided the rationale for her being asked to serve as the vice president nominee (Hilley. pp. 91-92).

In her well crafted and beautifully delivered acceptance speech, viewed by the entire world, she made her convictions clear, and emphatically proclaimed her readiness to serve. With charisma and class she stated: "We are expected to govern with integrity,

167

good will, clear convictions, and a servant's heart. I pledge to all Americans that I will carry myself in this spirit as Vice President of the United States. This was the spirit that brought me to the governor's office, when I took on the old politics as usual in Juneau, when I stood up to the special interests, the lobbyists, big oil companies, and the good-ole-boys network. Sudden and relentless reform, never sits well with entrenched interests, and power brokers. That's why true reform is so hard to achieve. But with the support of the citizens of Alaska, we shook things up" (sic) (Ibid. pp. 92-93).

From that moment forward there was a strong shift in journalistic integrity. Almost collectively, and in unison, they made a decision to go after this former beauty queen, and now high level representative of the Republican Party. On the one hand, they decided to use her attractiveness against her by suggesting smarts and intellect could not reside, with any competence, in a public figure without there being flaws in her knowledge base. Then they wrongfully attacked her clothes and contrived penchant for shopping at high fashion stores. The high heels she wore were too chic, her glasses were too stylish, her hair style was plain. And when the truth came out about the clothing allowance, it was dismissed. Of course by then the damage was done, systematic ridicule and abuse of this dedicated public official prevailed.

How tragic, then Charlie Gibson treated her as he *thought* he would treat a coed in a university government policy course by talking down to her, and lecturing her on government. But I can assure all who read these words, that only Sarah's graciousness to a guest, and good manners, prevented her from giving him a piece of her mind for being so condescending. The coeds today, by and large, do not sit still for professorial challenges to their intellect; nor do they hesitate to share with all who will listen that being a woman does not disqualify them from having independent thoughts, or making tough decisions for the well-being of those who depend upon them, either in the public or private sector, as well as at home.

This brings us to the third Couric question, on budget priorities. Couric: "Why isn't it better, Governor Palin, to spend $700 billion helping middle-class families who are struggling with health care, housing, gas and groceries? Allow them to spend more, and put more money into the economy, instead of helping these big financial institutions that played a role in creating this mess? The criticism of Sarah's answer to this question took on epic proportions. She stated, "That's why I say, I, like every American I'm speaking with, we're ill about this position that we have been put in. Where it is the taxpayers looking to bailout? But ultimately, what the bailout does is help those who are concerned about the health care reform that is needed to shore up our economy. Um, helping, oh, it's got to be about job creation, too. Shoring up our economy, and putting it back on the right track. So health care reform and reducing taxes, and reining in spending has got to accompany tax reductions, and tax relief for Americans, and trade – we have got to see trade as opportunity, not as, uh, competitive, um, scary thing, but one in five jobs are created in the trade sector today. We've got to look at that as our opportunity. All of those things under the umbrella of job creation" (sic) (J. Fallows, website).

One of Governor Palin's many detractors, James Fallows of the *Atlantic Magazine*, including critic-in-chief, Jack Cafferty of CNN have pointed to this answer; as well as those previously mentioned, including her reference to Russia and Putin, as demonstrations of Sarah's lack of preparedness to serve. But in actuality, it is the talking

169

heads/journalists, who should wear the dunce cap(s), because by attempting to make a

sitting Governor with executive experience and high voter approval ratings look the fool,

they showed exactly why their ratings are as low as the United States Congress, and

former President George W. Bush. Keep in mind, that Obama, McCain, Biden and Bush

are/were members of the Legislative and Executive Branches of government with

concomitant approval ratings so low as to be an embarrassment.

And Fallows, Cafferty, Couric, and the others feed off each others desperate

attempts to raise their ratings, for the higher the ratings, the more money they earn, and

the more secure they are in their jobs. If this means that they must work overtime in

attempting to make someone look like a fool, then so be it. In this instance, and at this

point in time in history, their target was Sarah Palin; they had to bring her down to make

themselves look good. Jealousy certainly was a factor, as well as an acute need for

acceptance by their media colleagues. But it was Sarah's ratings that was higher than all

of theirs combined, so the fools were those asking the questions who lacked credibility in

the first place.

Now with these plausible motives and agendas well established, we can return to

an examination of Governor Palin's responses to Katie Couric's question. I will,

however, concede the fact that the hesitation phrases of "Uh" and "Um" that the

journalists, and I use the term loosely, intentionally left in Sarah's answers were done to

show uncertainty in her stated positions. But millions of others use these same exact

phrases each and every day, including the great orator President Obama, when we are

attempting to give thought and measured significance to an important question(s).

Sarah's biggest problem was that she did not fully complete the thoughts that she had

170

verbalized to Couric's questions. But each issue in itself had been discussed in connection to the finance institution bailout. And with her forward thinking, Sarah also managed to let us know the risks to the workers as it relates to the auto industry. No one can doubt the role and importance that health care plays in the industries' bottom line, and now it factors into their deficit and retiree benefits.

Furthermore, the auto industry must now look to reform to stabilize its product (cars), and market shares. Indeed, trade and competition, whether it is national or international, will impact on jobs, and yes, this has been, and will be a "scary" time for all those connected to the auto industry, financial institutions, mortgage lenders, and the American workers. So what indeed was Sarah's problem? As far as I can tell she was guilty of showing compassion for those most hardest hit by this recession – The *American Worker*. Moreover, if Sarah's answer in linking health care to the struggling industries and workers, with the bailout, makes you believe that she is uninformed, then so too is *Time Magazine*. In its December 2008 issue, two major articles provides support for Governor Palin's response. James Carney of *Time* states, "Struggling companies may be forced to cut or kill their employee coverage just to survive. And while the cost of Obama's [health] reform is high – an estimated $75 billion a year – a big price tag hasn't kept Congress from raiding the Treasury to fix the economy's many other ills" (p. 57).

So much for Sarah's incompetence. These domestic type questions are Governor Palin's strong areas anyway, as they are/were with many of her gubernatorial contemporaries and predecessors. But once again we can turn our attention to the Alaskan voters who have far more insight into Sarah Palin's competence than those news

171

media talking heads whose first response after seeing her was to scheme and develop strategies to tear her down. One would think that an award winning journalist as Cafferty would have at least learned the value of objectivity, and therefore, on balance, would have weighted other evidence of Palin's competence without using the slanted Couric episode to determine that she is "scary." He also labeled her interview as pathetic. However, there seemed to be a general consensus that she gave a bravo performance at the Republican Convention in Minnesota, and more than held her own with Biden in their one and only debate. Oh, no! None of these issues mattered. Even film star Matt Damon weighed in by concluding that Sarah being a heartbeat away from the presidency is a "scary" proposition, and that she would be "dangerous" for America.

Others who wanted to exact their pound of flesh from Governor Palin were those who also considered themselves feminists. In their view, Sarah could not possibly be a feminist because she is a conservative that does not believe as they do on issues of Pro-choice v. Pro-life or gun-ownership and the economy. Hell she even hunted moose. Now, no self respecting feminist would be caught dead in winter gear and a camouflage suit; toting a high powered Winchester or Browning rifle, and then sighting down a moose at 200 yards in the wilds. She should be out carrying a sign in one of many demonstrations declaring that it is a woman's right to determine her own direction in life, and proclaiming empowerment/self-determination is also a woman's right, quite ironic, isn't it? Therefore, in this hypocritical view, they thought they were defining Sarah Palin. But of course to them there are limits to who these rights should be extended, and Sarah Palin is just not the "type" of woman who fits the mantra of feminist. Well bell hooks has something to say about such inconsistent hypocrisy. She argues:

172

"Revolutionists [substitute 'change agent' if this term carries too much power for you] seek to change reality, to make it better. Therefore revolutionists not only need the revolutionary philosophy of dialects [language peculiar to members of a group, e.g. feminist]. They need a revolutionary ideology, i.e., a body of ideas based on analyzing the main <u>contradictions</u> of the particular society which they are trying to change, projecting a <u>vision</u> of a higher form of reality in which this <u>contradiction</u> would be resolved. Support of anti-intellectualism in feminist movement is a good example of ideology that undermines and impedes progress ...Most women are deprived of access to modes of thought that promote the kind of critical and analytical understanding necessary for liberation struggle. This deprivation leads women to feel insecure about intellectual work and <u>to fear grappling with new ideas and information. It may lead us to dismiss as irrelevant that which is relevant because it is challenging"</u> (pp. 114-115) (underline mine).

It is no doubt that bell hooks could very well support Sarah as a sister-in-arms (no pun intended), for what she has achieved in life, by making bold decisions for her family and constituency. If Governor Sarah Palin does not fit the mold of a feminist, then I daresay, who does. But Gloria Steinem appears to be a Matt Damon in drag, as she strongly asserts her opposition to Sarah, not just based on differences in ideology, but rather denying Sarah the right to be different from her with a set of ideas all of her own choosing. Nor did Sarah walk lockstep in the mold that Steinem preordained as appropriate in order to fit her idea of feminism. Therefore she once remarked, in a *Los Angeles Times* op ed piece no less, that all Palin and Hillary Clinton have in common is a chromosome.

She further added, "I get no pleasure from imagining her in the spotlight on national and foreign policy issues about which she has zero background, with one month to learn to compete with Senator Joe Biden's 37 years experience ...She was elected governor largely because the incumbent was unpopular, and she's won over Alaskans mostly by using unprecedented oil wealth to give a $1,200 rebate to every resident" (*Los Angeles Times*, September 4, 2008). With this comment; Steinem exhibits an extreme naiveté, if not ignorance of politics. Sarah met many challenges in Alaska that Steinem

herself has pointed out. And if running against the record of an unpopular incumbent is

not a smart political move, then Obama would not be president, nor Clinton, nor Reagan,

and many others would not have a chance to win public office.

Steinem's comments were far more extensive and strident in the op ed piece than

those I mention above; and she left little wiggle room for dissenters who opposed the

Democratic Party process which gave the nomination to Obama over Hillary Clinton.

Her comments to the Hillary supporters who were contemplating voting for McCain in

protest that it "would be like saying, 'somebody stole my shoes, so I'll amputate my

legs'" (Ibid.). Yes, she has a way with words, this founder of *Ms. Magazine*. I believe,

however, that in the spirit of feminism in which she is a major player, had she chosen to

be a supporter, not of Palin's politics, but of Palin's strength, character, and contribution

to women homemakers, and those in the workforce, she would have added immeasurably

to the ideals in which she espouses. But when she spoke favorably of the Joe Biden's

gaffe machine, and made experience a major issue, she negated the relevance of her

endorsement as a feminist because women, for generations, have been overlooked by less

experienced men, and/or those men who are prone to making mistakes.

And women of course are held to a different and higher standard. For example,

Biden makes ethnic humor jokes and remarks, he has insulted Jews by embracing

stereotypes, insulted Blacks when he mentioned Barack is "clean and articulate," and has

"mangled historical facts …his gaffes piled up at such a rate [during the campaign] that

the Republicans dedicated a website to tracking them. His emotional reactions

sometimes appear to drive him to fudge answers. When CBS's Katie Couric prodded

174

him about an Obama ad that was criticizing McCain for not knowing how to use a computer, Biden called one of his own campaign's ads 'terrible,' and declared that if he'd known about it beforehand, 'We'd never have done it.' Later, he not only had to soften his criticism, but also had to admit that he had never even seen the ad. [And with respect] to President Bush's response to the financial crisis, he also told Couric that when the stock market crashed in 1929, 'FDR got on television' and explained to the American people what happened. And of course Couric never challenged Biden on these facts!! In fact, Herbert Hoover was president and radio was the medium of the era" (Biden Gaffes website).

Certainly it should be clear to even the most casual observer that had Sarah been prone to these types of mistakes, errors, and missteps, she would have suffered the most humiliating criticisms that could be imagined in the free world. But the double-standards, during the campaign, were not only blatantly obvious, they served to underscore the real need for the feminist movement of which Hillary Clinton has helped shape throughout her illustrious career.

Section III: Hillary Clinton

Madam Secretary, Hillary Rodham Clinton, formerly U.S. Senator Clinton, did not receive the same type of interrogative questioning on her competence as did Sarah when she was running for president in 2007 and 2008. The press wouldn't dare challenge Hillary's abilities given her years of service, but they felt right at home hitting her on a very personal level, inconsistent with Obama's questioning. While her experience was on par with the males in the campaign, and exceeded Barack Obama's, it became very frustrating for her candidacy and supporters to witness the double standards, and to see

175

her victimized by media assaults and caricatures which had nothing to do with her candidacy when it was just the two of them remaining. In gambling parlance, and even in the language used on Wall Street, it became clear that "The fix was in." By the rules suited to his candidacy, except for Michigan and Florida, Obama began to collect delegates from the caucuses, while Hillary was strongest in primary states to the degree that in the end her total vote count was higher.

But the delegate count was clearly in Obama's favor. Even longtime close allies of the Clinton's, e.g., New Mexico Governor Bill Richardson, bolted from her and her campaign, in obvious betrayal, to join Obama. The Democratic Congressional leadership began to push uncommitted delegates to make a decision, and their language suggested a strong preference for Obama because a number of them wanted Hillary to quit the race. And because she did not, there were more criticisms leveled at her. A primary media antagonist again was critic-in-chief Jack Cafferty. His problem is either women candidates, or women in general; it is difficult to tell because he rarely has anything nice to say about either.

Cafferty was very fond of labeling Hillary, probably as much, if not more so than Sarah Palin. As with many other misogynists, his disdain for women in power, or seeking power, transcended ideology; meaning that their problem with women is the first thing on their agenda. In viewing CNN, and reading messages posted to his blog, it was obvious that he had a following of hate Hillary and Sarah groupies. Of course this probably does not come as a surprise, but what may be revealing is that these gender based attacks use mostly similar terminology in describing or characterizing women, e.g., calculating, untrustworthy, and manipulative to name a few. Even women adopt the male antagonist line of thinking, particularly when it comes to Hillary. They use the same phrases and methods of attacks without giving any thought to where the line originated. For instance, one woman commented, "Politically and personally, she's trying to take on the male persona, and she isn't a woman in the way I want a woman candidate to be" (http://www.feministe.us/blog), which is quite difficult in itself to explain. For women, competence standards have become parallel bars for both conservative and liberal women.

Another posting, but in support of Hillary which adds an insightful perspective, stated "She's got to walk the same line as any other woman who's trying to get ahead in a male-dominated field, and she's being subjected to the same impossible standards of being tough, but not too tough, feminine, but not too feminine, etc. And she, like a lot of other women, just can't win" (Ibid.). One other comment from a misogyny blog demonstrates the level of personal cruelty in which the attacks can take in referring to Hillary as a bitch, that thing, cunt, whore and slut, terms generally reserved for "other" evil women that people don't like (Ibid.).

There has not been any evidence to show that Hillary has been anything but a class act since coming on the national scene in 1990-91. Her colleagues sing her praises, and so too does most of her constituents. Yet the hate continues. And added to that morass of nonsense is Cafferty's insistence of labeling Hillary a narcissist with an agenda of attempting to destroy the Democratic Party because she stayed in the race to fight until the end; as if he is a card-carrying Democrat who really gives a shit, such a hypocrite. A woman who fights just as hard as a man for something she believes in is held to a different standard.

177

This helps to explain why Cafferty has never had anything nice to say about her. As a journalist you would think he would be more objective. And because she refused to give up, she and President Clinton earned the label of narcissists. As a 19th Century term coined by British sexologist Havelock Ellis, narcissist is taken from the Greek youth supposedly enamored with his own reflection. "Freud later wrote that narcissists are virtually untreatable" (J. Hoffman, 2008). And of course a cocaine addict, Freud, would certainly understand this phenomena probably better than any other clinician. It has "deep roots in psychoanalytic literature, [and] appears to have become a popular descriptor so bloated as to have been rendered meaningless. Dr. Susan Jaffe, a Manhattan psychoanalyst [has stated] that it sounds more impressive to say that someone is narcissistic rather than a jerk …For though the word has a derogatory stamp, the very people we label narcissistic often are those who attract as well as repel us" (Ibid.). Indeed the popularity of the term has become a sound bite for the media talking heads who are mostly unfit and unqualified to use the term in reference to others. Unfortunately the label sticks, and then Hillary Clinton has additional baggage to tote around. Her strength is absolutely impressive, to say the least.

Now U.S. Secretary of State Hillary Clinton, nominated by the same person who bested her in the presidential race can use her talents, expertise, and experience to further serve our nation and the world. She will continue to be an excellent role model for other young women who are meeting challenges in the workforce, in the community, and even at home. And as previously stated, while her and Sarah are at different points in the ideological mix of things, they have demonstrated respect for each other which their supporters will do well to emulate. It would be an extraordinary event if the two of them

178

could develop some type of organizational effort that would have education of women at its base to teach them how to handle the negative abuses and terms thrown their way upon entering the public arena. In the final analysis, men like Cafferty, in spite of themselves, may learn a thing or two about class; and how to behave with dignity and professionalism, while being fair and non-antagonistic towards others with no regards to gender.

Section IV: The Fourteenth Amendment (XIV)

As previously discussed, the 14th Amendment to the United States Constitution is one of three Civil War Amendments, along with the 13th and 15th. But the 14th is said to be one of the most litigated amendments in the Constitution because of its special provisions of equal protection of the law, and due process. Section 1 in its entirety states: "All persons born or naturalized in the United States and subject to the jurisdiction thereof, are citizens of the United States and of the state wherein they reside [citizenship clause for former slaves]. No state shall make or enforce any law which shall abridge the privileges or immunities of citizens of the United States; nor shall any state deprive any person of life, liberty, or property, without due process of law; nor deny to any person within its jurisdiction the equal protection of the laws." Then Section 5 for emphasis on the authority of Congress adds: "The Congress shall have power to enforce, by appropriate legislation, the provisions of this article." Thus the Civil Rights Act, Affirmative Action, and Voting Rights Act, as well as other laws strengthened, and added clarity to the amendment when it became necessary.

I have added this amendment to this discussion for the expressed purpose of demonstrating its importance solely to the feminist movement. I place emphasis on the

179

term "solely" to illustrate that there has been a historical connection between race and gender insofar as civil rights are concerned. And the thought of White feminists not advocating for Black rights has been somewhat of an anathema to the movement even though women's liberation had far more White members than Black. This is not to say that Black women were detached from the feminist movement, but rather middle class White female values seem to be out of touch with the dual problems of racism and sexism which Black women have endured for hundreds of years. As bell hooks so succinctly states, "White women and Black men have it both ways. They can act as oppressor or be oppressed. Black men may be victimized by racism, but sexism allows them to act as exploiters and oppressors of women. White women may be victimized by sexism, but racism enables them to act as exploiters and oppressors of Black people [which is often shown by erroneously claiming Affirmative Action to be preferential treatment, making erroneous charges against Black men, and the Daughters of the Confederacy an offshoot of the KKK, suggesting that Black women be excluded from the 19th Amendment]. *Both groups have led liberation movements that favor their interests and support the continued oppression of other groups.* Black male sexism has undermined struggles to eradicate racism just as White female racism undermines feminist struggle. As long as these two groups, or any group, defines liberation as gaining social equality with ruling-class White men, they have a vested interest in the continued exploitation and oppression of others" (p. 16).

This is exactly the reason why throughout the long 2008 presidential campaign, while Hillary first, then Sarah, both were combating sexist stereotypes from the media, and the population in general, the other men in the campaign, including Obama , during and after the nomination, remained mostly silent and allowed it to happen. He first benefited from the hate messages hurled at Hillary, then he benefited from the misogynist actions turned on Sarah Palin. However to his credit he did have reason to speak out in defense of Hillary when Father Pfleger made disparaging remarks about her during the height of the campaign in May of 2008. However, the primary at this time had all but been decided.

Interestingly as these negative messages received more traction in the nation, Obama polls numbers would climb. Certainly there was a direct inverted relationship between the two issues, the more negative and hateful the statements made about Hillary and Sarah – the better Obama would do in the polls, a phenomena argued by bell hooks. The same phenomena occurred with the fantastically talented country music group The Dixie Chicks; but they were vindicated by justice when the lies of the Bush Administration were disclosed. When they criticized the "Bush Doctrine" of first strike/preemptive warfare and imperialism as it related to his Iraq policy, they were called every dirty name reserved for women that people hate.

Epithets were hurled at them by former fans and some of their industry contemporaries; initially their record sales declined because their music was not being played on the radio. As the hate messages increased, some of the other performer sales, who criticized them grew at a similar rate. Hate is a very strong motivator and sordid family value and belief system!! The Dixie Chicks "took the risk and had faith that they were right." They did not sell out their values as feminists (*Shut Up and Sing*, 2006). And eventually they ended up with the number one record in the nation, and they did not need radio to do it. Their fans flocked to their concerts, their popularity has increased,

181

and they did not betray their friends, values, or our nation. They are true feminists and patriots. Thus once again demonstrating the power of character within those who are feminists.

The importance of blending the feminist gender issue with that of race was a strategy by the feminists which they believed to be instrumental in achieving their goals. However it was not a contrived or phony coalition effort for they believed that there was a commonality in their objectives. This is one of the primary reasons that Obama did so well with White females at the polls. A feminist had this to say, "One of the things I've learned in my 8 years of studying the second-wave feminist movement (and the feminism that evolved out of it) is that White feminists cannot focus on gender and sexism without attention to race and racism if they want to make this a movement as vibrant and colorful as the world is. I think that AS FEMINISTS, we cannot afford the perception that we only care about discrimination against (White) women" (feminist website). There is a real and genuine passion in her words, and this message is the one that has resonated throughout our nations.

But on the other hand the contentious Democratic Party campaigns provided another view of showing feminists coming together to challenge the status quo, or what can be referred to as the "'good ole boys' network." Who can forget the Rules Committee meeting when a Black woman displaying an intercultural show of solidarity of feminism in support of Hillary Clinton, stood with her hand on her hip and scowling at the committee in defiance of their rules proceedings. Her animus was clearly shown as they disenfranchised the voters of Florida and Michigan which resulted in Obama winning the nomination. Leading up to this event, Jack Cafferty was relentless in his misogyny, as Hillary took the brunt of his demagogic hate for the better part of six months. However no better class was shown than Hillary Clinton when she stepped to the podium and conceded the nomination to Obama. We all can learn something about grace and class from her and Sarah, in particular, Jack Cafferty.

The 14th Amendment provided the foundation for all of the above actions coupled with the First Amendment of free speech. So while the feminists and racial minorities had a guaranteed right to run for political office unencumbered by barriers to voting, those who would choose to tear the candidates down with negative speech also enjoyed constitutional protection. What a truly great country this is with all of its faults and terrific checks and balances. They work in tandem to even protect those who are marginalized because of non-mainstream professions, such as sexual talk radio, internet, and gentleman's clubs, as well as prostitution in some states. The women who have chosen to engage in this lifestyle may not be looked upon with favor by many in the population; but make no mistake about it, they too are feminists exercising their right to make choices for themselves in terms of their livelihood and/or recreational activities.

But isn't it interesting that the derogatory language used to characterize and label these women are also the same negative terms and words that are thrown at Sarah and Hillary. It either shows how low they see them, or for that matter, any woman who does not measure up to their standards will be so labeled, and so be it. In either case, Hillary and Sarah, and even those marginalized women are right to ignore those who hate them. There is also one other consideration, in that those who are marginalized, have taken the power from those who would use those derogatory terms to define them, because they often use the same words to describe themselves. Taking the power away from your detractors certainly accomplishes one thing for sure, it pisses them off. And some of them though are not ones that take kindly to being ignored – because their mental stability is in question in the first place. Yes, exercising one's Constitutional rights in America has always come with risks.

For another example, let's examine a scenario which the forefathers could not have foreseen when they enacted the 14th Amendment. For one thing, they certainly were not supportive of women's rights or any semblance of a feminist cause, particularly when women could not vote by norms or by practice. D.J. Connolly in pushing forth the notion of equal opportunity theorizes, "Suppose that the forefathers had been warned, back in 1868, that the Supreme Court would one day use the 14th Amendment to force places like Virginia Military Institute (VMI) [with a 150 year old history and tradition of military education for men] to admit young women." Do you suppose that the 14th Amendment would have been ratified? Would it had made it through the Congress before going to the states for ratification? Connolly concludes that would never have happened because "The people back then would have thought women in military school(s) was a terrible idea. They also did not trust the Supreme Court, which they viewed as a 'diseased member of the body politic that was at risk of amputation.' America had just suffered through a civil war in which some half million people died. The Supreme Court, [it was thought], helped cause that war," because of its rulings on States Rights (10th Amendment) and the power of the federal government (D.J. Connolly website).

What is revealing by this scenario, as presented by Connolly, is that we have heard conservative presidents and candidates make note of the fact that they did not want a justice who will legislate from the bench. In other words, according to Reagan, Bush I and II, and John McCain had he won the presidency, wanted justices to remain true to the original intent of the Constitution, as written and envisioned by the founders. Thus, using that logic, the 14th Amendment should not provide equal opportunity for women, and women's rights would have failed the same as the ERA (Equal Rights Amendment) had in the states in which it came up for ratification, such as Florida in 1978, and Maine in 1984. But the Supreme Court at that time was doing exactly what Reagan and Bush opposed, they broadly interpreted the 14th Amendment, and voted to secure gender equity in the VMI ruling.

To better understand the implications of the VMI ruling and its relationship to the 14th Amendment and the ERA, Connolly provides the following, "In 1997, Justice Ruth Bader Ginsburg gave a talk at the University of Virginia Law School. There she was quoted as saying that she still wanted the ERA in the Constitution as 'a symbol.' However, Justice Ginsberg allowed that it didn't really make much difference. She stated that 'what has evolved' was pretty much the same as the ERA ...Justice Ginsberg had written the VMI decision; her opinion laid out the 'constitutional' principle that the 14th Amendment outlaws almost any state action or program which does not treat men and women the same" (Ibid.). Therefore while gender equity is officially the law of the land, thanks to the equal protection clause of the 14th Amendment, we still have a long way to go in practice as the experiences of Sarah and Hillary will attest. As quoted by bell hooks, each of these dynamic women were victimized by "Progressive Dehumanization," meaning as the campaigns went further, the personal assaults on them grew more frequent and strident (p. 3). The author hooks likens this experience to the brutal psychological treatment and attacks on prisoner's self-concept. There is also a certain

185

element of isolation that the targets of this abuse will have to endure. When put in this context, the bravery and character of the women pioneers is without question, and without peer.

Chapter Six – Endnotes

Carney, James (2008). "Why Reform's Moment Is Now," in *Time Magazine*, December 1, 2008.

Dixie Chicks (2006). "Shut Up and Sing." Home Box Office Special.

Hilley, Joe (2008). *Sarah Palin: A New Kind of Leader*. Zondervan Publishers, Grand Rapids, MI.

Hoffman, Jan (2008). "Here's looking at me, kid – are we narcissists?" *New York Times News Service*, Monday, August 4, 2008.

hooks, bell (2000). *Feminist Theory: From Margin To Center*, 2nd Edition. South End Press, Cambridge, MA.

Pop: Memorable Moments Defined '08 Campaign, "Katie's Comeback" and "Sarah/Tina/Palin/Fey." *The Flint Journal*, November 12, 2008.

Steinem, Gloria (2008). "Gloria Steinem on Sarah Palin," *Los Angeles Times* (Opinion Page). September 4, 2008.

Websites:

http://jamesfallows.theatlantic.com

http://www.boston.com   Biden Gaffes

http://www.cnn.com   Jack Cafferty

http://www.feministe.us/blog

http://www.geocities.com/djconhoo/ERA   D.J. Connolly "The Stealth Equal Rights Amendment"

http://www.shelfari.com

Democratic presidential candidate Hillary Clinton
greets supporters as she arrives at a rally.

Democratic vice presidential candidate Sen. Joe Biden, D-Del., and Republican Candidate Alaska Gov. Sarah Palin shake hands Thursday before the start of the Vice presidential debate at Washington University in St. Louis, MO.

CHAPTER SEVEN

Examining Barack Obama's "Machiavellian" Message of Hope and Change

Section I: Cultural History/Conceptual Knowledge

Throughout this text I have discussed the importance of concepts as they relate to the central persons who have been the focus of this discussion. Words do have meaning, for language provides the essence of who we are as people, and defines our relationship to groups, individuals, families, organizations, even political parties, and between nations. We progress through our ability to communicate to establish trust, and it becomes our bond and is a demonstration of our character and integrity. Therefore the significant argument to be made is really can we be trusted? Can others believe what we say? And for those who have chosen the path of politics, and entered the political arena, gaining the public trust is an important prerequisite to success. But the manner in which one defines success is crucial to the political process. As an illustration, in the matter of state diplomacy, the late British actor, Richard Harris, playing the part of English patriot and military tactician Oliver Cromwell of 17th Century fame, in a line from the film of the same name, he stated, "When men run out of words they reach for the sword. Let's hope we can keep [the two parties] talking" (1970).

But a statement to ponder, do personal reasons drive ambition, and then is ambition the means by which there is a fulfillment of service to the broader needs of the community, state, or nation. How people see their elected officials, and how they interpret their commitment to service, and whether or not there is an established trust or bond will determine their tenure in office; and as heretofore explained, will go a long way in erasing or at least minimizing the negative effect of stereotypes. This is of course important to our thesis.

And as previously stated, no one individual, group, or political party has a corner on the market of character, trust, or service. It becomes a matter of shared values and expectations. Annie S. Barnes writing in her book *Everyday Racism* has this to say, "People of integrity can be found in every part of the political spectrum, from the most conservative-minded people to the most progressive …[and] a person's political viewpoint is no indicator of his or her ability to behave with dignity, respect, and fairness toward others" (2000, p. 21). This is to say that until proven or shown otherwise, Republicans as well as Democrats can govern with equal public trust and responsibility. However the problems the Republicans had in the 2008 political cycle was the one of retrospective trust, accountability, and expectations.

The previous administration had so destroyed the public's ability to place confidence in another Republican, that it made no difference how honorable and ethical John McCain and Sarah Palin were, it made no difference how much integrity they had, their fate in terms of losing the election was probably sealed from the very moment it was found that George W. Bush and his administration lied about the weapons of mass destruction in Iraq. Nor did it help the Republican cause when full disclosure, and transparency, also became victims of the administration. America was truly suffering from Bush and Republican fatigue, and John McCain and Sarah Palin had to spend an inordinate amount of time attempting to rehabilitate the Republican image in the eyes of the public. This became an almost impossible job, particularly in light of the financial collapse that occurred.

191

The challenge for the Democrats was to make sure they would field candidates who could take full advantage of the suicidal attempts that the Republicans were engaging in, and not get in their way while they were at it. Thus fulfilling the old adage of when your adversary is trying to commit suicide, it is best to stay out of their way. It was well documented that John McCain was an honorable person, and his selection of Sarah Palin as a running mate, while a bold political move, did also place them both in the progressive column of the history books in spite of their conservative values. Had the Bush lies and the financial collapse been taken out of the campaign picture, there just may have been a completely different outcome. But then again, there was the candidacy of Obama to account for in 2008, and given the campaign that he ran, no matter what the issues, the Democrats could very well still be in control of the Presidency and Congress. These are scenarios which have to be evaluated if the Democrats want to retain control of Congress in 2010, and the White House in 2012.

So we will spend time in this chapter examining a few relevant racial and political scenarios, but only as they relate to Obama and the concepts that became an issue in 2008 because I am certain that they will resurface in 2010 and 2012. For example, there will be a repeated debate on the value of community organization, ACORN, and voter registration, spreading the wealth/socialism, the deficit, transparency, and of course, the previously named, "war on terrorism." These issues will be further examined by using a mid-term evaluation method introduced by the Obama administration. But for now it would be wise to become better acquainted with Obama himself, his cultural history, and ideology, which will provide us with a better yardstick for understanding of the complicated philosophical context in which his decisions will be made.

During the 2008 campaign a number of things were said and done from which we can use as a measuring stick of his character and integrity. However campaigns are never the sum total of who a candidate is, nor do they provide us with an accurate gauge of who they will be during their tenure in office, whether it is four, or eight years. Certainly the experience of Richard Nixon and the Watergate fiasco is an excellent example of the significance of this statement. How they might operate under stress, and indeed their personalities do come into play during campaigns; but without question, it is different in campaigns where their personal desire to be elected will put into motion apparatuses which are nowhere near as complex, as making decisions for a nation, with quite possibly global implications. Campaigns can help us judge character and integrity which are two important traits for any president, or for that matter, any person, public or private. Beyond that, as already stated, who we will vote for becomes a matter of individual history, culture, conscience, and values.

Findings in a number of surveys have concluded that Americans tend to vote for individuals who not only share their values, but who may also share their cultural roots or ethnicity (see for example A. Mohammad in endnotes). In the 2008 campaign cycle these factors were shown to be suggestive of another dynamic as demonstrated in the exit data displayed in Chapters 3 and 4, because a significant number of White Americans voted for Obama. Furthermore, it is well known that President Obama is biracial, and for general information, the nomenclature "mixed" is insulting, and the term "mutt" is offensive; and neither would appear on a demographic profile form or survey unless it is generated by White supremacists or bigots such as those William Kristol identifies with, who have already equated Blacks/African Americans with lower animal species.

Regardless of what Kristol and others may say with respect to the "mutt like me" comment made by Obama, there is nothing funny about it, but certainly it would be embraced by far-right conservatives like Hannity, Limbaugh, George Will and Kristol who so desperately want to discount race as a factor in American relationships where progress is determined by Whites with power.

Race and racism for Kristol, are factors of little consequence. So with respect to race relations, he embraces the Obama presidency with some satisfaction, initially, for it proves in his mind, his weak theory that racism is on the wane, and/or should be discounted as an important issue in 21st Century America. And in retrospect, I believe if Obama had it to do over again he would not make that type of negative statement in reference to his race/ethnicity; he would choose his words more carefully because if not, by extension, they cast dispersions on his daughters. Also on another important ethnic/race issue, Barack Obama has his roots in the continent of Africa in the country of Kenya, from his father's heritage, where he has identified family members, and from his American mother's side of the family, who is White, he has relatives in the United States. He thus has roots on the continent of Africa, and has generational experience with Europeans, vis-à-vis, colonization linked to White 15th Century global imperialism.

And the same imperialism that colonized and partitioned the African continent, also enslaved millions of Black Africans by chaining and brutally transporting them through the middle passage, to the Western Hemisphere. This enslavement irrevocably altered Black culture including language, religion, family and intra group relations, as well as the relationships with succeeding White generations. Therefore those with the colonization experience have a different history than those with a heritage of slavery.

Those with the former experience, and are immigrants to America, such as Obama's father, or are Americans by birth such as Barack Obama, through his mother, have been able to retain their original African name, and therefore they are African American through family roots and by name. On the other hand, those with the heritage of slavery, all have slave names, unless they have changed it, and they do not have any direct links to the continent of Africa, no family ties, and no identity from any country on the continent.

Ours, meaning those with a rich legacy found in our slave heritage, is a recognition of the difficulty and challenges of adaptation handed down from our ancestors. Being proud of our ancestral heritage which was shaped by the middle passage is who we are as Black Americans; historically we have also been marginalized in a hostile land. Survival as Americans meant adopting new cultural traits, i.e., language, religion, education, and family relationships, including interaction with the political and economic institutions of the antebellum society in which we reside. All of these socio-cultural factors for redefining ourselves makes us distinctly "Black" Americans, not African Americans. Robert Guthrie, psychologist and author of the pivotal book, *Even The Rat Was White*, makes similar observations to the ones that I have described above. Guthrie notes, "It seems necessary to me to capitalize the word 'Black'… when the word refers to a specific people. While it may be an 'exact synonym for African American,' I find the syntactical application of the word Black easier to use," (1976, p. xvii).

Moreover, another powerful testimony to these cultural identity facts is provided by John McWhorter. Writing in the *Los Angeles Times* he argues the following, "It's

195

time we descendants of slaves brought to the United States let go of the term "African American," and go back to calling ourselves Black – with a capital 'B'… Living descendants of slaves in America neither knew their African ancestors nor even have elder relatives who knew them …A working-class Black man in [Detroit] has more in common with a working class White man in Cincinnati than with a Ghanaian or [Kenyan for that matter]" (2004). Then when speaking of Obama's election to the Presidency, columnist Clarence Page of Obama's home town of Chicago had this to say, "Barack had an advantage in his quest, I suspect, in his lack of a family ancestry in American slavery, a defining characteristic of most [Black] Americans. Being raised by his White mother and grandparents in 'multi-racial' Hawaii and Indonesia, he was spared the 'post-slavery traumatic syndrome' that for many of us [Black] Americans has been a 'cultural crippler'" (2008).

As a student and professor of Black Studies, I take exception to the "cultural crippler" comment made by Page. Certainly in the Black community there are significant challenges that must be addressed but these issues have *not* made us culturally defective in our slave heritage. Quite the contrary, these issues are the result of being relegated to an inferior status because of enslavement, and it has been our culture that has sustained us during some of the most trying times of murder, degradation and oppression. In spite of what some may say, our family network is a source of strength whether immediate or extended, our institutions of faith comforts us, and politically we are more astute than years past.

Educationally and financially there is much work to be done, and yes, we suffer in the job market because of a number of factors that have absolutely nothing to do with

Black culture, even though there are those Black persons, who conservatives love, such as Bill Cosby and Ward Connerly, that will have Americans believe otherwise. To proselytize that Black Americans do not take enough responsibility for what ails us as a people is an absolutely ludicrous assertion. And culturally speaking, if there is a crippling effect, it is the American society as a whole. I hope that Mr. Obama does not share the view of Page, Cosby, and Connerly, and that he will listen to the consul of Reverend Jesse Jackson, and the minister he has marginalized, Reverend Jeremiah Wright so that truer transparency will prevail to address the structural abuse that has given rise to socio-economic and educational disparities. But a discouraging factor is that he has commented that he does not want his daughters to benefit from Affirmative Action. And with respect to Affirmative Action, his puzzling views on this, and similar public policy matters, continue to shift. For example, the government transparency that he championed is beginning to vanish under the numerous czars that he has appointed, 32 to date and still counting. I wonder how he thinks he became president, if not for Affirmative Action.

President Obama, but previously candidate and Senator Obama, used the phrases of "Hope" and "Change" to great benefit. Throughout our history these terms have been used by others as cultural benchmarks to promote ideas related to myths and beliefs designed to exploit Blacks and others who may be suffering from similar bouts of apathy and marginalization. This means if the orator can be successful in encouraging a sizeable population to embrace their notion of hope, and change, then the orator's recognition and stock becomes greater. Some of these individuals have been labeled as shysters, snake oil salesmen, or just plain con artists or pimps. To erase these labels, sincerity must be proven over time. As I have previously noted, a political campaign is different than

197

governing. The thing that would be disheartening, and most assuredly troublesome, would be for the true believers to wake up one morning to the realization that they have been hoodwinked, had, or in essence, "conned." Much to the chagrin of John McCain, it took Americans six years to awake from the romanticism and then malaise of Bush. As George Bush learned, the American people may be quick to forgive, but have a long memory with respect to lies and deceit by their leaders, as Nixon's and Bill Clinton's experiences will attest.

But for a better understanding of presidential experiences, one author writes of the pitfalls and successes of "rookie" presidents and places them in three neatly conceptual packages. Thus, in order to get a fix on the type that Obama may be, will require us to examine each category to determine if there is a fit of some sort. Beverly Gage writing in *Time Magazine* discusses a first type which she explains are those from the military.

The most well known of this grouping are Zachary Taylor, Ulysses Grant, George Washington, and of course the one we know the best with a stellar career, and a somewhat lackluster presidency, is Dwight Eisenhower (see the appendix for discussions on these and others to be soon named). But Eisenhower did initiate an intervention of sorts on race problems in the south, and warned Americans about the "military industrial complex" which the government and American citizens would have to reign in to prevent unchecked power and greed. The next category, according to Gage, are the technocrats which is descriptive of William Howard Taft, Herbert Hoover, and Jimmy Carter. All three have one notable characteristic in common, they each served only one term as president. Their bureaucratic view of the presidency, related to their extensive backgrounds and experience, did neither their administrations nor the nation much good in terms of "rallying support for their programs."

Indeed experience is a major factor in the selection of any leader for most any program, organization, or political post. But the experience must prove to be of benefit and not a hindrance. For example the captain of the Titanic had forty years of experience, but as stated in the film, it worked against him because he did not use his experience to take the necessary precautionary measures to save his ship, crew, and passengers. Therefore something positive can be said for first timers or rookies, with obvious constraints and caveats, but experience should still reign supreme. I would think the preference would be a seasoned professional over a rookie. In every arena, whether public or private, this statement holds true. A glaring exception was the 2008 presidential election.

The final category as identified by Gage are the charismatic youngsters. Included in this grouping are Teddy Roosevelt, John Kennedy, Bill Clinton, and of course Abraham Lincoln. Grant argues that they "have been the most ambitious of presidents, championing *transformative* [we will revisit this term soon] programs for national change. They have also marked their presidency with their outsize personal traits [Teddy Roosevelt – The Big Stick and Hunter risk taker, JFK and 'ask not what your country can do for you, but what you can do for your country' and the space program and Camelot, Clinton and new Democratic conservatism and 'Hope,' Arkansas, then Lincoln and the Civil War and the question of State's Rights and slavery" (p. 98). Barack Obama has the potential to fit nicely in this group given his beginning of developing such a broad political base and diverse national coalition, with hope and change as his rallying themes.

While Obama has selected Lincoln as his model, Gage argues that "A more exacting model for Obama may be the rookie Democrat Woodrow Wilson, who logged a scant two years as governor of New Jersey [which did give him executive experience that Obama did not have until elected President]. Like Obama, Wilson spent his adult life immersed in university politics" (Ibid.). But with respect to Obama's university background, the press failed to report that he did not hold a tenured professorship which is a major difference from an adjunct appointment. Refusing to explore this part of his resume, and paucity of scholarly publications, again shows neglect on the part of the press, which can only be interpreted as willful because it would have served to further harm his candidacy by drawing further distinctions between him, and his closest rival, Hillary Clinton. Gage further adds the very contentious "ism" of socialism in discussing the Wilson Presidency. She states that "Wilson managed to survive Wall Street corruption and plutocratic [government by the wealthy – a wealthy class that controls government (sound familiar)], greed [and the ensuring] political storm, and [managing to] win reelection by forging a judicious path between laissez-fair [free market], and socialism. What's more he did it in an era when 'socialism' was a genuine grass-roots movement rather than an empty political charge" (Ibid.). In begging to differ with Gage, even the notion of socialism brought up in polite circles, in the distant and more recent past, would create quite a furor; and then suspicions of one's lack of allegiance to American democratic values would be enough to bring all sorts of sanctions down on the suspected transgressor.

This is the major reason why the Obama campaign did their level best to distance themselves from the errant message of "spreading the wealth," and the attacks on Joe

"The Plumber" were not coincidental. They were designed to send a strong message that "The One" would not tolerate criticism, even if it came from a Mr. Citizen Nobody, who had the audacity to ask a question that would expose the deeper ideological philosophy of then candidate Obama. And by the way, an ideology, in part with respect to government assistance, that I happen to be in agreement with, along with millions of other Americans as the outcome of the 2008 election has shown. But trying to sidestep the obvious negativity of these issues does create a more significant problem of forthrightness, if not lingering questions of veracity, which will only worsen if/when a controversy of any significance will develop. For example, TARP (Troubled Asset Relief-Program) was argued to be a blight on the free enterprise system, as well as Obama seizing control of the auto industry and financial institutions.

While concepts are changed, and names are altered to bring them in line with American democratic values, it is left up to the orator, in this case the President, to imbue confidence in the direction in which the country is moving; something of course the previous administration loss the ability to do after suspicions of veracity became apparent. In the Norman Kelley text entitled *The Head Negro In Charge Syndrome*, he quotes from the famous medieval philosopher and educator Niccolò Machiavelli in which he articulates five qualities a leader must have to maintain the confidence of the constituency. These traits are being: merciful, faithful, humane, sincere, and religious (prelude).

During the campaign Obama displayed a unique ability to be all things to all people. Furthermore, by crafting a bipartisanship administration with a strategic emphasis on negotiation and compromise, he hopes to move his legislative agenda forward. The question arises, will that be enough to satisfy the party faithful and placate those persons on the right, to the degree that they won't create mischief, and muddy the waters before he can fully act on his agenda to "change" America. The term "transformative" continues to surface in reference to him and his skills to reach out to others. In Colin Powell's endorsement of Obama, the former Secretary of State, and former Chairman of the Joint Chiefs of Staff in the Clinton and Bush administrations, on Meet the Press, put it this way, "Obama [is] the 'transformational' leader who [will] electrify our country and the world ...and that he has successfully crossed ethnic, racial, and generational lines, the epitome of the true non-racial candidate" (*Jet*, 2008).

The term "transformation" emerged again in Kelley's discussion of powerful dynamic Black leaders such as Reverends Jesse Jackson, Al Sharpton, and Minister Louis Farrakham. He spoke of another transformational wave of Black progress that transcended decades beginning in the 1970s (p. 30). Adding a theological perspective to the significance of the term, Paul writing to the Romans, where a transformational change was definitely needed, stated, "do not be conformed to this world, but be transformed by the renewing of your mind" (Romans 12:2). This passage was also used by Dr. King as he reflected inward while attempting to reach those who were walking lock-step in erecting racist barriers to Black progress. To overcome oppression of any kind requires individual acts of decency and personal responsibility. For example, bell hooks speaks of the transformation of society as it relates to the feminist movement with respect to ideas and theories (p. 114); and so, too, does Marable and Mullings as they present three social visions which have framed the basis for Black activism: integration, nationalism, and transformation (2009, p. xxv).

202

As we have discussed, President Obama has somewhat of a scholarly background, and from his prepared speeches and community organization, and legal expertise, it is clear that he is well steeped in theoretical frameworks. Furthermore, he is grounded in concepts that have aided in his ability to understand exactly what needs to be said, and at the most opportune time for his audience to get the full impact of his message. As we saw at the Democratic national Convention in 2004, when he made his debut on the national stage, he possesses a certain charisma which moves his audience in the direction he wants them to go, in the manner of other great orators, whether they espoused good or evil. But governing requires more than words, and Richard Wolfe and Karen Springen writing in *Newsweek* captured the full socio-political and cultural implications of his delivery and style.

The two authors collaborated to provide the following discussion, of course interspersed with my analyses. "Obama's desire to bring people together may make him seem high-minded and likeable, but in trying to be all things to all people [holding a fragile coalition together] he winds up avoiding difficult decisions [acting as the ultimate accommodator]. On the stump, he speaks in the grandest of terms, but in practice he inches his way toward a goal [which can be maddening to individuals or groups who have long suffered oppression – as the late great Supreme Court Justice Thurgood Marshall stated in an answer to a question about moving too fast on desegregation of schools – Eisenhower's position. Marshall said 'I believe in gradualism, but it has been some 90 odd years [circa 1953] since the Emancipation Proclamation in 1863. And I think 90 years is pretty gradual']. At times Obama has settled for a piece of what he set out to achieve in hopes of getting a little bit more the next time around [adversaries will figure this strategy out in short order, and then in negotiations they will have the upper hand. The constituents will feel they have been short changed, if not forgotten, because no one really bothered to ask them as to how much of the pie they would be willing to accept, and the sacrifices they have come to expect from previous administration(s) will be the norm in today's political environment as in the defunding of the HBCUs]. If Obama is selling any transformational revolutionary idea, it's a celebration of compromise that's a rare concept in Washington when getting nothing done is seen as a victory, and giving up an inch to the other side [represents] a defeat" (p. 39).

They continue by adding this cogent historical perspective, "Since the founding, the American political tradition has been reformist, not revolutionary" (Ibid.), as Obama told *Harper's Magazine* in 2006. Furthermore, "What that means, is that a political leader to get things done, he or she should ideally be ahead of the curve, *but not too far ahead.*" He added, "I want to push the envelope, but making sure that I have enough folks with me that I am not rendered impotent" [this is straight out of the Machiavelli school of political leadership text as articulated by one of Obama's academic mentors, Saul Alinsky which we will discuss in the following section]. He further makes the logically obvious observation by stating, "No one ever won a presidential campaign with the slogan, 'Incremental Change For Working Americans,'" (Ibid.). This gives rise to the notion that the population is being conned, or at least being carefully manipulated in a strategic sort of way. And this inclusive, soft-pedaling approach of take what you can get style, was met with mixed results during his tenure in the Illinois State Legislature, and his short service as a United States Senator (Ibid.). See also the following table on Obama's Senate voting record in the 109th Congress as compared to former Senator

204

Hillary Clinton. As shown, she voted along party lines less than did Obama, but she missed more voting opportunities than he did. However, she had significantly more bills sponsored, and co-sponsored than Obama , which could be telling as he attempts to implement his policies. Therefore "transformation" in this view may possibly be signaling a cunningly cautious, if not hesitant approach to policy-making, while providing voters with the *belief* that he will be a bold new leader. Therein lies the contradiction, for the charisma, that sends chills up the leg of conflicted and bias journalists such as Chris Matthews of MSNBC Cable News.

Once again we will return to Machiavelli to explain the nature of expediency when attempting to remain true to the five qualities of a leader as presented earlier. Machiavelli tells us that "a prince [leader] must take great care that nothing goes out of his mouth which is not true to these qualities [merciful, faithful, humane, sincere, religious], and to see and hear him, he should seem to be [all of them with the addition of integrity as a stand-in for sincere]. And nothing is more necessary than to 'seem' to have this last quality, for men in general judge more by eyes than by hand, for everyone can see, but very few have to feel ...let a Prince therefore aim at conquering and maintaining the state, and the *means* will always be judged honorable and praised by everyone, for the vulgar is always taken by appearances and the issue of the event, and the world consists only of the vulgar, and the few who are not vulgar are isolated when the many have a rallying point in the prince" (in N. Kelley, prelude). Therefore, attempting to maintain the allegiance and confidence of the many, requires obedience, primarily to religion and integrity with equal attention paid to the other three qualities.

Measuring Legislator Effectiveness/Partisanship
Capitol Records
Obama and Clinton Records in the 109th Congress

	Obama	Clinton
Votes on Party Line	94.8%	93.0%
Votes Missed	11	16
% of Votes Missed	1.7%	2.5%
Bills Sponsored	66	90
Bills Co-sponsored	255	497

Sources: The Washington Post Vote Data Base
Library of Congress
Newsweek, Jan. 21, 2008

Herein lies the challenge because the nature of politics will often lead to the

violation and/or twisting the values (the vulgar) for the sake of expedient political

gamesmanship, where it is often believed that the *Ends Do Justify The Means*. So

squaring this with the five qualities becomes a major dilemma for those reported to have

a "good heart?" If the heart remains true, the masses will follow, but there will be leaders

who have lost favor with the masses by breaking faith with the leadership qualities. We

see this occur in one lost election after another. But in examining the legislative

partisanship table we observe that Obama, in his short senate tenure, has had some

successes in reaching across the aisle to fashion legislation to serve the greater good, and

not seen as totally serving the legislators themselves. In the previous chapter, we heard

how faith sustained Sarah Palin, and provided the foundation for her service to others.

This, in essence is, understanding the good and decency in others, based on the five qualities of leadership; so therefore it is commendable to reach across the aisle to accomplish the greater good without following the faulty premise that the end *can* justify the means.

To provide examples of this notion, and additional guidance and insight as to how goals may be accomplished in a positive manner, let's turn our attention to the 2008 campaign and a few outcomes of the Obama election. Some will call them loose ends, while others may discount them altogether, but they are worthy of our discussion because they all factor into the Obama legacy, e.g. at least five major things are true now that were not true prior to Obama's election:

First, we have the obvious which is the election of the first African American to the presidency. There will be political demagogues to exploit the issue of race and to pander to the base fears of our nation, with respect to racial division. There is no integrity in this political strategy, and at some point race hatred will take over reason and good judgment. The penchant for violence and race hatred is evident throughout the history of America; and so-called persons of goodwill have succumbed to lost conspiracies and demagogy where they perceive their interests are threatened. As argued by Ashahed Muhammad, "In a country where Whites have enjoyed power and privilege, Black advances that smash the idols of White superiority or threaten White power have produced often violent backlashes [particularly] where there is a perceived threat to some White people [to their privileges and values]. The real sad thing is that the social element which is most frightened by the election of Barack Obama is the group that is going out and buying guns" (November 10). The "scary" notion is of those who would threaten the President's life, also bring dishonor on our nation by attempting to undo the impressive beginning we have made in projecting a positive image abroad, and his potential for serving as a role model of sorts, for our youth today.

Second – Overt political misogyny, as in racism, is shown to be a remaining curse on our nation, but with the Republican Party now making history with Sarah Palin and also Michael Steele (the first Black chairman of the Republican National Committee, [RNC]). It is shameful how those who dislike women seeking power, continue to justify their animus towards them with lowball tactics befitting of the White supremacists who thrive on hateful schemes. For instance, in a special double issue of *Newsweek Magazine* dated December 29, 2008 and January 5, 2009, it displays captions of those persons who were prominent in the news, and 2008 events. For Sarah Palin the caption read "Ill-informed, inarticulate shopaholic has ego bigger than Alaska – and she is still the darling of the GOP." Clearly, *Newsweek* was fulfilling its position of hatchet publication on the Republican Party that is until the Democrats do something to make themselves fall in disfavor. Objectivity and truth are not the media's strong suit where Governor Palin is concerned. For example a reasonable explanation was provided for Sarah's clothing allowance provided by the RNC, and if there had been anything untoward occurring, I am certain it would have been widely reported in the news. But still they continue to make negative reporting of Sarah an art form, with a relentless mission to destroy her which speaks volumes about the mental makeup of those involved in the attacks.

Also speaking of her being ill-informed, no doubt they were mostly referring to the Katie Couric interview. It is fascinating though that there was limited mention of the fantastic job she did in the Vice Presidential Debate, and there was limited coverage of the numerous gaffes made by Vice President Joe Biden. Also interesting is that the magazine captioned Tina Fey opposite Sarah Palin, and she received high reviews for, of course, making a mockery of Sarah's personality and image. Misogyny is the only logical way it can be explained and/or characterized. And interestingly in a prompt about face, Hillary Clinton has now become their darling with her narcissism label a thing of the past, I guess. Furthermore, I imagine Hillary must have received therapy, or the diagnosis itself was faulty, which strengthens our argument of misogyny because those so-called responsible journalists and their editors move between fact and fiction with the skill of self-righteous bigots.

Third – Affirmative Action has taken another negative hit because experience was minimized in the voter's decision, due to slanted media coverage and the ensuing debates. Clinton was soundly criticized for raising the issue of experience in her ads. Joe Biden also brought it up, and in 2004 Obama himself, in a taped interview, stated that he would not have enough experience to run for President in 2008. He had the right to change his mind, but these factors were made irrelevant during the campaign. Experience is a major factor for Affirmative Action – now less qualified persons over minorities and women will be eligible for positions without being disqualified for lack of experience. It was taking place before the campaign, but care had to be exercised in the selection of a candidate that did possess less experience. For instance, in December 2008, Auburn University selected a White head football coach over a Black coach with more experience. Former pro basketball player Charles Barkley, an alumnus of Auburn complained about the process, and pointed to the experience factor.

However Charles was an ardent supporter of Obama, and he never once raised the experience issue during the campaign as a reason *not* to vote for Obama. Auburn's coach was confirmed without much fanfare, and no other references were made to his lack of experience when compared to the Black candidate. I am certain we will see an increasing number of these cases in the coming months and years, and the Supreme Court may have a larger role to play in the future where challenges of fairness, justice, and experience, vis-à-vis, the 14th Constitutional Amendment, will become more commonplace with the newest nominee to the Court, Judge Sonia Sotomayor playing a pivotal role, and hopefully assuring that Affirmative Action and those who have been disenfranchised will receive a fair hearing. However she has been targeted for making a statement of logistical fact in that her background has better prepared her to make decisions than those that would be made by a White male who has not lived the richness of her life experiences. Certainly this is a principle of Affirmative Action in which the Obama administration had saw fit to back away from in its literal form. However those who have lived a life of meager beginnings, as a minority in America, knows full well the challenges that she had to overcome to reach the level that she has, so therefore she understands issues that a White male with natural privileges, because of phenotype, just has no grasp on as it relates to justice and fair play.

Interestingly, Hannity, Limbaugh, O"Reilly, Levin, Ingraham, and Coulter, can readily see racism in Sotomayor, while refusing to acknowledge its presence in the privileges that they and other White Americans have enjoyed for centuries. Reverse discrimination is such a ridiculous oxymoronic claim to make. There is a very true expression that is applicable to this issue which is: "The nature of any kind of privilege whether it is heterosexual, male or racial, is that it is INVISIBLE to those who possess it".

Fourth – Associations of a personal nature matters less than they previously did before the issue was raised of Obama's acquaintances and/or friends. The whole notion of guilt by association became less of a factor as the President successfully deflected allegations that he shared some of the values of those persons that he knew in Chicago, and that helped him with his career. The Reverend Wright issue was a total different matter altogether, because character charges could be leveled at the President given the manner in which he cast Reverend Wright, a longtime personal friend and religious advisor, aside for political purposes. This opens up the leader-quality paradigm in terms of integrity and faithfulness. He may have had more faith in the American people, in that regard, to trust his judgment of knowing right from wrong, in his determining the best interest of our nation as he has done in other matters of a socioeconomic nature, and appointments. Inconsistent decision making is a trait common to rookies. However this may be a naïve position, but we will never know because the damage was done to Reverend Wright's national image precipitated by Obama's concomitant reactions to statements which he has heard Reverend Wright make for years from the pulpit and other venues. This indeed opens up another crack into the character of the President. From this point of view then there is yet one other issue to consider which is informing our children that their acquaintances do matter, and who they "pal around" with has a bearing on what people might think of them, and their judgment; and certainly, if their acquaintances are doing wrong it essentially serves to harm their image. Perceptions are reality which you may not agree with, but the perception itself must be dealt with in one way or another; and we observed the manner in which Obama choose to deal with the perceptions of his relationship to Reverend Wright.

Fifth- America is rapidly moving to an expansive government ownership model, which some have labeled socialism. The 60% ownership of General Motors, along with the Chrysler and Fiat deal, and the power being exercised over the finance and insurance industries are examples of the phrase "spreading the wealth around" which was prominent during the 2008 campaign. Moreover the car and financial czars provide the president with a great amount of power and latitude to make grandiose decisions that contribute to the transformation of American society. Furthermore the national health insurance initiative provides yet further evidence that the government will become far more active in the lives of American citizens which makes a lot of people, mostly conservative Republicans very nervous.

It is essential then that the president puts forth an air of confidence devoid of arrogance. Therefore with respect to the qualities of integrity and faithfulness, those who work with the President/leader on a regular basis must trust him/her; and the constituents, in this case the American people, must have confidence in the judgment of our leader. A helpful paradigm, that follows, is provided by experienced leaders who leaned on the following traits to build positive coalitions without sacrificing their character or integrity (Gage, B., 2008). Thus, in a sense, becoming transformative.

First, show respect. "When you are asked by the media whether you have earned a mandate, do not take the bait. Be gracious in victory [humility is a virtue]. Nothing energizes the opposition party more than the opportunity to defeat a president who claims a personal mandate [put the ego in check; no quicker downfall can be had than an inflated ego with an arrogance of preeminent invincibility]. This will help to take care of the image of elitism" (Ibid.). Moreover, at times it may help to shun the cameras as opposed

212

to being drawn to them as a magnet. Thus minimizing the perception of self-indulgence or adulation, as when complemented about a speech, Obama couldn't resist the response of "I have a gift", as opposed to a simple "Thank you. You are very kind."

Second, build trust. "Demonstrate that your talk of bipartisanship is not just talk" (Ibid.). Appoint a bipartisan cabinet which President Obama has attempted to do. However the far right will always be skeptical of anything the president does, so he must take care in adhering to the leadership qualities. Justice, in one way or another, in most cases, will eventually prevail if one is wrongly persecuted. But it would be quite a noble gesture for the leader to reach out and support those who have been wrongly persecuted by others, and the media. Thus demonstrating leadership by standing up for those whose voices have not been heard is an extremely positive move to make; but the leader would have to be strong enough to accept the risk of helping those who are in disfavor or marginalized, which Obama has shown a lack of will to do because thus far he is ruthlessly political in his decision-making characterized as Machiavellian.

Finally, "in legislative negotiations, let everyone taste victory [spread the praise= wealth]. Don't aim for compromises in which two sides battle over the narrowest sliver of the pie – and then cut it in half [an adversary's agenda may be that they couldn't care less about the pie, but rather creating mischief is their ultimate goal. And they will search for anything that the opposition will value, no matter how big or how small – they do not embrace the leadership qualities]" (Ibid.). There are two old adages which are applicable to this issue: (1) Don't get into a pissing contest with a skunk; (2) You can wrestle in the mud with a pig, and you both will get muddy – but the pig likes it!

Now we will turn our attention to philosophical ideologies which have been the

basis of the conceptual foundation by Obama that has factored in the decision making

process. This understanding becomes crucial as we move forward in analyzing agendas

and how they became crystallized, prioritized, and then operationalized.

Section II: Philosophical Transformative Ideology: From Machiavelli To Alinsky

This section will be an in depth look at ideological formation and a few key

theorists who have played a central role in our understanding of the methods the Obama

team used during the 2008 campaign. The ideology of programmatic and systems change

is rooted in the theory and philosophy of Community Organization. Furthermore it is

coupled with the principles and practices of leadership. Thus from an organizational

standpoint, to help ensure both short and long term success, the analytic framework

coupled with data analysis, may at times utilize opposing points of view to strengthen the

direction in which it has been determined is the best way to proceed. To further make

this point, we are fully aware of the organizational machine that the Obama team put

together that won him the presidency. The programmatic methods they used embraced

the principles and value of service, resulting from the ideas, theories, and knowledge of

Community Organization and Leadership, then culminating in the outcome of

transformational systems change for American progress as confirmed by the vote on

November 4, 2008. But *transformation* itself is a big word for a social scientist, that

carries with it enormous challenges, outcomes, and responsibilities. The question

becomes is the leadership up to the task?

Put yet another way, capturing the essence of service requires utilizing the

knowledge base of theory and practice, in Community Organization and Leadership to

214

achieve the outcome of *transformational* change. This process is team driven, and is best operationalized with a leader who embraces the Participatory Management Style of shared decision-making, and eschews autocratic problem-solving. However in terms of the Presidency, the "buck" stops in the Oval Office is an applicable phrase made popular by President Harry Truman. President Obama has demonstrated a preference for this organizational method. And the Executive Branch and some top Cabinet appointees are evidence of this because each are strong decision-makers in their own right; and as stewards they should provide the President with excellent counsel. As an example, Joe Biden and Hillary Clinton were two of his most ardent critics and adversaries during the long 2008 Presidential Campaign, and now they are team members. And where then do the American people fit in this complex paradigm for change. How much pain are they expected to feel, and how patient are they required to be during this process; when the inevitable grumbling begins, prior to the outcry, who at the table will honestly articulate the nature of the dissatisfaction.

A very controversial author, Jerome Corsi, after publication of his book, *The Obama Nation*, the play on words by Corsi was intentional, helped to catch the attention of Obama critics on radio and television. But in his book there were a few excellent points made which I will use as a basis for discussion of theorists whose approaches have proven to be almost legendary, i.e., Niccolò Machiavelli whose pivotal work, *The Prince*, has been the source of political reference and debate since its publication in 16th Century Italy; and then Saul Alinsky, whose theories and methods of practice I studied in grad school, from the books *Rules For Radicals*, and *Reveille For Radicals*. According to Corsi, in documenting that Obama immersed himself in Alinsky's work provided an

215

excellent rationale for his utilizing community organization practice methods. Corsi, with good justification, argues that Alinsky's Community Organization tactics have been used for several generation "leftists" going back to his early efforts to organize Chicago's Back of the Yards meatpacking neighborhood in the 1930s. Alinsky died in 1972, more than a decade before Obama moved to Chicago to learn his methods. Still Alinsky's impact on Obama is clear. We need look no further than Alinsky himself to find out where Obama got his mantra of "Change" (2000, p. XV).

Long before Obama came on the political scene, Alinsky became famous for making "change" his credo. For some three decades before Obama was born, Alinsky had been defining the political meaning of change for those activists who Corsi labeled as "radicals" for good reason because it was adopted from Alinsky's book entitled *Reveille For Radicals*. "Change" for Alinsky invoked the concept of radical socialism in that it meant the redistribution of wealth. For Obama, according to Corsi, the meaning is the same, however by shielding his usage of the term he avoids having to be explicit about the specific goal behind the theme of change in the context of "spreading" the wealth (Ibid.).

However while Corsi spends a significant amount of time attempting to make Obama into this "scary" socialist boogeyman, there are those students of Alinsky, this author included, who embrace the concept of change in a similar *transformational* context as discussed in the previous section. I am certain that Secretary Powell's endorsement of Obama was *not* a testimony to ensure that we all should brush aside our form of government to embrace Leninism or Marxism as Corsi's argument would suggest. In the spirit of the work of Alinsky, the instruction of students as

216

interventionists through his methodology is designed to help those in need to achieve some modicum of the "American Dream." Therefore by providing assistance for them and their families is the humanistic and politically responsible thing to do, and is in keeping with the leadership qualities – meaning proactive change. But Corsi methodically characterizes Alinsky's work, which he accurately attributes to Obama's knowledge base, as "…creating change through a set of carefully calculated power politics tactics where the end always justified the means" (pp. 130-31). Therefore in this definition of a Machiavellian approach to decision-making is, "Suggestive of or characterized by expediency, deceit, and cunning" (Heritage Dictionary).

If this is so, then Alinsky's work takes on a somewhat different, but still significant meaning. *In Rules For Radicals*, for example, Alinsky sought to articulate his methodology of Community Organization for future generations of *"leftists."* And what then is a leftist? Corsi adds, "Alinsky taught practitioners of his methods the importance of raising the consciousness of the economically disadvantaged who were typically [identified as] minorities" (Ibid.). This helps to clarify and provide justification for Obama's organizational work on Chicago's south side. In Corsi's somewhat narrow definition, though he omits other groups who have been historically disenfranchised by the very political institutions which were, and are, designed to "promote the general welfare" as articulated in the preamble to the U.S. Constitution, e.g., gays/lesbians, and segments of the poor, single parents, ethnic/racial minorities as well as all Americans who have faith in our system of government, meaning all persons and groups, which were part of the Civil Rights Era. We should once again be reminded that dissent is patriotic no matter what political party is in office.

217

Corsi further adds that Alinsky's "goal was to stir the pain of economic suffering in order to create awareness in an economic underclass of its members' disadvantages" (Ibid.); as if there is some diabolical scheme to promote an underclass Bolshevik type of revolution. He, meaning Corsi, does accurately add, "From there, the community organizer's job [is] to mobilize this discontent into political power. Alinsky's goal was to set in motion a *peaceful* revolution, using [and this is critical] the *ballot* box, *not* bombs or bullets, to wrench power from the hands of [insensitive and greedy] capitalist elites and business leaders currently in charge," e.g., American International Group (AIG), and other financial and mortgage institutions, to name a few (p. 131). We have to be careful here because this power politics goal could be so easily misunderstood, as Corsi does in his observations. For example, on the one hand, given the outcome of the 2008 presidential election, it can be emphatically stated that Obama was indeed successful in operationalizing Alinsky's model, while embracing Machiavellianism in form and substance.

But on the other hand, it can also be argued that a troubling issue emerged during the campaign with respect to the Obama supported voter registration group ACORN, which is the notion of subterfuge as they conducted registration drives in various regions and states of the nation. For the Obama campaign to deny that ACORN's purpose was *not* designed to raise voter participation which would ultimately translate into votes for Obama, at the polls, is simply ludicrous; and I hesitate to think that anyone could be so naïve as to believe otherwise. Of course subterfuge is not a new strategy as it has often been used as a political tactic. But hidden agendas which rely on deceit is an insult to the intelligence of the American voters, and may create a Bush-like backlash if the Obama

218

team, down the road, does not exercise greater caution and move away from the tendency of arrogance and *"strategic"* denials interpreted as outright lies with respect to power grabs, and decion-making.

ACORN is more suited for these low-ball activities as an outgrowth of the Alinsky method of Community Organization where embracing "subterfuge" is a form of intellectual jujitsu, and not a coincidental outcome. It is a design planned method of intervention. "Deceit" as a strategy is an intentional lie, but a fine line for intervention purposes separates the operational aspect of the two terms. For example, where "subterfuge" is defined as a strategy, "deceit", on the other hand, creates an atmosphere of distrust interpreted as a trick or being false in your beliefs or actions. And here, my explanation of the terms could be interpreted as either subterfuge, or deceit, in the true form of Machiavelli, because I intentionally omitted the term deception from the initial definition of subterfuge. These fine line strategies moving between ethical and unethical beliefs and/or practice are certainly within the Alinsky defined methods of intervention underscored by the Machiavellian philosophy.

To effectively deal with the power structure which has nearly unlimited resources at its disposal, along with an entrenched system of oppression, those who have chosen to take this difficult path for true *transformational* change must have, in the Alinsky thought and model, an aggressive playbook that will push acceptable practice(s) right to their limit. Thus, the confusion of ACORN and its registration procedures, at first blush, do seem somewhat unwarranted or suspicious. But it is a fact that with the interstate investigations launched by the FBI, because of these suspicious practices, no actual voting laws were initially thought to be broken, nor were there any pre-election indictments handed down which changed in 2009. Utilizing Alinsky's methods, and unfortunately in the minds of ACORN volunteers, the ends did justify the means because Obama was elected the 44th President of the United States; and more so, the first African American to ever hold that high office. And ACORN did play a vital role in the electoral process. A truly historical event!! (See ACORN endnotes).

Corsi, furthermore, correctly observed that the role of the White middle class would be central to the organizational effort to create a fundamental change in the response of American institutions, in particular, finance and government (p. 132). To reiterate this point, Corsi quoting Alinsky states, "Organization for action will now, and in [the future] center upon America's White middle class ...that is where the power is ...When more than three-fourths of our people from both the point of view of economics and of their self-identification are middle class, it is obvious that their action or inaction will determine the direction of *change*" (p. 132). Therefore the effective organization of minorities and those in poverty, in order to bring about the desired change must include the middle class. And based upon the outcome data reported in previous chapters, Barack Obama followed this organizational philosophy to perfection.

Also interestingly, a Fox news poll conducted in November 2008 reported that 47% say that race relations will get better in the next few years, while only 14% believe they will worsen. Additionally 30% stated that they would be scared if McCain would win the election, compared to only 23% who would be scared if Obama would win. The next data set is very telling in that 75% of those voters polled believed that the Supreme Court would be a major factor in the election. Of course these data reflect middle class values and concerns (November 4, 2008). It is no wonder that Obama won by such a decisive margin, and that so many White Americans cast their vote for him.

Interestingly, as has been observed, Obama possesses an elitist nature which is endemic to his general character and disposition. However during the 2008 election cycle, because of the severity and nagging effects of the challenges facing our nation, voters had a tendency to overlook certain character flaws by this politician because they truly believe that he is capable of making substantial changes in their lives. But the tendency to overlook negative personality traits, or those perceived as such, will erode as other issues are addressed. People must have something to criticize, and there still remains the stereotype of the "Uppity Negro" or "Magic Negro," which many conservative Whites and racists, and even some Blacks will use as an example of the President being out of touch with the common American. George W. Bush suffered this fate, but it really did not harm him until well into his second term; however by then so many additional problems were occurring, and the fact that he would not be a candidate in 2008, meant the stigma would be transferred to McCain and Sarah Palin which is why, among other trivial matters, the clothing and shopping issue became such a big deal. The strategy was to discredit Palin in the hope of peeling away enough misogynist White votes to make a difference in the election's outcome, and the plan worked as previous data shows.

Partisan bigotry also surfaced in December 2008 by way of a jingle "inadvertently" released to the tune of *"Puff the Magic Dragon"*. The replaced lyrics were *"Barack the Magic Negro"* etc. Some folks found it humorous, while many White and Black Americans failed to be amused. It was both insulting and racist, which shows

221

there is an overtly bigoted element of our society that masks some pejorative feelings, and beliefs. These attitudes most assuredly will continue to resurface as time moves forward.

Returning to our original point on elitism of which racism is connected insofar as Barack Obama is concerned, according to Corsi's quoting of Alinsky, and which I happen to agree, "he taught that politics camouflaged as community organization [of which Obama is adeptly astute in theory and practice] was the only effective way that the social elites could mobilize the have nots [the disenfranchised, see also Chapter Five], to take power from the haves" (pp. 132-33). As we make our conceptual case on this issue, please keep in mind the aforementioned five leadership qualities that effect the organizational apparatus, and the decision-making responsibilities of those in position of power. To this end, Corsi also acknowledges that "Obama went to school on Alinsky. [And that] he advanced to the point where he was able to teach in a classroom setting [these principles] to new organizers" (p. 133).

Interestingly Hillary Clinton was also a student of the Alinsky Model of Community Organization, and in her 1969 thesis while at Wellesley College she wrote a seventy-five page tribute to his work (Ibid.). So it is not surprising that she too ran a successful primary campaign for the 2008 Presidential Election, with a populist message, for which she was rewarded by more popular votes than Obama. But unfortunately because of questionable party rules, the proverbial glass ceiling for women would not be broken insofar as the presidency is concerned in the 2008 election. Adding to this outcome was the disenfranchisement of Michigan and Florida voters, and the matter of race trumping gender all seem to work in tandem for Obama to emerge as the party's

222

nominee. Thus, the end justifying the means, giving rise to the great historical event, our first African American president, which of course could very well have been our first female president, or vice-president.

To provide clarity to this discussion, Corsi adds this astonishing Alinsky observation in which "he quotes himself by saying 'Let us not forget at least an over-the-shoulder acknowledgment to the very first radical: from all our legends, mythology, and history (and who is to know where the mythology leaves off and history begins – or which is which), the first radical known to man who rebelled against the establishment, and did it so effectively that he at least won his own kingdom – Lucifer [this cautionary statement is intended as a warning to illustrate how the best laid plans can go awry, and noble endeavors and ventures can turn to egotistical and selfish motives and works of evil, i.e., Satan]. Alinsky tells us that he [understood the pitfalls] and learned from Lucifer, the Prince of Lies [deceit and subterfuge], and modeled his writing [and theories as previously stated], after Niccolò Machiavelli, the original architect of power politics, taken from his book, *The Prince*. Thus *Rules For Radicals*, and the 'call for change was the reveille' that Alinsky held for those who would follow his methods" (pp. 133-34). As a prelude to the following discussion, I would like to make it very clear that one should keep in mind that a fine line *does not* exist between fact and fiction and embellishment of the truth and lies.

Niccolò Machiavelli (1469-1527), an Italian philosopher born in Florence is best known for his treatise on political expediency entitled *The Prince*, published in 1513. It was a political exposé on deceit and cunning among the elite. It characterizes the rise to power of a little known political figure as he claimed the highest office in the land, as did

Obama. He discusses power plays, strategies, and pitfalls. The parallels and the bridge of *The Prince* to Alinsky's philosophy becomes clear when Anthony Grafton (see endnotes), in The Introduction to *The Prince* states "In insisting that no single quality could be identified as virtue and pursued in every situation [see again leadership qualities], Machiavelli then became the political teacher of Europe" (p. XXVIII), as well as a principle theoretician for this body of work.

The following phrase is crucial to Corsi's claims and to my assertions on the connection between Alinsky and Machiavelli. Grafton writes, "Generations of readers in courts and universities learned from him to scrutinize the making of political decisions with a hard new realism, and a clear sense that some forms of deceit [emphasis mine], are not to be avoided by any ruler who hopes to survive" (p. XXVIII). Certainly in terms of this treatise, the underscoring of "deceit", not subterfuge, was as central to the McCain campaign as it was to Obama's given the magnitude of the problem with respect to his reaction to Reverend Jeremiah Wright. And then there was the Obama comment about the Stimulus Bill, and the optimism of job creation as it related to the Caterpillar Corporation. Was this an honest mistake or an intentional lie intended to *deceive* the American people and bolster his image? It was the Caterpillar CEO, however, who contradicted Obama. Therefore one of the nation's largest corporation's chief executive took issue with the President making an errant statement on a glaring unemployment problem that reflected poorly on his character/judgment, and image. Of course this will come back to haunt him in the future. If one has a problem telling the truth, sometimes it makes sense to shun the cameras. It is amazing why so many politicians do not understand and embrace this simple fact. But there they stand, telling one lie after

224

another, while the cameras are rolling, and the playback always seem to be so much worse than what it was intended to be at the time of the telling. And it is preserved there for all time. If you don't believe me, just ask Richard Nixon "I am not a crook", or Bill Clinton, "I did not have sex with that woman".

The same as with the media, the truth gets sacrificed for sound-bites. And the truth is always a casualty where ratings are concerned; we have observed this in the constant barrage of half truths and lies directed at Sarah Palin – the same as was done to Hillary Clinton. No wonder the ratings for many news services, both electronic and print, are in a free fall. Suffice it to also say that character became an issue in the treatment of Reverend Jeremiah Wright by both the media and the Obama campaign. The reaction of the former was expected, for we have seen callousness on the part of journalists for generations; however, the Obama response was cold and calculating (deceit or subterfuge?), and for those of us who know Reverend Wright, he deserved far better treatment from one of his own – a mentee, than to be held up to public ridicule. In Machiavelli's own words, he offers this somber caveat that, "...men willingly change their ruler, expecting to fare better ...but they only deceive themselves, and they learn from experience that they have made matters worse" (p. 8), i.e., in the words of Reverend Wright and Malcolm X, "The chickens coming home to roost." This was in essence the same statement that was made for a reaction to American policy abroad that was coined by the Central Intelligence Agency (CIA), called "Blowback." This concept has been around for years without any consequences befalling the agency for its use or its meaning (see Chalmers Johnson in Endnotes). But the hue and cry of outrage against Malcolm and Reverend Wright was mostly due to the fact that they are Black more so than any other single issue.

The operant term of "ruler change," with respect to America, was a matter of practical and constitutional necessity as G.W. Bush could not, fortunately, run again for President. But the continued confidence of the general population in Obama will have much to do with his displayed obedience to the leadership qualities put forth in *The Prince* ("The One," to be discussed soon). And questions as to whether or not problems will worsen, is a futuristic claim that can only be determined by events which are planned, or otherwise unconnected, and unexpected, with the outcome of *transformation* or *"Blowback"* hanging in the balance.

In terms of power, as it relates to the relationship between nations, the work of Machiavelli does ring true today as it did in the 16th Century when he asserted that, "...as soon as a powerful foreigner invades a country, all the weaker powers give him their support, moved by envy of the power which has so far dominated them" (p. 11). If one recalls, Joe Biden predicted that there would be a test of Obama's leadership, resolve, and fortitude by some nations that has experienced, in its view, a disrespect of their sovereignty or standing in the world by our government. Obama's character and judgment will be the quality which will determine whether or not our nation is up to these future challenges.

And then again, regarding continued leadership and the people, Machiavelli offers this sobering truth and caveat across centuries past, "When things are quiet, everyone dances attendance, everyone makes promises, and everybody would die for him so long as death is far off. But in times of adversity, when the state has need of its citizens, there

226

are few to be found. And this <u>test of loyalty</u> is all the more dangerous since it can be made only once" (Ibid.) (underline mine). And once the loyalty challenge leaves questions to an unnerving aspect of one's character, then the following precept of this Machiavelli paradigm helps to compensate for the shortcomings by adding, "Therefore a wise 'leader' *must devise ways by which his citizens are always, and in all circumstances, dependent on him, and on his authority; and then they will always be faithful to him" (p. 35,* emphasis mine). But a collapse in public confidence, owing to deceit, may not be far in the future as Bush discovered. *Dissent then is not so admirable or patriotic when looked at from the other side, huh?*

And when, if ever, is the faithfulness returned? And on this question we can only glean answers by examining past performances; so in this respect, as it relates to Barack Obama, the future is uncertain, particularly with Reverend Wright, Chicago politics, and socialism as reoccurring issues for the media and others to debate. A statement made by retired Admiral John Nathan, helps to bring into focus a theme from Obama's book, *Change We Can Believe In*, that, according to the Admiral, "The qualities of an individual that allows him or her to lead can include experience" [a questionable attribute when it was applied at the time prior to the election on November 4, 2008, given the fact that the admiral cites as evidence then Senator Obama's brief tenure on the Senate Foreign Relations Committee]. He continues by adding, "...the most important qualities of a good leader are integrity, character, and judgment. These are the qualities we need in our President. In my naval career I have had the opportunity to assess many men and women on their potential to lead in times of peace, war, or crisis. Barack Obama is a leader. He will lead America well" (Three Rivers Press, NY. pp. 101-102). Please note the similarities of Admiral Nathan's assertions to Machiavelli.

Indeed, over the upcoming years these are the issues that will continue to be contentiously question and debated. On the matter of exercising good judgment, the question remains in the minds of some that Obama's past associations refute that claim. Additionally integrity and character are tied to the attribute of loyalty, and as I have previously asserted, the jury is still out given his betrayal of Reverend Jeremiah Wright, and his "kicking to the curb" a longtime supporter and one time Secretary of Health and Human Services nominee, Tom Daschle (see Endnotes), for purely political reasons. We must also acknowledge the fact that his cadre of supporters, many of whom have been with him for a number of years, ACORN included, may wonder about their future, while his credibility as someone that Americans can trust does raise questions. But recall, immediately after nine-eleven (9/11), and at the beginning of the Iraq War, George Bush's ratings soared to the upper 70th percentile, and more, depending on the polls and at the time they were generated. At the end of his presidency, public opinion had turned against him with 75% of Americans registering disapproval of the job he was doing, they simply wanted him out. President Obama can learn something extremely important about the presidency, and the American people by examining Bush I and II and Clinton's tenures in office. There is a learning curve already in operation because now Obama's speeches, (to many to be sure), with respect to war, sound eerily similar to George W. Bush; surprisingly given his criticism of Bush. Moreover when a policy fails you learn to invoke the name of your predecessor, and lay the blame at their doorstep. And therefore, with respect to the economy and terrorism, so Bush did to Clinton, and now Obama is doing likewise to Bush.

Section III: Obama and Post Racial America?

The lead-in of this section is an oxymoron. America is irrevocably linked to its racist past and present; and then given the tenor and so-called humor attributed to the Republican National Committee in its so-called parody of a song about Obama, and Obama's mutt comments about himself and others, demonstrates how much further we have to go in the future before racial wounds are healed. Please keep in mind that our schools are more segregated now than they were at the time of *Brown v. Board of Education* in 1954. And school segregation is an indicator of residential segregation, and also mentally how we still see each other in terms of developing relationships. Super conservative, Bill Bennett, who appears on cable shows as a political analyst, and has a radio program on satellite Sirius, spoke of aborting Black babies to lower the crime rate; and Mike Church, also on Sirius talk radio, refers to House Speaker Nancy Pelosi as Nazi Pelosi, and Rush Limbaugh labels women in the women's movement as Feminazis. These are tough demagogic comments serving as testimony on the state of America's race and gender relations. Furthermore 66% of those persons surveyed in a *Fox News* poll stated that they believed things will get worse in our nation. Indeed, when the economy is sour other sins of our society are magnified (March, 2009).

On the matter of stereotypes and egos, Barack Obama claims that he does have a very healthy ego, which may spell trouble for him down the road because of the added admiration factor shown by others in dubbing him with the nickname, "The One." It also appeared on his website. This is a troubling perception because there are those

229

"...mostly conservative Christians [who] believe a great battle is imminent ...[with] Obama being a sweet-talking world leader who gathers governments and economies under his command to further his own evil agenda. 'In this world view, the spread of secular progressive ideas is a prelude to the enslavement of mankind' explains Richard Landes, former director of the Center for Millennial Studies at Boston University" (*Newsweek*, 11-24-08, p. 18).

Another observation by other Christian conservatives believe that Obama is the Antichrist defined as an "enemy of Christ; a great antagonist expected by the early church to cause chaos and corruption in the last days before the Second Coming – a false Christ" (The American Heritage College Dictionary). Matt Staver who holds the post of Dean at Liberty University's Law School, states that the people who believe such about Obama are "not nuts. They are expressing a concern, and a fear, that is widely shared" (L. Miller, 11-24-08, p.18) (emphasis mine).

The importance of this discussion on ego, and self-indulgence insofar as the presidency is concerned, is to make clear the looming problems for anyone who seeks the presidency, but particularly Obama given the historical nature of his accomplishment. There will constantly be steady sniping at his presidency for the very reasons contained in this treatise. There is always a tremendous learning curve in any first term administration, the question becomes; will Obama be given an opportunity to benefit from the mistakes that will be made, and I assure you that there will be quite a few. However, if I might make one suggestion, it will be that he rids himself of the nickname "The One." Oprah Winfrey did not do him a favor by placing that tag on him because it conjures up images in the minds of people which he cannot possibly live up to or achieve.

President Barack Obama

Photo: www.whitehouse.gov

231

The only thing special about Obama is phenotype, and the presidency; anything beyond that is an illusion, a myth of accomplishments destined to be beyond human potential. And therein lies the problem, i.e., unrealistic expectations which an inflated ego may not be able to reconcile in an environment of race hatred and mistrust. Obamamania will not last. The media giveth, and the media taketh away. Americans are an impatient people, particularly where their pocketbooks are concerned. The referendum on history and economics will soon be played to its conclusion, and the matter of race will reemerge with a vengeance, I suspect.

There is this view held by some Black and White Americans that we have moved into a post racial society because of Obama's election. But Ta-Nehisi Coates writes in *Time Magazine* that, "It pains me to deliver this sobering news to those who think Obama will wave his hand and erase whole ghettos: Barack Obama is a Black President, not Black Jesus. In fact, the very idea that Obama should *transform* [there is that word again] African Americans into the Black Waltons is flawed. It rests on the notion that the Black community, more than other communities, is characterized by a bunch of hapless lay-abouts who spend their days ticking off reparations demands and shaking their fist at the White man. The truth is, that the dominant conversation in the Black community today is not about racism, or victimization, but about self improvement" (p. 33). There is a double message imbedded within the Coates discussion. First, I would like to know exactly who he has been conversing with to reach the conclusions that racism and victimization are not primary topics of discussion within the Black community, or colloquially speaking – "The Hood." Just what does he think Blacks talk about when we hear songs come over the airwaves, written and promoted by White folks in positions of

232

power and authority, which are racially demeaning and insulting to the Black community as a whole. To what does he think Blacks attribute our double digit unemployment, which is nearly twice that of most White Americans? Does he think that Blacks have lost their ability to reason?

And with respect to the law breaking element: in every culture, in every society and community, throughout history, there has always been a small percentage who are either criminals and/or "free-loaders," many of whom are portrayed in both the Old and New Testaments; who will "work" the system to their advantage, and cry foul for no justifiable reason whatsoever. It is unfair, and downright wrong, for Coates or anyone else for that matter, to suggest that Blacks in general suffer from a chronic lack of determination to succeed; for the same reason that it is wrong to paint all Whites as racists. The stereotype does not fit, and it never has. It is only a handy emotional provoking means to turn race hatred and/or misogyny, into language weapons where the group so offended will curse those who inappropriately use the labels for their own benefit, or justification, e.g., the oxymoron "reverse discrimination" which negatively effects both minorities and women, with only those who have enjoyed racial/gender/heterosexual privileges making the complaint.

What we do know for sure is that those who have power, whether White or Black, or male or female, are always reluctant to share it; or change the way it operates to provide others less fortunate with the same opportunity that they have enjoyed for years. When Obama says share the wealth, in the Alinsky model, *he is not talking about taking anything away from anyone.* His premise is that there are plenty of American resources to help others in need. The resource distributional system can be altered to the advantage

233

of all. His supporters argue that our cultural *transformation* is not an illusion, it can be a reality if we have the will and patience to work with the president to eradicate the vestiges of hate, suspicion, and mistrust which has divided us for hundreds of years with charges of character and socialism notwithstanding.

But if the rocky start by Obama, owing to those persons he has cloaked himself with, ACORN included, is any indication of the leadership to come, then the next four years, and possibly the next eight (2012 or 2016) will not be a "change we can count on," but rather a shaky legacy as a referendum on politics as usual as we have seen in his various appointments rife with patronage and privilege; and a callous disregard for the legal standards that we all must adhere to in terms of paying our taxes without evasion, folks lacking experience, cleaving to lies, and shallow excuses to deflect criticisms which will come with more frequency. He also has retracted campaign promises where lobbyists are brought into the administration as bona fide public servants. This does call into question the judgment of those involved. But betraying them after an appointment has been made is another issue altogether (see endnotes), because it is difficult to argue that he did not know of their shortcomings prior to the appointments. Is the leader naïve, or a liar?

The Machiavelli philosophy on leadership within our expanded discussion on trust and character has provided the basis for our analysis and conclusions by keeping in mind the following debacles: the Roland Burris appointment to the U.S. Senate by the embattled impeached Illinois Governor Rod Blagojevich, the Caroline Kennedy aborted appointment to the New York Senate seat underscoring further mockery of the Democratic Party process and its feminism hypocrisy as it relates to experience and the arguments made against Sarah Palin, and the withdrawal of the Bill Richardson appointment as the Secretary of Commerce due to ongoing legal problems, and the debate and reversal of support for Burris by Obama and Senate Democrats. All of these issues taking place just prior to the swearing in of the new president suggested something other than projecting confidence in Democratic leadership which is a fair expectation for Americans to have of a new leader, or for that matter, any leader.

David Broder in a *Washington Post* article makes a similar point by stating, "Richardson was a familiar fellow traveler on the 2007-08 presidential campaign trail, and Obama should have known that there were reports of a grand jury investigation of pay-for-play in New Mexico [quite similar to Illinois]. As for Blagojevich, Obama had to know, from his years in Springfield [Illinois capitol city] and Chicago, about the governor's tawdry and ruthless reputation" (1-11-09). However Broder was willing to give Obama the benefit of the doubt by adding that "Obama seriously underestimated Blagojevich," which could possibly have been the case; but whether he did or did not know of the governor's methods of governing is of little consequence because unfortunately the cracks in leadership have begun to materialize. And it doesn't help that his next attempt at filling the Commerce Secretary post fell through with a Republican claiming that he could not be a team player with Obama's administration. The problem with Tom Daschle's appointment again raised the specter of trust, loyalty, betrayal and judgment.

As Broder states, "The lesson that other politicians have drawn is that Obama may not always be able to count on his congressional allies, and they may not be able to count on him. That is not the way he wanted to begin" (Ibid.), because leadership is a matter of character and trust as we have argued throughout this treatise. A similar statement was

made in *Time Magazine* which is a fitting conclusion to this chapter. The author

eloquently argues the point that for those politicians in which we have entrusted our

government for change, and a new refreshing and different dialogue, "Instead of serious

leadership, Congress gave us the Burris showdown in which gall challenged sanctimony,

while insincerity vied with incompetence" (D.V. Drehle, 1-6-09). And there will be

battle royals over the Supreme Court nominees; a true clash of ideologies, and an

exercise of strategic power politics will ensue. The winners may ultimately become the

losers depending upon the mood swing(s) of the population. But in the final analysis the

nominees will be confirmed much to the chagrin of the minority party and their

opposition.

Racist Backlash Likely After Obama Election (SPLC).

AP Photo Crockett County Sheriff Office

White Supremacist, Daniel Cowart, is accused of going on a national killing spree, shooting and decapitating Black people and targeting Democratic presidential candidate Barack Obama, according to federal authorities.

Hate is an infectious disease, passed from one generation to the next.

Obama Candidacy Exposes Race Hatred In America

By Ashahed M. Muhammad and Richard Muhammad
Updated Nov. 10, 2008

SHAWN ROBERT ADOLF   THARIN GARTRELL   NATHAN JOHNSON

Shawn Robert Adolf, age 33
Tharin Robert Gartrell, age 28
Nathan Johnson, age 28

Authorities Smash Alleged Obama Assassination Plots
(Intelligence Report, SPLC, Winter 2008, Issue 132, p. 3)

238

Beginning of the End
for Hillary's campaign

Rules Committee Anger
AP Photo: LM Otero

44th President of the United States
AP Photo: Jae C. Hong

The First Family
AP Photo: M. Spencer Green

Chapter Seven – Endnotes

Barnes, Annie S. (2000). *Everyday Racism*, Sourcebooks Publishers, Inc. Naperville, IL.

Broder, David (2009). "Reversal Over Burris Shows Obama's Weakness With Democratic Allies," *Washington Post* Writers Group in *The Flint Journal*, 1-11-09.

Chappell, Kevin and Associated Press (2008). "Obama Gets Powell Endorsement..." in *Jet*, Nov. 3rd. pp. 11-12.

Corsi, Jerome R. (2008). *The Obama Nation: Leftist Politics And The Cult Of Personality*, Threshold Editions Publisher, NY.

Drehle, David Von (2009). "The Moment," in *Time Magazine*, 1-6-2009, p. 13.

Gage, Beverly (2008). "Do Rookies Make Good Presidents," *Time Magazine*, November 17th.

Guthrie, Robert (1976). *Even The Rat Was White: A Historical View Of Psychology.* Harper and Row Publishers, NY.

Harris, Richard (1970). "Cromwell" Film on the 17th Century English statesman.

hooks, bell (2000). *Feminist Theory: From Margin To Center*, 2nd Edition. South End Press. Cambridge, MA.

Johnson, Chalmers (2000). *Blowback: The Costs and Consequences of American Empire.* Henry Holt and Company, NY.

Kristol, William (2008). "What A Puppy Proves About Obama," *The New York Times News Service* in *The Flint Journal*, November 11, 2008, p. A9.

Machiavelli, Niccolò (1513). *The Prince.* Published by Penguin Books. Translated with notes by George Bull, "Introduction" by Anthony Grafton, London, England; NY

Miller, Lisa (2008). "Is Obama The Anti-Christ?" in *Newsweek*, November 24, 2008.

Muhammad, Ashahed (2008). "America's Trial: A Post-Racial Future Or More Racial Division," *Associated Press* and *Final Call Newspaper*.

Page, Clarence (2008). "Jackson's Tearful Reaction Eloquent," *Tribune Media Services*, in *The Flint Journal*, Nov. 11, 2008, p. A9.

Wolfe, Richard and Karen Springen (2008). "The Incremental Revolutionary," *Newsweek*, Jan. 21, 2009.

Narrative Endnote on Tom Daschle, Biden, Gregg, and Character

Early in the Presidential campaign, former U.S. Senator Tom Daschle was one of the first well known persons to back Obama when he announced his candidacy for president. Daschle was instrumental in garnering delegates for Obama including the Kennedys. Obama nominated him for Department of Health and Human Services Secretary, and then it was revealed that Daschle had a tax problem. It took less than 3 days for him to withdraw his name, and Obama went on TV to chide Daschle for his non-payment of taxes until his nomination was secured. One analyst observed that this is an Obama pattern, which is to "kick supporters to the curb" once trouble appears. As humans we all have flaws, but in the words of George C. Scott playing the great general George Patton, "I may have many flaws Brad, but ingratitude isn't one of them, I owe you a lot." Obama could very well have said this to Reverend Wright, and Senator Daschle. Betrayal of a friend and supporter, particularly when they may need you the most, is a reflection of one's character. Obama also found it necessary to "diss" the Vice President Joe Biden at a press conference. It was an overt act of ridicule and dismissal of a Biden comment which left some members of the press corp wondering about the truth and their relationship. Now enter U.S. Senator Judd Gregg, a New Hampshire republican who was nominated to serve as Commerce Secretary. He withdrew his name due to irreconcilable differences on fiscal matters, while the Obama administration criticized him for pulling out, another lost nominee. A disturbing pattern of inept leadership with trust and character flaws has developed for Obama which is not the foundation of hope and change the American people had wanted. It is not enough that he kicks supporters and mentors to the curb once trouble materializes; he then publicly criticizes them on their shortcomings with the end result of deflecting responsibility from himself and keeping his judgment from being questioned or suspect. Recall again the comment about Caterpillar, the Stimulus Package, and rehiring laid-off workers; Obama's misstatement, deceit/lie?

Blowback Defined: (Charles Johnson)

"A term which officials of the CIA first invented for their own internal use… It refers to the unintended consequences of policies that were kept secret from the American people. What the daily press reports as the malign acts of 'terrorists' or 'drug lords' or 'rogue states' or 'illegal arms merchants' often turns out to be blowback from earlier American operations" (p. 8). Also included in this definition would be 9/11 – the Twin Towers, the Pentagon, and the fourth plane takeover and crashed by Arab terrorists – "The chickens coming home to roost," referring to President John Kennedy's assassination, and 9/11 – consequences as stated concomitantly by Malcolm X, and Reverend Dr. Jeremiah Wright. A different phrase/term but has the same meaning which conjures up double standards/ demagoguery, with the attempt to demonize Black activists, and label them unpatriotic.

244

Acorn Investigations:

There are approximately 13, 00 ACORN workers nationally. ACORN does not support Republican candidates, but is the recipient of federal dollars. Their national policy, according to spokesman Scott Levenson, is not to violate state or federal voting laws, however the following was found: Nevada employee was fired for voting fraud. In Missouri, eight pleaded guilty to election fraud. In Washington state, seven employees were indicted and pleaded guilty to voter fraud. In Colorado, two pleaded guilty for perjury in false registrations. Over 14 different states there were found voting irregularities, including Wisconsin, and New Mexico. Many of these states, as you can see, were hotly contested battleground states during the 2008 presidential election. In Philadelphia, Pennsylvania, there were 8,000 fraudulent voter registration forms discovered. While charges were made in 2008, this has been a long-term issue with ACORN. The organization remains in the cross-hairs of the media where reporting of financial mismanagement and fiscal irresponsibility, and violation of election and voting laws are commonplace. The fiduciary responsibility of its governing board has been called into question by a few board members themselves (Contentious interview of ACORN national spokesman, Scott Levenson on the FOX channel Glenn Beck and Bill O'Reilly shows, May 2009. Also interview of two ACORN board members who have complained about the lack of transparency in the financial books of the organization).

CHAPTER EIGHT

EPILOGUE

Throughout this text I have discussed history and contemporary politics of our nation as they pertain to issues of race, gender, and leadership. We have taken excursions through the Revolutionary War, and passed through the Civil War, while examining legislation and policies, or lack thereof, which impacted on the ability of our country to live up to its noble values of life, liberty and the pursuit of happiness. We have witnessed political chicanery, and true examples of noble service. The election of 2008 underscored all that is good about America, while also demonstrating an element of meanness that reflects the saddest part of our evolution as one people. Racism and misogyny over the ages, has not disappeared, giving rise to gross hypocrisy, that has manifested itself to the degree that it becomes an insult to the American people. And how obvious the differential behaviors and practices are when put in the context of time, laws, policies, and constitutional amendments as shown in the various time lines throughout the text.

Of course one of the major reasons this ugly underbelly of our society is shown is that we have diverse individuals now running for high-levels of public office, where heretofore, it was believed to be an impossible occurrence. Some years ago, it was a Black woman who was first to be on the ballot for president in all fifty states. Then another Black woman vied for the nomination in a major party.

Afterwards we have witnessed a Black male candidate in two successive presidential elections contend for the nomination, and a second Black male and Black female in another major party primary, another woman became a major candidate, then a major breakthrough occurred, a woman was tapped to be the vice-presidential running mate of the Democratic party.

246

While it was the Democrats that made these landmark gains, the Republican Party stood on the sidelines of progress. Then something very unusual happened that threw a monkey wrench into all of the well-laid plans of erecting barriers intended for discrimination. Each party nominated someone that would make history, i.e., the Republicans had for the first time nominated a woman as the vice presidential candidate, and the Democrats selected an African American as their presidential standard-bearer.

Over the years the adversarial relationship between reactionaries and progressives, and the hypocrisy charged to the Republican Party, was easy for Democrats to claim and to accept, and even equally to understand; for they were the political pariahs, mostly Republican conservatives who eschewed any semblance of progressive values unless it came from within the ranks of their own party members on issues such as pro-choice and gay rights (Arlan Spechter and Arnold Schwarzenegger are two good examples). Now it was the Democrats turn to show the nation that they could be just as hypocritical and discriminating as the Republicans were argued to be over the years. The Democrats also demonstrated that they have learned to be just as mean and vicious in their campaign attack ads, which was the territory that they had previously carved out exclusively for Republicans; for it was them that had not hesitated to use race-baiting as a campaign strategy that helped to win Bush I the presidency.

But now it was the Republican nominee that had the sights of hate leveled full bore at her. But interestingly, within the Democratic Party, this dislike for women in power, and the hypocrisy it showed, was already part of the political landscape. Members of the Democratic party began to detest what they saw in their party, and the betrayal of Democratic ideals was being charged which forced many of them to leave the party after decades, and even generations of membership. Once a long term held value has been cast aside for corruptible ideals, to

247

recapture what has been lost will be a long term process, if possible at all. However if it can be done, the Democrats have the people at the top of the party who have the ability to understand what has been lost, and the wherewithal to bring transparency, and some political credibility back into its system.

There are honorable people on both the Democratic and Republican side of the Congressional aisles. What is unfortunate is that they will stoop to the lowest tactics during campaigns, and excuse themselves by stating, "well its politics," as in the apology offered to Bill Clinton by a Black Congressman for the charges of racism leveled him during the 2008 campaign with the excuse, "We just wanted to win really bad" (FOX News, 5-28-09). I believe that there are individuals who would make great public servants, but have declined to serve as an elected official because of what they might find it necessary to do – or even tempted to do – for the sake of winning, e.g., betraying old friends, saying negative things about their competitor, sometimes knowing it to be untrue, accepting money from the lowest individuals on the food chain, and looking the other way to the corruption they are involved in while hoping none of it comes to light, and making promises which they know very well they cannot keep. There are two very cynical and quite possibly erroneous views of politicians which dominate public scrutiny. One is put forth by a line in the suspense cold war film "Red October." The National Security Advisor tells Jack Ryan that, "I am a politician Jack which makes me a thief and a liar. When I am not kissing babies, I am stealing their lollipops ...and you, Jack, are expendable." The other view holds that "Politicians are all a bunch of crooks. If not, why then would they spend hundreds of millions of dollars to get a job which only pays a few hundred thousand dollars a year?"

248

With these negative caveats stated, and precautionary arguments put in place, we can move forward with a more positive message. I am of the mind that we must be well informed and wary of the potential that people have to stoop to the lowest level of our human existence to achieve their personal goals and selfish aspirations. I also believe that there are literally millions of Americans who not only want to see our leaders rise above these lower expectations, and achieve the greater good for our nation and our purpose on earth. We have seen many examples of individual heroism in our military men and women, in our first responders, police and firefighters, our health care professionals, in our teachers, and regular everyday workers who do a tremendous job in caring for their families, and contributing their skills in volunteerism to their communities and our nation. They deserve a political system that is fair and just, and which embraces the great values put forth in our Constitution. Many opportunities exist for the greatness of our nation to shine through, and capture a better life for our children, both at home and abroad. This only will come about through leadership, and in that regard, our elected president and other officials can provide hope for the future. But Bush-like power grabs, expansion of government, overly taxation, and increasing debt are not the changes Americans will accept for any length of time.

Yet Barack Obama's candidacy and run for the presidency was remarkable. He fashioned a fusion/multi-cultural coalition throughout our nation that made his candidacy truly unique for an African American, or for that matter, any politician. His administration has embarked on the difficult task of attempting to repair our nation's credibility at home, and our image abroad. Both values must blend together if we are to achieve the goals his administration has laid out before us. The President put forth an ambitious agenda which he claims to be is transparent and measurable. In his interview as Person-Of-The-Year for *Time Magazine* he provided a lengthy performance checklist to be completed by voters in two years which I

strongly suggest that we revisit for its stated purpose. He presented the following with my

discussion (ideological) comments in brackets to illustrate the complexities of the agenda:

"1)   Have we helped this economy recover from what is the worst financial crisis since the Great Depression? [Issues which will come into play are socialism v. capitalism. The free market in our democracy, and constitution issues regarding taxation, and stimulus packages given to corporations that are/were in deep financial trouble, Troubled Assets Relief Program will be at the center of the debates.]

2)   Have we instituted financial regulations and rules of the road that assure this kind of crisis doesn't occur again? [Discussions centered on Wall Street v. main street – financial abuses/bailouts, power grabs and overreaching/constitutional authority and subsequent congressional debates.]

3)   Have we created jobs that pay well and allow families to support themselves? [Discussions on union concessions/contracts v. right to work states, e.g., Michigan v. Arizona, outsourcing, protectionalism/tariffs, foreign trade e.g., NAFTA, and ideologies on government intervention and personal responsibility are magnified.]

4)   Have we made significant progress on reducing the cost of health care and expanding coverage? [Precipitating universal healthcare/socialized medicine, i.e., with the Japanese and European models debated using the inefficiency of Europe, contrasted by the longevity of Japanese citizens within their national health system. There is also the debate as to whether health care is a right or a privilege, two contrasting ideologies.]

5)   Have we begun what will probably be a decade long project to shift America to a new energy economy? [At what expense to manufacturing, e.g. auto industry and regulation debates. How might industries emerge from bankruptcy, stronger and more competitive without further government control and intervention. And have investors gained a renewed confidence in the auto industries.]

6)   Have we begun what may be an even longer project of revitalizing our public school systems? [Precipitations charter schools v. public school debates, equity financing, private and public schools assessment accountability discussions.]

7)   Have we closed down Guantanamo in a responsible way, put a clear end to torture and restored a balance between the demands of our security and our Constitution? [How do we define those in confinement, are they prisoners of war or detainees

250

with jurisdiction in military tribunal or civilian court – thus addressing the constitutional question: then what do we do with the detainees, NIMBY = Not In My Back Yard becomes a relevant issue. But Senator Lindsey Graham, hoping to bring some clarity/closure to the discussion adds, "Both sides are wrong. There needs to be a hybrid system" (Joe Klein, *"Terrorism on Trial*, Time Magazine, June 1, 2009).]

8) Have we rebuilt alliances around the world effectively? [What of our image and global economics? Israel security and the enemy of my enemy is my friend debate/treaties are important considerations. What of the continued role of NATO = North Atlantic Treaty Organization debates?]

9) Have I drawn down U.S. troops out of Iraq, and have we strengthened our approach in Afghanistan, not just militarily, but also diplomatically, and in terms of development? [Drug legalization v. interdiction v. education are important debates. There is the question of poppy, Afghanistan's cash crop, supply and demand for drugs at home; and the isolation of Iran in a nutcracker between Iraq, Pakistan and Afghanistan may become an international concern. How might we avert an ever-growing political and military quagmire with dire consequences for our nation, our troops, and the Afghan people.]

10) And have we been able to reinvigorate international institutions to deal with transnational threats, like climate change, that we can't solve on our own? [Thus precipitating short v. long term economic impact debates with possible assistance to developing nations, and effective use of the UN.]

11) And, outside of specific policy measures, two years from now, I want the American people to be able to say – Government's not perfect; there are some things Obama does that get on my nerves, but you know what – I feel like the government is working for me. I feel like it's accountable. I feel like its transparent [trust, character, and American values are important considerations]. I feel that I am well-informed about what government actions are being taken. I feel that this is a President and an administration that admits when it makes mistakes and adapts itself to new information" (D.V. Drehle, *Time*, p. 54). [Analysis: Arguments of constitutional violations, punitive tax levies, socialism, and controlling/managing private enterprises. Overreaching, power grabs were similar criticisms of G. W. Bush. Now the issues of double standards/hypocrisy, and transparency are problematic for the Obama administration. Therefore it bears repeating, dissent is patriotic, no matter which political party is in power.

In terms of the realm of possibility, Obama may not achieve all that he has set out to do, and he does have some character flaws particularly shown in betrayals which needs to be addressed; but at least he has a plan that is arguably centered on the American people as

251

a whole, and not just the wealthy few such as the Bush administration's energy initiative at the beginning of his first term in office. Chaney held the high powered *closed-door* meeting with energy executives, and soon thereafter the oil and gas prices began to rise to unconscionable levels. But on the other hand, Vice President Joe Biden held a *closed-door* meeting with union leaders, and who knows what was on that agenda. So much for the notion of Democrat transparency. What's up with these vice presidents and their *closed-door* strategy meetings with special interest groups? However, I believe in general, with the obvious caveats, our country is looking to the future with optimism and anticipation. At this point of course our choices are limited, unless of course we adopt the posture of Hannity, O'Reilly, Levin, Beck, Limbaugh and the others. No one can doubt the obvious fact that a new day has certainly dawned in America, and a historic event has occurred. We do, however, have the ability to *learn* from our past. Americans can be proud of what has been achieved in electing the first African American president, Mr. Barack H. Obama. May God bless you, your family, and our nation.

GEM

Chapter Eight – Endnotes

Drehle, David Von (2008). "Why History Can't Wait," in *Time Magazine*, December 29, 2008-January 5, 2009.

Mr. President

AP Photo/Alex Brandon

APPENDIX

THE PRESIDENTS

(Brief Biographies and Initiatives)

The President's discussion has brief biographies adopted from the *Universal World Encyclopedia*, and the *American Heritage Dictionary* with the final six presidential biographies adopted from the *Wikipedia* websites. Please note that each president had/has some unique issues, if not drama surrounding their Presidency with race, conspiracies, war, and political economy taking center stage. Over all the years of the presidencies, through all of the legislation, controversies, and scandals, not one was related to assisting women specifically in achieving justice and equality beyond privacy legislation and the 19th Constitutional Amendment. Even the Family Leave Act during the Clinton administration was not totally a gender issue, which of course is debatable. While Jimmy Carter appointed a record number of women, Blacks, and Hispanics, still gender based issues dealing with discrimination was not a core policy issue. And therefore misogyny along with racism in America continues.

1. George Washington (1789-1797). His high courage and strong, but disciplined will brought endurance and purpose to the course of American independence. From a well-deserved retirement he was called to preside at the Constitutional Convention. Unanimously chosen the first President of the United States of America, unanimously re-elected, he declined a third term. And he argued against any notion of establishing an American monarchy, installing him as king.

2. John Adams (1797-1801). Was one of the most learned of the public men of his day. The fervent patriotism of John Adams gave direction to the Continental Congress, certainly to the Declaration of Independence. Served as Vice President, the first man to be so honored. As a candidate of the Federalist Party, he defeated Thomas Jefferson in

1776, and became the only man to serve 8 years as Vice President and then to become President.

3. Thomas Jefferson (1801-1809). Authored the Declaration of Independence. He had a genius for using his varied abilities to strengthen his own leadership and to improve the public welfare. It was Jefferson's sense of the need for security and expansion which helped in obtaining approval of the treaty for the purchase of Louisiana.

4. James Madison (1809-1817). Previously prepared for the ministry. In the writing of the federal constitution, and in the struggle over its ratification, Madison reached the peak of his public achievement. He earned the title, "Father of the Constitution." No man did more to perfect the instrument itself or to obtain its acceptance. He did not like the political arena and welcomed retirement.

5. James Monroe (1817-1825). President Washington appointed him minister to France. Under President Madison he served as Secretary of State and as Secretary of War. Few men have been better qualified by training and experience for the national presidency to which he was elected by the Democratic - Republican Party in 1816. There was no opposition to his re-election four years later. The chief events of Monroe's administration were the pronouncement of the independent position of the Western Hemisphere (later to become famous as the Monroe Doctrine), the Anglo-American place pledge over the Canadian border, the Florida Purchase from Spain, and the Missouri Compromise.

6. John Quincy Adams (1825-1829). John Adams was a great American, but perhaps in both learning and achievement his son, John Quincy Adams surpassed him. Exceptionally brilliant, he was secretary to the U.S. minister to Russia at fourteen. President Washington appointed him minister to Holland, then in turn he became minister to Prussia, England, and Russia. Helped to bring an end to the War of 1812. Nominee of the National-Republican Party in 1824. The election failed to return a majority, and Adams was chosen President by the House of Representatives. His concept of public service has been rarely, if ever, surpassed. He was more interested in being right and in the general good than he was in gaining popularity and in extending political patronage. Defended Cinque and other captives of the slave ship Amistad before the U.S. Supreme court in 1841. Won their release and freedom.

7. Andrew Jackson (1829-1837). A renowned Indian fighter. Became a national hero from the amazing victory of American frontiersman over British regulars at New Orleans in 1815. Impulsive and headstrong, his flaming energy carried him into quarrels, duels, and political conflicts. Nicknamed "Old Hickory." Jacksonian Democracy was a political triumph for the common man. It developed the "spoils system," strengthened the federal government over the states.

8. Martin Van Buren (1837-1841). By the age of 18 years he was an active party worker. In 1821 he entered the U.S. Senate. For 2 months he was governor of New York, but resigned to enter the Cabinet of President Jackson as Secretary of State. Two years later he was chosen Vice-President. His loyalty and skills endeared him to President Jackson. But Jackson inheritance weighed down his presidency and prevented his re-election.

9. William Henry Harrison (1841). From 1801-1812 he was governor of Indiana Territory. After the War of 1812 in which he distinguished himself, he served in both houses of the Congress. The Whigs persuaded Harrison to be their candidate in 1840 with John Tyler as he running mate. President Harrison died of pneumonia one month after his inauguration. His grandson, Benjamin Harrison, also became President.

10. John Tyler (1841-1845). Became president by succession from Harrison's death. Consistently John Tyler opposed policies which strengthened the national government at the expense of the states. Although a Democrat, Tyler's forceful opposition to "Jacksonianism" had in the eyes of the Whigs, made him appear desirable for the Vice Presidency. His independent nature was shown in his decision to be President in the fullest sense and not merely a substitute as provided in the Constitution; thereby he set a precedent that has become the rule. His administration was marked by controversies with Congress, and by the trend toward territorial expansion. Texas was annexed shortly before the end of his term.

11. James K. Polk (1845-1849). An important issue in the campaign of 1844 was westward expansion, and closely bound up with it was the problem of the extension of slavery. His administration became famous for the addition of Texas, California, New Mexico, Utah, Nevada, and the western part of Colorado to the U.S., then also the Oregon question was settled. In 1835 he became Speaker of the House. The only Speaker ever to reach the presidency.

12. Zachary Taylor (1849-1850). In the War of 1812 he served with distinction. His brilliant defense of Fort Benjamin Harrison against a large force of Indians won him much acclaim. Nicknamed "Old Rough and Ready," was a popular hero by 1848, and the Whigs chose him for their Presidential candidate. An honest soldier with no political ambitions or obligations, he protested against the "Spoils System." It seemed that he might ease the tensions between the North and South when suddenly he was stricken with fever and died – a little more than a year after his inauguration.

13. Millard Fillmore (1850-1853). Came to the presidency by the accident of President Taylor's death. Came from a humble farm life. His political competitors were men of unusual gifts in oratory when debating skill was at its political peak. The highly controversial Compromise of 1850 received his support. He also signed The Fugitive Slave Law which further fueled controversy. Failed to obtain re-nomination from the waning Whig Party.

14. Franklin Pierce (1853-1857). When the Whigs nominated General Scott in 1852, the Democrats sought a rival candidate, experienced in politics with military glamour, and with political appeal to both Northern and Southern Democrats. That candidate was Pierce. Made the Gadsden Purchase from Mexico, opened up Japanese ports to American traders, furthered plans for the first railroad across the continent to the Pacific, and approved the Kansas-Nebraska Bill, an act which brought the question of slavery extension squarely before the people. Was not re-nominated for a second term.

15. James Buchanan (1857-1861). He started his political career as a federalist, but soon switched to the Democrats. President Jackson appointed him minister to Russia. Was

President Polk's Secretary of State; and President Pierce made him the minister to Great Britain. Slavery and State's Rights became flaming questions during his administration. Although he was convinced that slavery was morally wrong, he believed that, under the Constitution, he could not interfere with slavery or prevent secession. Tried to maintain a balance between pro-slavery and anti-slavery factions, but was unable to forestall the secession of South Carolina on December 20, 1860.

16. Abraham Lincoln (1861-1865). Whenever *men* speak of great leaders, the name of Lincoln is heard. No national leader has come from more humble beginnings, and none has achieved a more revered memory. He was a storekeeper, postmaster, and surveyor. Earned high regard from his neighbors as "Honest Abe." He opposed the extension of slavery in the famous Debates with Stephen A. Douglas. Also believed that Blacks were inferior and should not be granted the same rights as Whites. Stated later that the nation could not survive half slave and half free. Elected in 1860 and the Civil War followed his election/inauguration. Assassinated in 1865 by John Wilkes Booth. Five days after lee's surrender.

17. Andrew Johnson (1865-1869). His wife taught him to read and write and arithmetic. Became interested in politics as a Jacksonian Democrat. Although a sincere Southerner, he would not accept secession. Lincoln's death thrust him into a situation for which he seemed unfit. Politics led to impeachment proceedings, these failed by one vote. He was not re-nominated.

18. Ulysses S. Grant (1869-1877). Was a dismal failure at farming, at selling real estate, and at clerking. Became a military leader who saved the Union. Accepted the surrender of

General Robert E. Lee at Appomattox in 1865. Nominated in 1868. His administration faced complex problems of reconstruction in the south, serious questions of finance, and foreign policy.

19. Rutherford B. Hayes (1877-1881). Brave exploits in his war record. In the Presidential campaign of 1876 he defeated Samuel J. Tilden (D) by one electoral vote in a disputed election decided by Congress after a deal he made to remove the federal troops from the South called the "Hayes Bargain" which ended Reconstruction in 1877. His administration was peaceful and honorable. He fought for an improved civil service; and he opposed political patronage.

20. James Abram Garfield (1881). Life was hard on the frontier, worked at odd jobs. He taught country school. In 1880 Republicans factions, after much difficulty in selecting candidates, compromised by nominating Garfield. On July 2nd, a few months after his inauguration, Garfield was fatally shot by Charles Guiteau.

21. Chester Alan Arthur (1881-1885). The choice of Chester Arthur in 1880 as nominee for the vice-presidency was the result of a settlement between two Republican factions. Thus the incident of compromise plus the accident of President Garfield's death brought Arthur to the Presidency. The solemn obligations of the presidency changed Arthur's attitudes and actions. He served with ability and distinction. He supported civil service reform a change from his previous position and put the welfare of the country above party ambitions. Thus he was not re-nominated.

22. and 24. <u>Grover Cleveland</u> (1885-1889 and 1893-1897). His zeal for good government

was rewarded further by his election in 1882 to the New York Governorship. In 1886 he

became the first president to be married in the White House. Re-nominated in 1888.

Republicans won the election. Nominated again in 1892, won easily. No compromiser,

he frequently incurred the ill will of those who opposed his policies, but his honesty and

unwavering courage were ably applied. During his tenure in office he vetoed a total of

443 spending appropriation bills submitted to him by Congress (Mike Church, Patriot

Radio, February 2009).

23. <u>Benjamin Harrison</u> (1889-1893). Was the second Harrison to become President. His

grandfather was the 9th president. The Republicans searching for a candidate with good

political traditions, preferably from the Middle West (Midwest), found Harrison to be the

right man. He was the 4th general to become President since 1868.

24. <u>Grover Cleveland</u> (1893-1897). (See previous profile.)

25. <u>William McKinley</u> (1897-1901). Was the third President to be assassinated. Shot by an

anarchist, Leon Czolgosz, September 6, 1901, at the Pan-American Exposition, Buffalo,

New York, he died eight days later. His administration was distinguished by victory in

the Spanish-American War, annexation of Hawaii, and acquisition of the Philippines. In

1900 McKinley was elected to a second term.

26. <u>Theodore Roosevelt</u> (1901-1909). Was born in New York City, where his ancestors of

Dutch origin, had lived since 1644. Overcame physical handicaps. When the Spanish

War came, he was the Assistant Secretary of the Navy, a post he resigned to organize the

1ˢᵗ U.S. Cavalry (Roosevelt's Rough Riders). In 1901 McKinley's assassination made
him President, and in 1904 he was elected President. His term was noted for "trust
busting" vigorous foreign policy, and for the Panama Canal Project. In 1912 he ran for
President on the Progressive ticket, but was defeated.

27. William Howard Taft (1909-1913). Nine years as Chief Justice of the U.S. Supreme
court and four years as Chief Executive of the United States made him the only American
who has been Chief of both judicial and executive branches of the national government.
In 1900 he was appointed Civil Governor of the Philippines and in 1906 took temporary
charge of affairs in Cuba.

28. Woodrow Wilson (1913-1921). A cultured home formed his character with wisdom and
refinement. The Democrats, looking for a candidate of liberal views, selected Wilson as
their leader in the 1912 campaign and the Taft-Roosevelt feud insured a Democratic
victory. In Wilson's first term important legislation affected banking, trusts, tariff, labor,
and income taxation. Wilson's personal strength and his sincere attempts to avert war
won his re-election in 1916. Despite Wilson's efforts the inevitable war came, and he
was compelled to give leadership for the great task of victory. As a world leader his
fourteen points formed a basis for peace, and he insisted upon a League of Nations,
which the U.S. alone of the great nations, rejected.

29. Warren Gamaliel Harding (1921-1923). Lifetime of newspaper work. Failing by his
Republican activities, to please his Democratic employer, Harding gained independence
by purchasing the *Marion State* paper, an enterprise which became a major success. The
chief campaign issue that swept him into the presidency was the League of Nations, but

those who opposed it, or wished reservations won out. Harding's distinguished appearance, genial nature, and political experience forecast a normal administration, but instead came such things as the "Teapot Dome" affair and the President's tragic death. Two unworthy cabinet members were the chief figures in the oil scandal.

30. <u>Calvin Coolidge</u> (1923-1929). The news of Hardin's death came to Calvin Coolidge in the little farmhouse at Plymouth, Vermont, where he was born. His father, a local justice, administered the oath of office to the new president by the light of a Kerosene lamp. The vigorous words and effective actions which Coolidge as governor of Massachusetts applied to the Boston police strike rang favorably throughout the country. Coolidge brought native forthrightness, sparse utterance, and a thrifty economy to the White House. Drastic reduction of expenditures followed in all departments of the government. With rare political courage he vetoed a soldier's bonus bill. Elected in his own right in 1924, but declined re-nomination in 1927.

31. <u>Herbert Clark Hoover</u> (1929-1933). Studied geology and mining at Leland State University in Oregon. Became chief engineer for a mining company in Australia. Then he was director general of mines for the Chinese government. When World War I began, he was made chairman of the American Relief Commission in Belgium. In 1917 he was appointed Food Administrator for the U.S. After the Armistice he became head of the European Economic Council and gave several years to the relief of distressed peoples. In 1921 when Hoover accepted the Secretary of Commerce post, he was probably the most favorably known American throughout the world. Elected president in 1928. His term started smoothly, but was soon overwhelmed by worldwide panic. Unreasonable though

it might be, his administration was blamed for the disaster, the onset of the Great Depression and Stock Market Crash of 1929. He was defeated in 1932.

32. Franklin Delano Roosevelt (1933-1945). Fifth cousin of Theodore Roosevelt. Married Anna Eleanor Roosevelt. He was appointed Assistant Secretary of the Navy in 1913 serving until 1920, resigning to accept nomination of Vice President. Shortly after the Democratic defeat, he was stricken with infantile paralysis. Elected governor of New York for two terms. Received the presidential nomination in 1932. New social legislation followed. Re-elected in 1936; in 1940 (the first third term) and again in 1944. Japanese attacked Pearl Harbor, Hawaii on December 7, 1941. He met global war's demands by calling for overwhelming production at home and by participating in conferences in distant places with the leaders of allied countries. He died suddenly April 12, 1945. Roosevelt's three term presidency precipitated the 22nd Amendment to the Constitution which held that "No person shall be elected to the office of the President more than twice, and no person who has held the office of President, or acted as President for more than two years of a term to which some other person was elected President shall be elected to the office of the President more than once." This Amendment was ratified February 27, 1951.

33. Harry S. Truman (1945-1953). Was the seventh Vice-President to receive the presidential mantle by the constitutional provision of immediate succession. He accepted the heavy obligations with courage and resolution to complete successfully the plans already made for allied victory which included using the Atom bomb against Japan. Rejected from West Point due to faulty vision. Held jobs as drugstore clerk, railroad

timekeeper, bank clerk, and clothes salesman, took music lessons. Entering WWI as a private but rose to the rank of Captain. Elected president in 1948, and had to deal with the problems of post-war recovery. He led opposition to the spread of Communism in Europe with the Marshal Plan and in Asia with the signing in 1951 of the Pacific Pact and the Japanese Peace Treaty. He declined to be a presidential candidate in 1952. Fired the very popular Five Star General Douglas MacArthur for insubordination. The Cold War began on his watch.

34. Dwight David Eisenhower (1953-1961). He was a former member of MacArthur's staff, 1933-39. Advanced rapidly in rank prior to U.S. entry into WWII, he was supreme commander of the Allied Expeditionary Forces, he directed the landing on the Normandy beach in France. In December 1944, he was made General of the Army, the highest military rank. Served as Chief of Staff, 1945-48, he retired from military service to become president of Columbia University. In 1950 he accepted a new post as supreme commander of NATO forces, but resigned to become the Republican presidential candidate in 1952. Re-elected in 1956. Campaigned on a platform of peace and prosperity. When he left office after his second term he was then the oldest U.S. President in history. He warned that the nation should be aware of the "military industrial complex," its power and control must be checked. The nation unfortunately did not heed his warning. It is entrenched now as nearly a trillion dollar international enterprise with vast tentacles in the private sector. The Carlyle Group is one such entity with members/investors as former presidents, foreign policy dignitaries and citizens of foreign governments such as in Saudi Arabia.

35. <u>John Fitzgerald Kennedy</u> (1961-1963). The second youngest man to become president and now in 2008 there is Barack Obama also at age 44. Kennedy served with distinction during WWII. Afterwards had a brief but successful career in journalism. The year 1956 saw the publication of his best-selling Pulitzer prize winning book *Profiles in Courage*. That year he almost captured the Vice Presidential Democratic nomination. Received presidential nomination in 1960, and defeated Richard M. Nixon by a narrow margin. His presidency was marked with controversy over the beginning of the Vietnam War and racist politics and policies at home. The Civil Rights Movement was in full swing over his, Eisenhower's, and Kennedy's successor, LBJ's administrations. On November 22, 1963, while riding in an open motorcade in Dallas, Texas, Kennedy was assassinated. One person was held responsible for the assassination, Lee Harvey Oswald who was never brought to trial because he himself was murdered by petty criminal and gambler Jack Ruby as he was being taken to the court for arraignment. Ruby himself also met with an untimely death as he waited for trial. Conspiracy theories have become popular of his assassination largely due to film producer Oliver Stone's version in the film JFK. He presents a plausible scenario of a conspiracy which includes high level government officials.

36. <u>Lyndon Baines Johnson</u> (1963-1969). Had a tour of duty with the U.S. Navy in WWII. As Vice-President in the Kennedy administration, he was an important government representative abroad. He also became chairman of the National Aeronautics and Space Council. On November 22, 1963 after Kennedy's assassination, Johnson was sworn in as President in Dallas, Texas. He was elected president in 1964. During his administration, Congress passed a number of bills that he had requested to support his Great Society

programs that became bogged down due to the Vietnam War which escalated on his

watch. Medicare, antipoverty legislation, civil rights and aid to education were examples

of domestic legislation that also framed his administration. But Vietnam was the

controversy that sank his administration. He did not run for re-election in 1968.

37. Richard Milhous Nixon (1969-1974). He served with distinction in the U.S. Navy from

1942-46. Served two terms as Vice-President 1952-1960 in the Eisenhower

Administration. Ran for President against JFK in 1960, but lost by a margin of only one-

tenth of one percent. In 1962 was defeated for governor of California, returned to law

practice. Received the nomination for Republican candidate for President in 1968.

Campaigning on ending the Vietnam War in his first term. He made the campaign pledge

that any president that does not end the war in his first term, should be a one-term

president. Defeated Democrat Hubert Humphrey, he was re-elected in 1972, and due

to statesmanlike efforts of Henry Kissinger, his Secretary of State, the Vietnam War officiall

ended (1954-75). The country had been partitioned into North and South Vietnam but

reunited as one nation in July 1976. Because of the Watergate scandal, a second-rate burglar

of a Democratic office at the Watergate Hotel, the origin, conspiracy, and cover-up was

traced to Nixon. Congress recommended three articles of Impeachment. He resigned the

office of the Presidency, August 9, 1974.

38. Gerald R. Ford (1974-1976). First was Nixon's Vice-President, appointed after the

resignation of Nixon's elected Vice President, Spiro Agnew. Agnew was being

investigated on charges of extortion, bribery, tax fraud, and conspiracy. In October 1973,

Agnew was formally charged with having accepted bribes totaling more than $100,000 while holding a previous office in Maryland. On October 10, 1973 Agnew was allowed to plead no contest to a single charge that he had failed to report $29,500 of income received in 1967 with the condition that he resign the Vice presidency. Ford was appointed to his post under the terms of the 25th Amendment to the U.S. Constitution. And in the aftermath of the Watergate scandal, Ford then ascended to the Presidency after the resignation of Richard Nixon – the only President to have resigned the post. Ford was the only person not to be elected to either the Vice Presidency and the presidency, gaining both through resignations. As president he had enormous tasks of inflation, the economy, solving chronic energy shortages, and addressing the conflicts in the world. He reduced taxes on businesses, eased regulatory controls, and helped to persuade Israel and Egypt to accept an interim truce agreement. Continued "detente" (increased diplomatic, cultural and commercial contact) with Russia. However his pardon of Richard Nixon did not bode well for his presidential candidacy in 1976. He lost to Democrat Jimmy Carter.

39. Jimmy Carter (1976-1980). He "aspired to make government competent and compassionate, and responsive to the American people and their expectations. His achievements were notable, but in an era of rising energy costs, mounting inflation, and continuing tensions, it was impossible for his administration to meet these high expectations. James Earl Carter who rarely uses his full name, was a peanut farmer, and is devoted to his Baptist faith. Graduated from the Naval Academy in Annapolis, served as a Naval officer, he left the military and was elected governor of Georgia. He attracted attention by emphasizing ecology, efficiency in government, and the removal of racial barriers. He sought to improve the environment. His expansion of the national park system included protection of 103 million acres of Alaskan lands. To increase human

and social services, he created the Department of Education, bolstered the social security

system, and appointed record numbers of *women*, Blacks, and Hispanics to government

jobs. He helped bring cordial relations between Egypt and Israel. He established full

diplomatic relations with the Peoples Republic of China and worked towards the

completion of the nuclear limitations treaty with the Soviet Union (SALT – Strategic

Arms Limitation Talks). But the coup-de-grace of the Carter administration was the

consequences of Iran's holding Americans captive, together with continuing inflation at

home, contributed to his defeat in 1980. Even then, he continued the difficulty

negotiations over the hostages. Iran finally released the 52 Americans the same day

Carter left office.

40. <u>Ronald Reagan</u> (1980-1988). At the end of his two terms in office, he viewed with

satisfaction the achievements of his innovative program known as the Reagan

Revolution, which aimed to reinvigorate the American people and reduce their reliance

upon Government. As president of the Screen Actors Guild, Reagan became embroiled

in disputes over the issue of Communism in the film industry, his political views shifted

from liberal to conservative. He toured the country as a television host, becoming a

spokesman for conservation. On January 20, 1981 he took office, only 69 days later he

was shot by a would be assassin, but quickly recovered, and returned to duty. His grace

and wit during the dangerous incident caused his popularity to soar. A renewal of

national self confidence by 1984 helped Reagan and Bush win a second term with an

unprecedented number of electoral votes. Their victory turned away Democratic

challengers Walter F. Mondale and Geraldine Ferraro (the first female candidate on a

major political ticket). By ordering naval escorts in the Persian Gulf, he maintained the free flow of oil during the Iran-Iraq War. In keeping with the Reagan Doctrine, he gave support to anti-Communism insurgencies in Central America, Asia, and Africa. Over the Reagan years we saw a restoration of prosperity, and the goal of peace through strength seemed to be within grasp. However much of this prosperity was at the expense of the lower classes, and particularly Blacks and other minorities. There was controversy within his administration known as the Iran-Contra Affair. Major Oliver North was found guilty of illegally distributing arms to the Contra rebels. Also known as Iran-gate – a scandal in which members of the administration sold weapons to Iran and illegally used the profits to continue funding an army of rebels in Nicaragua.

41. George H. W. Bush (1988-1992). Held a multitude of political positions prior to his presidency, including Vice President of the United States in the administration of Ronald Reagan, and director of the CIA. Became the youngest aviator in U.S. history served during WWII. Became a millionaire in the oil business. Foreign policy drove the Bush presidency; operations were conducted in Panama and the Persian Gulf at the time of world change. The Berlin Wall fell in 1989, and the Soviet Union dissolved in 1991. He reneged on a promise not to raise taxes. He lost his bid for re-election to Bill Clinton.

42. William J. Clinton (1992-2000). During the administration of Bill Clinton, the U.S. enjoyed more peace and economic well-being than at any time in its history. He was the first Democratic president since FDR to win a second term. He could point to the lowest unemployment rate in modern times, the lowest inflation in 30 years, the highest home ownership in the country's history, dropping crime rates in many places, and reduced welfare rolls. He proposed the first balanced budget in decades and achieved a budget

surplus. As part of a plan to celebrate the millennium in 2000, Clinton called for a great

national initiative to end racial discrimination. Failed in his second year in reforming

health care, an initiative led by the First Lady Hillary Rodham Clinton. He shifted

emphasis declaring "The era of big government is over." He sought legislation to

upgrade education, to protect jobs of parents who must car for sick children, to restrict

handgun sales, and to strengthen environmental rules. Clinton was elected Arkansas

Attorney General in 1976 – the Governor in 1978 – lost a second term – he regained

office in 1984. Then ran for President and defeated George H. W. Bush and Third Party

candidate Ross Perot in 1992 election, with his running mate – Tennessee Senator Al

Gore. In 1998, as a result of issues surrounding personal indiscretions with a young

woman, Monica Lewinsky, a White House intern, he became the second U.S. President to

be impeached. He was found not guilty. He apologized to the nation and continued to

have unprecedented popular approval ratings for his job as President. In the world, he

successfully dispatched peace keeping forces to war torn Bosnia and bombed Iraq when

Saddam Hussein stopped United Nations inspections for evidence of nuclear, chemical,

and biological weapons. He drew huge crowds when he traveled through South America,

Europe, Russia, Africa, and China, advocating U.S. style freedom.

43. George W. Bush (2000-2008). Served as governor of Texas where he earned a reputation

for bipartisanship and promoting compassionate conservativism, while presiding over the

most state executions (152), of any sitting governor in recent American history (Sr. Helen

Prejean, 1-13-05, *"Death In Texas".*) Was a fighter pilot in the Texas National Guard

which enabled him to miss combat action in Vietnam. After working on his father's

successful 1988 Presidential campaign, he assembled a group to purchase the Texas

Rangers baseball team. He became the first Governor in Texas history to be elected to consecutive 4 year terms. On the morning of September 11, 2001, terrorists on our nation brought down the Twin Towers in New York City with two passenger airlines killing approximately 3,000 people. Another airliner hit the Pentagon, and yet another one's plan was thwarted when the passengers refused to go along with the hijackers/terrorists. He authorized an attack on the country of Iraq because he argued wrongly that Saddam Hussein had weapons of mass destruction and was part of the conspiracy that attacked our nation. A 9-11 commission provided recommendations to restructure our nation's security, and the Department of Homeland Security was initiated and authorized. Bush has had one of the lowest job approval ratings of any president in history. His slow response to Hurricane Katrina, the nation's largest natural disaster (New Orleans/Gulf Coast), August 29, 2005 also plagued his presidency with charges of race and class insensitivity. The Stock market tumbled on his watch, the worse losses since the 1929 Stock Market Crash. The economy and Bush's job approval ratings, and the Iraq War all worked to the advantage of Barack Obama who became the nation's first African American president, defeating Republican Senator John McCain and his running mate Alaskan Governor Sarah Palin who was the first woman Vice President nominee on the Republican ticket.

44. Barack Obama (2000-   ). The nation's first African American/Black president. Biracial of birth, born of a White mother and a Kenyan father on August 4, 1961. He attended Columbia University, but found New York's racial tension inescapable. He relocated to Chicago and worked as a lawyer and a community organizer helping poor and disenfranchised Blacks on Chicago's south side. He and his wife Michelle took up

residence in the up-scaled neighborhood of Hyde Park in Chicago. For 20 years he was a member of Trinity United Church under the Reverend Dr. Jeremiah Wright who became his friend and mentor. He learned Chicago style politics and became friends and acquaintance with some influential Chicago persons who later were used against him during his campaign for president. One person/friend after another he either had to repudiate any deep involvement with them or had to totally betray them as he did Reverend Wright, and HBCUs which he expressed no desire to help. Of course political expediency, for the self-proclaimed egotist, was the reason given to make the decisions about past friends and acquaintances because of ambition in his pursuit of the presidency. His paternal relatives still live in Kenya. Is the first American president to be born in Hawaii. As a child growing up in Hawaii his classmates knew him as Barry. Another of his nicknames is "The One." His prolific keynote address at the Democratic National Convention in 2004 was said to be one of the best addresses ever given and it launched him on the national stage. The first few weeks of his presidency were met with nomination problems and Congressional skepticism by the Republican Party for the largest stimulus/spending bill in U.S. history totaling $800 billion intended to resolve the finance, unemployment and recession problems which began in 2007. The federal debt over a trillion dollars has accumulated on his watch.

276

Bibliography

Ali, Omar H. (2005). "Independent Black Voices from the Late 19th Century," in *Souls*, Vol. 7, No. 2, Spring 2005. Columbia University, NY.

Anderson, Ralph and Irl Carter (1990). *Human Behavior in the Social Environment: A Systems Approach.* 4th Edition. Aldine DeGruyter, New York.

Articles of Confederation (1781). Continental Congress.

Asante, Molefi K. and Mark T. Mattson (1991). *Historical and Cultural Atlas of African Americans*, MacMillan Publishing Co., NY.

Bailey, Holly (2008). "Do the 'Wright' Thing," in *Newsweek*, Vol. CLII, No. 17, p. 44.

Barker, Robert (1995). *Social Work Dictionary,* 3rd Edition, Published by the NASW Press.

Barnes, Annie S. (2000). *Everyday Racism*, Sourcebooks Publishers, Inc. Naperville, IL.

Bates, Beth T. (2002). Review of Mark Solomon's, *The Cry Was Unity: Communists and African Americans*, the University of Mississippi Press, 1998, in *The Black Scholar, Journal of Black Studies and Research,*Oakland, CA

Boyd, Herb (2008). *"Obama and the Media"*, in the Black Scholar: Journal of Black Studies and Research, Vol. 38, No. 4, Oakland, CA

Bridges, Jeff (2000). "The Contender." Motion picture. Millennium Studios. Dreamworks Distributors, CA.

Broder, David (2009). "Reversal Over Burris Shows Obama's Weakness With Democratic Allies," *Washington Post* Writers Group in *The Flint Journal*, 1-11-09.

Caldwell, Christoper (2009). *"The Limits of Empathy"*, June, 2009, Time Magazine.

Camarota, Steven A. (8-2000). Census Bureau. Center for Immigration Studies.

Carney, James (2008). "Why Reform's Moment Is Now," in *Time Magazine*, December 1, 2008.

Chappell, Kevin and Associated Press (2008). "Obama Gets Powell Endorsement…" in *Jet*, Nov. 3rd. pp. 11-12.

_____ (2009). "Blacks Key to Obama Victory…" in *JET*, Vol. 115, No. 5. Boulder, CO.

CNN (March 8, 2000).

_____ (March 9, 2000)

College Encyclopedia (1968). Inter American Copyright Union, Processing Books, Inc.

Congresswoman Corrine Brown, Florida's 3rd District.

Constitutional Convention of 1787. Continental Congress.

Corsi, Jerome R. (2008). *The Obama Nation: Leftist Politics And The Cult Of Personality*, Threshold Editions Publisher, NY.

Cruse, Harold (1968). *Rebellion Or Revolution*, William Morrow and Co., NY.

Dees, Morris (2007). "Klan Group Under Fire," Southern Poverty Law Center, Montgomery, Alabama.

Diverse Magazine (2008). "Domestic Violence Facts," March 20, 2008.

Dixie Chicks (2006). "Shut Up and Sing." Home Box Office Special.

Drehle, David Von (2008). "Why History Can't Wait," in *Time Magazine*, December 29, 2008-January 5, 2009.

_____ (2009). "The Moment," in *Time Magazine*, 1-6-2009, p. 13.

Fanon, Frantz (1963). *The Wretched Of The Earth*, Grove Press, Inc. NY.

Gage, Beverly (2008). "Do Rookies Make Good Presidents," *Time Magazine*, November 17th.

Goldman, Jerry (1996). "The OYEZ Project." Northwestern University Website.

Grolier Multimedia Encyclopedia (May 1995). "Reaffirmation or Requiem for The Voting Rights Act." ACLU.

Guthrie, Robert (1976). *Even The Rat Was White: A Historical View Of Psychology.* Harper and Row Publishers, NY.

Hamilton, Alexander, James Madison and John Jay (1787-88). "The Federalist Papers." The New York Press.

Henline, L.M. (2000). *Southern Culture and Tradition* (see usersquest website).

Hilley, Joe (2008). *Sarah Palin: A New Kind of Leader.* Zondervan Publishers, Grand Rapids, MI.

278

Hine, Darlene Clark, William C. Hine, and Stanley Harrold (2009). *African Americans: A Concise History*, Prentice Hall Publishers, Third Edition, New Jersey.

Hoffman, Jan (2008). "Here's looking at me, kid – are we narcissists?" *New York Times News Service*, Monday, August 4, 2008.

hooks, bell (2000). *Feminist Theory: From Margin To Center*, 2nd Edition. South End Press, Cambridge, MA.

Ingraham, Laura (2008). "The Factor," Bill O'Reilly Show on *Fox* Television.

Isikoff, Michael (2009). *Newsweek*, March 16th.

Koyana, Siphokazi (2002). "The Heart of the Matter: Motherhood and Marriage in the Autobiographies of Maya Angelou," in *The Black Scholar*, Vol. 32, No. 2, Robert Chrisman, Editor-in-chief.

Kristol, William (2008). "What A Puppy Proves About Obama," *The New York Times News Service* in *The Flint Journal*, November 11, 2008, p. A9.

Los Angeles Times Newspaper.

Machiavelli, Niccolò (1513). *The Prince*. Published by Penguin Books. Translated with notes by George Bull, "Introduction" by Anthony Grafton. London, England; NY.

Matthews, Gerald E. (1995). A *Declaration Of Cultural Independence For Black Americans*, U.B. and U.S. Communications Systems, Hampton, VA.

_____ (2001). *Journey Towards Nationalism: Implications of Race and Racism*, 2nd Edition. Thomson Custom Publishers (Cengage), Mason, Ohio.

_____ (2001). "The Principles of Advocacy: Issues, Concepts, and Case Examples" in *Journey Towards Nationalism*, 2nd Edition, G. Matthews, editor. Thomson Custom Publishers (Cengage), Mason, Ohio.

_____ (2002). *E Pluribus Unum: Justice, Liberty and Terror*. Thomson Custom Publishers (Cengage), Mason, Ohio.

_____ (2004). *Hegemony: America's Historical Link To International Racism*. Thomson Custom Publishers (Cengage), Mason, Ohio.

_____ (2007). *Evangelism Or Corruption: The Politics Of Christian Fundamentalism*. Thomson Custom Publishers (Cengage), Mason, Ohio.

McMorris, Michael and Barbara F. Turnage (2001). "Continuity 2000: A Realistic View of the Historical Relationship Between Black Americans and the Police," in *Journey Towards*

Nationalism: Implications of Race and Racism, Gerald E. Matthews, editor (2001). Thomson Custom Publishers (Cengage), Mason, Ohio.

Miami Dade Newspaper (3-2001).

Miller, Lisa (2008). "Is Obama The Anti-Christ?" in *Newsweek*, November 24, 2008.

Montgomery, Leslie (1998). "Final Paper," BSW Program, Ferris State University, Big Rapids, MI.

Morris, Dick (2008). Sirius Patriot Radio. Conservative Talk Show.

Muhammad, Ashahed (2008). "America's Trial: A Post-Racial Future Or More Racial Division," *Associated Press* and *Final Call Newspaper*.

National Advisory Commission On Civil Disorders (1968). Bantam Books. New York.

National Urban League (2007). *The State Of Black America*, The Beckham Publishing Group, Silver Spring, MD.

New York Daily News, December 24, 2000.

Orlando Sentinel Newspaper, December 17, 2000.

Page, Clarence (2008). "Jackson's Tearful Reaction Eloquent," *Tribune Media Services*, in *The Flint Journal*, Nov. 11, 2008, p. A9.

Patterson, Orlando (2008). "The New Mainstream," in *Newsweek*, Nov. 10th. Vol. CLII, No. 19.

Pop: Memorable Moments Defined '08 Campaign, "Katie's Comeback" and "Sarah/Tina/Palin/Fey." *The Flint Journal*, November 12, 2008.

Prejean, Helen, Sr. (2005). *Death In Texas*.

Quarles, Benjamin (1987). *The Negro In The Making Of America*, 3rd Edition. MacMillan Publishing Co., NY.

Randall, Francis B. (1964). "Introduction" to *Communist Manifesto*, (1848). Simon and Schuster, NY. pp 20-22.

Reagan, Mike (2008). Sirius Patriot Radio, November 10, 2008.

Roberts, Cokie (2005). *Founding Mothers: The Women Who Raised Our Nation*, Harper Collins Books, NY.

280

Schmidt, Steffen W., Mark C. Shelley II, and Barbara A. Bardes (1989). *An Introduction to Critical Thinking in American Politics: American Government and Politics Today*. West Publishing Co., St. Paul, MN.

Sheafor, Bradford, Charles Rittorejsi, and Gloria A. Horejsi (1991). *Techniques and Guidelines For Social Work Practice*, 4th Edition. Allyn and Bacon Publishers, Boston, Mass.

Smiley, Tavis (2006). *The Covenant*. Third World Press, Chicago, Illinois.

Stampp, Kenneth (1956). *The Peculiar Institution*. Vintage Books, NY.

Steinem, Gloria (2008). "Gloria Steinem on Sarah Palin," *Los Angeles Times* (Opinion Page). September 4, 2008.

_____ (2008). Governor Sarah Palin critic who once commented that the only thing Palin has in common with Senator Hillary Clinton is a chromosome. How sad when Steinem was at the forefront of the feminist movement to give women a voice and equal opportunity, the epitome of Sarah Palin's achievement in her home state of Alaska, and now throughout the nation. Steinem is listed in the American Heritage Dictionary as a feminist and the founding editor (1972) of *Ms. Magazine*.

Stewart, James B. (1986). "Abolitionist Movement. The Readers Companion to American History" (see website).

Tilave, Jonathan (August 13, 2000). Newhouse News Service.

Twenty Fourth Amendment to the Constitution.

United States Constitution.

Universal World Encyclopedia, Consolidated Book Publishers, Chicago, Illinois.

USA Today, December 12, 2000.

_____, December 18, 2000.

Walton, Hanes, Jr. and Marion Orr (2005). "African American Independent Politics on the Left: Voter Turnout for Socialist Candidate Frank Crosswaith in Harlem and New York," in *Souls: A Critical Journal of Black Politics, Culture, and Society*, Vol. 7, No. 2, Spring 2005. Columbia University, NY.

Webb, Jim (2009). "Our Prisons," in *Parade*, March 29th.

Wise, Tim (2000). Independent News Media.

Wolfe, Richard and Karen Springen (2008). "The Incremental Revolutionary," *Newsweek*, Jan. 21, 2009.

Yohn, Keith L. (March 5, 2001). The University Record, Vol. 56, No. 23, p. 12.

Websites:

http://blackcommentator.com

http://en.wikipedia.org   (Congressional Black Caucus)

http://en.wikipedia.org/wiki/FourthAmendment
http://jamesfallows.theatlantic.com

http://knowledgerush.com   (History of African American Rep.)

http://www.geocities.com/djconhoo/ERA   D.J. Connolly "The Stealth Equal Rights Amendment"

http://www.nps.gov   Jim Crow Laws

http://racism.suite101   (8-30-08)

http://womenshistory.about.com

http://www.1kwdpl.org

http://www.boston.com   Biden Gaffes

http://www.cnn.com   Jack Cafferty

http://www.feministe.us/blog

http://www.highbeam.com   (racial redistricting)

http://www.history.rochester.edu

http://www.house.gov   (CBC – 111th Congress)

http://www.ibiblio.org

http://www.kansascity.com   (Illinois Governor appoints)

http://www.shelfari.com

http://www.wctu.org

http://www.womenshistory.com

http://www.theloop21.com (HBCUsfundscut)

Mo'Kelly Report website. HBCUs funds cut

Index

285

287

XYZ